My Time

ALSO BY ABIGAIL TRAFFORD:

Crazy Time:
Surviving Divorce and Building a New Life

My Time

Making the Most of
the Rest of Your Life

ABIGAIL TRAFFORD

BASIC
BOOKS

A Member of the Perseus Books Group
New York

Published by Basic Books
A Member of the Perseus Books Group

Books published by Basic Books are available at special discounts
for bulk purchases in the United States by corporations, institutions,
and other organizations. For more information, please contact the Special
Markets Department at the Perseus Books Group, 11 Cambridge Center,
Cambridge, MA 02142, or call (617) 252-5298, (800) 255-1514
or e-mail j.mccrary@perseusbooks.com.

Designed by Brent Wilcox
Set in 11.5-point Fairfield Light

Library of Congress Cataloging-in-Publication Data
Trafford, Abigail.
    My time : making the most of the rest of your life /
Abigail Trafford.
        p.   cm.
    ISBN 0-465-08673-X
    1. Middle aged persons.   2. Middle aged persons—
Conduct of life.   I. Title.

HQ1059.4.T7 2004
305.244--dc22

2003016775

03 04 05 / 10 9 8 7 6 5 4 3 2 1

For Abigail and Victoria

Contents

Acknowledgments   xi

PROLOGUE The *Jolt!*   xv

PART ONE **Hitting Second Adolescence**

1 Getting There   3

2 Breaking Away   23

3 Transforming Loss   41

4 Dreaming   63

PART TWO **Seeking Purpose**

5 Challenging Work   83

6 Giving Back   105

7 Expanding the Mind   123

8 Leaving a Legacy   145

PART THREE Nurturing Love

    9 Refreshing Friendships   165

   10 Exploring Romance   183

   11 Redefining Family   207

   12 Confronting the Spiritual Crisis   231

EPILOGUE *Another Jolt!*   255
Selected Bibliography   261
Resources   263
Index   265

Acknowledgments

First I want to thank my editors at the *Washington Post* for their support. The *Post* has been my workplace family for almost twenty years. It is where the idea for *My Time* got started. As a health writer, I could see how longevity was changing our lives. The concept of a vital new stage in life after 50 has been the subject of many columns that I have written for the *Post*. A number of people who appear in *My Time* have already been introduced to *Washington Post* readers in the pages of the Health section.

The book has two godmothers—Jo Ann Miller, my editor at Basic Books, who drew out the best in me, and Gail Ross, my agent, who believed it was possible. I am deeply grateful to both of them.

The research formally began during a sabbatical in 2000 with three fellowships—from the Harvard School of Public Health in Boston, the International Longevity Center–USA in New York, and the Program in Integrative Medicine at the University of Arizona Health Sciences Center in Tucson. My thanks go to Dean Barry Bloom and Jay Winston at HSPH; to Dr. Robert N. Butler, president of ILC; to Dr. Andrew Weil, pioneer of integrative medicine; and to Mel Zuckerman, founder of Canyon Ranch.

At the time, I did not have the "story"; I just knew something big was going on. So many people at these institutions gave me their expertise to figure it out. Slowly, slowly, during the initial months of exploration, I began to see that *My Time* constituted a totally new and separate phase in personal development. I had the backbone for a book.

To flesh it out, I attended several key seminars and meetings: "The Graying of America" conference at the Knight Center for Specialized Journalism at the University of Maryland; the "Coming of Age Conference" sponsored by Civic Ventures, a national nonprofit organization that encourages public service in the bonus decades; the 55-plus program at Chautauqua Institution in Chautauqua, New York, the summer center of arts, education and religion; the "Ms Senior America" pageant in Biloxi, Mississippi. All the while, I was conducting interviews for articles in the *Post*.

Throughout, I was supported by a network of family and friends. My two book clubs—one of couples, the other of women—provided regular hand-holding and many insights. So did the Cosmos Group, organized by Dr. Florence Haseltine, a monthly meeting of women in science and health at the Cosmos Club in Washington; and the September 11 Dinner group, a collection of friends brought together in the wake of the attacks that continues to meet about six times a year. Many, many people helped at every step of the way—reading copy, suggesting candidates to illustrate *My Time*, providing meals, insight, solace, and friendship: Henry and Deborah Allen, Merribel Ayres, Norman Birnbaum, Candace Boyden, Perry and Annie Boyden, Chris Clark, Buffy Colt, Ann Crittenden, Mary and Tom Edsall, Elizabeth Fox, Marc Freedman, Murray and Jeanne Gart, Robin Herman, Caroline Herron, Eloise Hodges, Pat Jackson, Yvonne Lamb, John E. Lawrence, Becky Lescaze, Noel Miller, Don Neff, Tom Peterson, Anne Marie Pittman, Trip Reid, Harvey Sloane, Crocker Snow, June Spencer, Jim and Maude Terry, Bonnie Trafford, Stella Trafford, Nicholas von Hoffman, Ann Waldron, Eric Wentworth, Clare Whitfield.

Special thanks go to the home team of editors—to my daughters, Abigail Miller and Victoria Brett, to poet Heddy Reid, who read many drafts and chose the epigraphs that introduce each chapter, and to Mary Hadar and Susan Dooley Carey who reviewed the final manuscript.

Finally I want to thank the people in this book—the My Timers who opened their lives to show the way to this unprecedented stage in the bonus years. Out of their generosity of time and spirit has come this powerful story of personal renaissance.

Thank you all very, very much.

The *Jolt!*

The afternoon knows what the morning never suspected.

SWEDISH PROVERB

You see them everywhere: two women in midlife traveling together, a group of men with craggy faces lingering over lunch, a couple holding hands at the matinee movie—or scrambling over rocks in the Grand Canyon. A husband, off with his church group to build houses in Mexico. A wife, off to a poetry retreat. The grandmother in high heels who runs for mayor.

They don't look old. They don't act old. They are fit, energetic—engaged and engaging. They have an aura about them that says: *I'm free. I've paid my dues. Now it's time for me to be who I am, do what I really want to do.*

Something huge is happening. A demographic wave has swept over the social landscape. It's not just that people are living longer—they are *healthier* longer. The biological calendar has been reconfigured so that people are physically younger than their chronological age.

This has created a whole new stage in the life cycle—a period of personal renaissance inserted somewhere after middle age, but before old age. No longer an isolated experience for a hardy few, this Indian Summer phase of life is becoming a global phenomenon. But what are people to do with these bonus decades?

It is not an easy period. There are layoffs and mammograms, retirement parties and forgetting where you left your keys. There are losses, too. The death of a parent, for example. For most, this new phase involves some crisis and a lot of confusion. Yet it also heralds unprecedented possibility.

I remember going to a college reunion when my classmates and I were young adults in that early high-stress zone of juggling children and marriages and jobs—and we were all pretty exhausted from meeting other people's needs. One woman stood up and wailed: "When is it going to be *my* time?"

My Time! *Jolt!*

The answer is: when the primary tasks of adulthood have been completed, for better and for worse. Children have been raised. Marriages have been made—and remade. Career goals have been achieved—or not. You've paid the mortgage, filled out your résumé.

And then what?

The question is at the crux of *My Time: Making the Most of the Rest of Your Life*. The book chronicles how people have confronted this new period. It's not just about seeking a second career or finding another spouse or finally going to Times Square. It's a complicated process of regenerating yourself and your life to take advantage of these extra innings.

Most people are unaware of My Time even as they stumble into it. I didn't have a clue. I was too busy. I had a husband, two daughters, and a high-pressure career as an editor at the *Washington Post*.

Besides, the passage to My Time doesn't happen all at once. It usually comes in spurts, much like puberty. There are jolts—events that signal that your life is changing. Some of the signs are wondrous, some are devastating. Often it's only in retrospect that you understand the jolts for what they are: proof that the long, indefinite stretch of middle adulthood is coming to an end and a new era is about to begin.

Looking back, I can see that I almost missed the first jolt. It was a small thing. I was offered the chance at another editing job at the newspaper. It was technically a bigger management job, but not as creative. I was torn. In a final push to convince me to compete for the job, the person who was interviewing me quipped: "I'm surprised someone at your age is getting this kind of chance."

At your age! *Jolt!* I was 50. The editor who made the remark was about the same age, but further along on the power track. Old? Last chance to move up on the power train! *Jolt!* Surprise! At your age!

I came home, distraught. My husband, ten years older, wiser—we were then in a good phase—put his arms around me. It was true. I was "old"—compared to what I had been when I started out, covering the Apollo moon landing program in Houston. Indeed, I am a senior citizen in the workforce. Anybody over 50 is considered a mature worker. The jolt had given me a whiff of how ageism operates in the culture. But it also was a personal awakening.

"What do you really want to do?" asked my husband.

"I'd like to write more. I miss it," I replied.

I didn't pursue the job. I got off the train and stayed in a job I loved for another decade. But a rumbling restlessness started in my chest. *What do you really want to do?*

◆

The emergence of an older, more vigorous population is the most significant social story of our times. As a health writer, I have seen how the longevity revolution has altered every aspect of the culture. Political leaders wring their hands over the swelling ranks of Medicare and bemoan the future burden on Social Security. At the same time, entrepreneurs have built a burgeoning anti-aging movement that offers everything from Botox injections and supplements to weight-loss regimens, spiritual retreats, life-long learning centers, and sex manuals—all targeted to people 50 and older. A vibrant leisure industry is turning the golden years into real gold for the national economy with cruises, travel packages, and retirement communities.

What's missing is a psychological road map for My Time. All around me, I see people struggling with the changes that occur in this period. They sense that previous generations never grappled with this conundrum. It has no name, no fixed shape. They start to wonder: *What the hell is going on here?*

Once I hit my mid–50s, the jolts come in a rush—a crescendo of life-changing gains and losses.

The most glorious event is the birth of my first grandchild. The call comes at 10 P.M. My daughter is in the hospital in Charlottesville, and the obstetrician wants to go ahead with an immediate Cesarean delivery. I jump in the car with a friend and we race down Route 29 in the fog to the University of Virginia Hospital. I am nervous. My daughter has gestational diabetes. The baby is going to be at least ten pounds. We arrive just as Brooks Trafford Miller takes his first breath. I look into his perfect face and am overwhelmed. A few months later, my daughter turns to me and says with a smile: "I get it now, Mom." We both laugh. We're on the same side now.

With this grand jolt, the family is reshuffled. The bond with adult children grows closer. And there's a whole new opportunity to love a child again—to put down roots in a new generation. My internal compass starts shifting to the future.

Yet, the wonder of becoming a grandparent is balanced by a catastrophic loss. My marriage collapses. It is a second marriage and a love match meant to last into the setting sun—the right blend of adventure and tenderness. But after many good years, my husband sinks deeper into despair, deeper into bottles of Tanqueray gin. We try to break the cycle. I find myself closing up on the inside and working too hard on the outside. The marriage is slow to die, with stops and starts, a seesaw of hope and sorrow. The bedrock of love endures—but not our life together. I experience the divorce as a death. Losing my husband breaks my heart, breaks my life. I am 55.

In the midst of this, my body rebels. I go to the gynecologist for a checkup and am told: *You have a polyp on your uterus and you need surgery.* Like the shake of a kaleidoscope, everything in my head disassembles and forms a new pattern as I confront the possibility of major illness. Cancer? Unlikely, replies the doctor. But it is a possibility and my mind starts racing toward the dark zone. The surgery, just before Thanksgiving, is an outpatient procedure. The news is good: The polyp is removed and proves benign. I have turkey dinner on a tray in the living room and recover quickly. But my sense of a vague, forever future is replaced by a more immediate sense of urgency. *What do you really want to do?*

Finally, my job changes. After almost fourteen years at the helm of the newspaper's Health section, I step down. The section needs a new direction. And so do I. After a short sabbatical, I return to the *Post* in a new role as columnist. This is the classic bittersweet turning point of mourning the past while dreaming about the future.

With all these jolts, I plunge into a chaotic phase of re-examination. It's not a question of simply starting over. I cannot re-roll the tape of my life the way I could in my 30s. After age 50, the book of adulthood is pretty much written. I am comfortable with the old script. Yet, a line has been crossed. I can't just go back and extend the status quo of the earlier years.

But how to go forward? I struggle with the double paradox of the bonus years: You have this wonderful opportunity to reinvent yourself. But you face what often seem to be insurmountable obstacles in a society that is still laced with aging stereotypes. You have to plan for a long life—much longer than previous generations could expect. You also know it can all end tomorrow.

You have more time—and no time to waste.

You finally get the freedom to do what you really want to do. But what exactly is that? Maybe you've been too busy to think about it.

How do you search for new ways to live and love and work at an age when your forebears would have been settling into a rocking chair? Indeed, they probably would have died long before. In 1900, life expectancy in the United States was only 47. Today, you might only be halfway through your life span.

Look around you. There are legions of men and women who are struggling with the existential questions posed by the bonus decades: What do you really want to do? What is My Time all about?

The emergence of this new stage in life is beginning to seep into the popular culture. Playwright David Hare explains it this way in an interview on his play—*The Breath of Life*—about two 60-plus women, starring Judi Dench and Maggie Smith: "Thanks to modern medicine and all that milk we drank after the Second World War, there's almost a new category of life in the West. You can no longer call it middle age, and you certainly can't call it old age. It's something in between—a period when men and women can look back and see the transit of what used to be a whole lifetime . . . and yet that backward view is from the advantage of an actuarial hope of another twenty years to come."

This "new category of life" is fast becoming a normal milestone, and it is reshaping the architecture of society. It is also a personal emergency in love, work, play, and spirit.

In the end, I talked to hundreds of men and women to understand this new stage. Some are on the brink of My Time, trying to sort out events that signal the end of middle adulthood. Others are fully engaged in their new chapter. Their stories show the potential for creativity and contribution in the bonus years—for having an impact in personal relationships as well as in public works. They are teachers, lawyers, nurses, doctors, stay-at-home moms, technicians, musicians, clerks, police officers, company managers, ministers, government workers. Most are from the middle and upper middle class.

The people who opened their lives and hearts to me wanted to share what they had learned. Over and over they asked: *Do you find this happens to others?* Slowly patterns began to emerge as I saw them face this new period with a combination of wonderment and anxiety. As a condition of the interview, people were permitted to review their story before it was published. This allowed them to talk freely about their experiences. In a few instances, names have been withheld and details changed to provide anonymity. Plot lines and quotes remain intact. While not a scientific study, the book, with all its stories, has something to tell you about My Time.

You protest. This is not the way it's happening for you. You're right. Everyone is different. You write your own script at this stage of life. But there are some predictable patterns. Without self-awareness and an understanding of the changes that are occurring internally and externally, you can flounder in these years.

I learned that you don't have to have a major crisis to feel unsettled. It's normal to have a period of anxiety and re-evaluation. I also found that loss, however devastating, can turn out to be the liberating event that helps you begin the process of reinvention.

The window of My Time is thirty years or more—from about age 50 to 80. Most people go through a transition period similar to adolescence. You have to break away from traditional adulthood the way teenagers break away from childhood. You try out different options—a new job, a course in pottery, some volunteer work, a different house—the way adolescents go off to school and take summer jobs. Experimenting is a means of figuring out what you want to do in your bonus years.

It can be dangerous to stay in the rut of middle adulthood and not move on. You pin your identity on being a "former"—former fire captain, former ambassador, former spouse-of. Or you wait too long to make the break and then find it's too late to do what you want to do. It's easy to slip into a state of functional stagnation in a job or a relationship. Or you can become stuck in your own thinking about life. You hang on and drift. But that means you're wasting your precious gift of time.

The perils are real. Not just missed opportunities but suffering. The highest suicide rates, for example, are found in white men over 65. Why this surge in self-destruction among those who have been most privileged in the culture? The immediate explanation is usually untreated depression or some other medical problem. But in the larger context of the longevity boom, the statistic sounds an alarm: If you can't find new purpose and pleasure in the bonus decades, you can get trapped in a biological purgatory. You feel too old to live, but too young to die.

It doesn't have to be that way. For many people, these bonus decades are a period of liberation and contentment. Losses are balanced by gains: the deepening of love, more purposeful work, greater opportunities to be creative, have fun, and help others. You are relieved of the burdens of early adulthood. What's to stop you now? Mostly, you hold on to your health. You've finished the tasks of the middle years. You have nothing to lose. You're free. As Janis Joplin belted out in her gravelly screech: *Freedom's just another word for nothing left to lose.* And everything to gain.

◆

How do you know if you're into My Time? It's a slow complicated process and it can sneak up on you.

I go to Asia on vacation. I have settled into a different rhythm with new energy. This is a magic trip of adventure and reflection.

On a clear October day, I visit the ancient city of Kyongju in South Korea and walk up the mountain through the woods to the great, giant Buddha that sits in a grotto. For a long time, I stare at this massive granite figure from the eighth century A.D. Then out over the mountains to the East Sea on the horizon. And back to Buddha, sublime in grandeur and simplicity.

As I stand there alone amidst the chatter of schoolboys and the smell of fallen leaves, time stops. In the gaze of the Buddha, I am suspended. Here is the calm of eternity, where the past is validated and the future cherished. One part of my life is over; another is beginning. Both flow into each other. But instead of a straight line, the two halves form a circle—the future shifts from getting ahead to getting whole. In the quiet of Kyongju, harmony triumphs over power, tranquillity over success, creativity over status—and love over everything.

I walk down the mountain in a state of exuberance.

It has been five years since the rush of jolts began, ten years since that offhand remark from a colleague. So much has changed inside and out. Finally I am free. This is going to be My Time.

PART ONE

Hitting Second Adolescence

1

Getting There

And the trouble is, if you don't risk anything, you risk even more.

ERICA JONG

RESTLESS. NOT SO YOUNG, but restless. People ask you: How are you? What are you doing? And now they really mean it. *Is your health holding up? Your job? Your family?* Oh, fine. Everything is fine. Here you are, barreling over the 50-year yard line—busy, busy—cruising along toward Medicareland. Heading toward . . . what?

What?

The rumble starts in the chest. What are you going to do with the rest of your life? Are you that old? Old enough to start thinking about it? Young enough to make a plan? You don't feel old. You don't look old. But the kids are gone. The house is quiet. And at the office . . . the new boss is younger than you are! Someone mentions the R-word . . . *retirement*. Do nothing for the next thirty or forty years? You can't. It's not just the uncertain economy. You need to work; you want to do *something*. But you're restless. Even a little bored—at work and at home.

3

You get scared. The nightmare stereotype pops up in your brain: What if you end up like those lonely old sad sacks playing bingo day after day after day.

Not you. You're not sad or lonely. You're busy. Everything is just fine. In fact, you've never felt so good. Or looked so good. Or had so much time to enjoy life.

But now, what?

There's a low-grade drumbeat of anxiety spreading across the land, a background noise of restlessness that affects people of a certain age. It's not a bad noise; in fact, it's a normal response to a challenge that the psyche recognizes as new and potentially threatening. Indeed, it is a social symptom of the most profound evolutionary change occurring in the human species: longevity. Instead of winding down after age 50, you're having to gear up. Longevity's imperative is regeneration.

But, how? How do you master the art of reinvention?

Jimmie Grace Van Vacter, 71, of Homer, Alaska, is proof that it's never too late to start a new life. A rare beauty with platinum hair and a doll-like smile, Jimmie Grace has attitude. As she explains: "I'm friendly." She exudes warmth—a soft-tough pioneer charisma that reflects her childhood on a ranch in Texas. This makes her a wonderful nurse in the long-term care unit of the Kenai Peninsula hospital.

She didn't become a nurse until age 60. (She was the oldest in the class and was named student-of-the-year.) She moved to Alaska only two years ago. And that was after several previous lives.

For Jimmie Grace, like many women of her generation, marriage came before career. And then marriage turned out to be the route to a career. She gained much from her husbands. The first marriage at age 18 in Oklahoma ("He was my first love," she recalls) ended in divorce but gave her two children. A second marriage in West Virginia to a White Knight Wild Man ("He really had rescued me") also ended in divorce, but gave her another son. A third marriage back in Oklahoma ("Not a love match," she says) ended with his death from heart disease—he was good to her in his own way.

Each ending led to a beginning. In the first marriage, she learned to stand up for herself. In the third marriage, she learned about self-respect. In the second marriage, she learned the oil and gas business.

At the age of 50, after the end of her second marriage, she returned to Oklahoma and became a business tycoon. "I bought out a bunch of wells that were not producing. I was president of the corporation. We did well with it," she says. "My being a woman at that time got me through the door. I really knew oil and gas."

And then, after ten boom years, she lost it all. A bad deal on the sale of the company. "I never got it back. I learned an important lesson: You can't always win," she says.

Suddenly she was 60, wiser and poorer. "I thought to myself: Maybe I should do something real, maybe I should get a real job." So she went to nursing school. For a few years, she worked in a nursing facility in Oklahoma. After her third husband died, she became a traveling nurse.

One day, her daughter, who is also a nurse, read about the shortage of nurses in Alaska. Why not? Why not go to Alaska as replacement nurses for three months? *If not now, when?*

In 2000, mother and daughter and grandkids went to the Kenai Peninsula in southern Alaska.

"It's such a wonderful place," says Jimmie Grace. Growing up, she wanted to be an opera star, but got married instead. Now she sings to her patients. "If I couldn't make them better with medication, I could sing to them," she says. One woman lay unconscious for a week. "I took her hand and sang 'Amazing Grace.' Her lips moved to the words," she says. Another time, she sang the Lord's Prayer. "Life has been good to me," she says.

She has her family. She has her work. She has her beauty. She has her beaux. There's one in particular. "He makes me laugh."

She has the My Time attitude. "At this age you can be who you are," she says. "When I was young—you dread getting older. I've learned that age gives back so much more than it takes away. It gives you a confidence in yourself and in the Good Lord. You love and respect people more. Life is not a competition. It's being who you are and allowing the other person to be the same. Age teaches you."

◆

It's just dawning on Americans that this new stage of adulthood has been created in the life cycle.

Television star Jane Pauley spoke for many when she announced that she would leave NBC after twenty-seven years with the network, and do what? "I keep walking by bookstores and seeing titles talking about second acts in life," she told the *New York Times*. At 52, she's wondering: "What's next, or even, what is it I really want to do?"

All around you are people who have turned the bonus decades into a personal renaissance. Think Jimmy Carter, global peacemaker who won the Nobel Prize at age 78—more than twenty years after losing the White House. Think Bonnie Raitt, 52, in her album "Silver Lining"—*We're gon' have the time of our lives*.

Think your neighbor.

Think yourself.

The rumble starts in the chest again. And the anxiety dreams at night. You aren't thinking about the future. There is no crisis to force you to change. You may be happy where you are. But the ground is quietly shifting beneath your feet. And then comes a dream that wakes you up.

One woman describes it this way: "In real life, my company was taken over by another," she begins, "but I was told my position was secure even though I'm in my late fifties. In the dream I go to the office and find it completely rearranged into regimented rows of desks. . . . My office is gone! The place is filled with strangers! I can't find my desk, and I'm in the middle of a project that I worry I won't be able to finish. The only actual offices are inhabited by white-haired men in hospital beds. . . . I kept screaming—*Where is my desk?* No one cared. I woke up in a cold sweat. The dream stayed with me all day. I said to myself—*I better start to think about what's next.*"

"It's not like we have a lot of role models to show us the pathways," says James Firman, president of the National Council on the Aging (NCOA). When you celebrate your 50th birthday, "you're starting the second half of your life," he says. "You have some money. You have some control. You have opportunity." But no one told you that you have to write a new script for these "extra" years. "This concept hasn't sunk in yet," he says. "We're all lost as a generation."

Not so long ago, official retirement was an endpoint. Leaving the job after decades of service meant a gold watch and a few golden years of leisure. "You didn't do anything. That was fine," continues Firman. You didn't live very long after you stopped working. You deserved the rest.

Now a whole generation is waking up to the fact that the rules have changed. If you take early retirement at 55, you can expect to live—and live well—for another three or four decades. An entire life span in centuries past. "What am I going to do? What's my purpose? That's a fundamental question," says Firman.

"This is about reinventing yourself in a new stage of life. It's a gift—years of opportunity, years of health. But there's no clear path."

Reinvention starts in your head.

Physician Jonelle Rowe remembers the first jolt. A professor of medicine, she was teaching interns and residents how to allocate their time in the real world of medical practice. She went to the blackboard and drew three interlocking circles: one for her children, one for her husband, one for her work. A resident stood up and asked her: *Where's the circle for you?*

Jolt! "There was no me," she says.

No room for a "me" in the zoom zone of early adulthood when your focus is on others. And then those stresses ease up. The children leave home. The résumé gets filled out. The marriage is down to the two of you. Or down to one. Now you have time to think about things.

"All of a sudden, there is a me," explains Jonelle, 62, a pretty woman with red curls, who ran a hospital neonatal unit at a medical school in Connecticut. Five years ago, her marriage broke up and she left academic medicine to work on women's health issues at the Department of Health and Human Services. Her son and two daughters are grown. She's just bought a house, her very own place for the first time. Her goals reshuffle.

Jonelle likes her house, filling it slowly with spare modern furniture. She likes the network of close friends that she's created, the new opportunities for love and relationships. She likes making a difference in women's lives through public health measures. She likes walking along the river in springtime and savoring the sense of possibility. The three circles have merged into one: My Time.

Still, she's restless. Still, she wonders about *What, next?*

"It's wrapped up in my mortality. Time is limited. Whatever that time, you really want to use it. How do you want to spend your life? We're in a position to make choices," she says. "There is something about this being our Last Hurrah. Double or Nothing!"

What do you really want to do?

✦

The script goes like this: You go to the doctor for a checkup. A little creaking in the knees, some hearing loss. The jolly doctor smiles and says: "At this rate, you're going to live to be 100."

This is not a joke. Scientists predict that if current anti-aging experiments in mice were to work as well in humans, the life span could creep up to 110. Financial planners already advise clients to calculate their economic needs as though they were going to live to 100. You'd hate to run out of money at 95. Or out of meaningful things to do. Or meaningful people to love.

A hundred years ago, there was no My Time. Life expectancy at birth was less than 50. Today it's more than 77 years. Among people over 80, the United States has the highest life-expectancy rate in the world.

But quantity of years is only part of the longevity revolution. The real transformation is in the *quality* of later years. This is the new concept of "health span." While extending life span is about adding calendar years to the end of life, extending health span is about adding quality years in the middle of life. Health span, not life span, is the real bonanza of the aging boom. "We've created ten years of health span. That's huge," says John W. Rowe, the physician who headed the MacArthur Foundation Study of Aging in America.

And the best is yet to be. Researchers are learning how to manipulate the "normal" changes in the aging process and prevent the loss of physical strength and short-term memory. Animal studies suggest ways to increase muscle fiber and regenerate cells in the brain. Social research is beginning to identify emotional, spiritual, and lifestyle factors that extend health span. Doctors, in addition to treating disease, increasingly deal with such basic functions as memory, vision, hearing, reaction speed, immune system, and sexuality.

John Rowe calls this new focus of medicine the "eighth day of creation." An extra ten years of good life on average could become an extra twenty. For some people, it already has. This is a world where 80-year-olds look and function like 60-year-olds. And 60-year-olds come across as 40-year-olds. This biological bonus is redefining what is old—and what is young. In the process, health span is rewriting the script of every aspect of your life, from work and family to politics and sex.

That makes you a biological pioneer. By 2010, there will be eighty-five million Americans between the ages of 50 and 75, nearly one-third of the population. You are part of an historic stampede into the bonus decades.

Yet, the potential of My Time has largely gone unrecognized—by the general public and by older individuals themselves. A pop culture focused on youth remains trapped in obsolete notions of what it means to be "elderly." "We've added muscles—for what? Added brain cells—for what? Added years—for what?" asks Rowe, who became president of Aetna health insurance company in Hartford. "There's a structural lag," he continues. "Society's approach to the elderly has not kept pace with the development of the concept of health span."

You have to figure out how to beat the structural lag by yourself. You are a *Chrono Rad*—a *chronological radical* who is smashing conventional chronology. Rowe points to the famous image of Whistler's Mother—dour-faced, head covered with a lace cap, looking downward, sitting in a chair waiting for death? This traditional poster child of old age was only 67 when her portrait was painted a century or so ago.

Now Granny is out of the rocking chair. She's going to graduate school. She's modeling clothes. She's running for office. She's introducing her grandchildren to hip-hop. She's going to Mexico with a lover and sending e-mail messages back to the kids. . . . And, so is grandpops.

Whatever happened to the grand old stereotypes of growing old?

They're out the window. The longevity revolution has spurred a social revolution. You may not know yet what you're going to do in your bonus years, but you can hum along to the Freddie Mercury hit song from the 1970s: *We Are The Champions . . . And we mean to go on and on and on and on.* Mercury was ahead of his time.

✦

But you don't *just* go on and on. The jolts accumulate. Jolts in love, in work, in body, in spirit. Jolts of loss are messengers of closure, totems of finality. Jolts of joy are tidings of possibility, trinkets of opportunity. You swing between the poles of endings and beginnings.

Sometimes it takes a big jolt to get the process started. You need an outside event to trigger the process of reinvention. The journey of self-exploration is still long and slow. You don't know where you will end up. Or if you will have a good ending. That's what taking risks is all about. When you start to change, you don't know where it will lead.

Harvey L. Rich, 57, looks like a French artist—sparkly brown eyes, a speckled gray beard, the Left Bank black sweater. Indeed, he's learned to speak French. Even his smile has the Gallic mix of wit and irony. And he now lives part of the year in Paris.

This is a long way from the streets of Chicago where he grew up poor—"My parents sold rags," he says—and a childhood with a father who was always afraid—afraid there wouldn't be enough to eat, afraid "they" were going to get him—and a mother who had a zest for life but resented being a woman. And it's a long way from the salons of Washington, D.C., where Dr. Rich is a member of the American Psychoanalytic Association with a model network of successful colleagues and friends. He is still a loving husband and proud father of two sons—but he lives in a new world.

The big jolt occurs when he starts to go blind at age 54. Turns out he has a rare genetic condition that tears the retina. Despite several operations, he loses sight in one eye. The doctors tell him he'll probably lose it in the other one, too. "What am I going to do as a blind man?" he says.

First thing that comes to mind is that he can always touch type. In his training to become a physician, the typing course he took in high school has proven more useful than learning how to tie surgical sutures in medical school. He types up notes on patients, he types papers for publication. He doesn't have to look at the keys. So maybe it won't be so bad, not being able to see. It could be worse. Day after day, he sits at the computer and types out his thoughts—not too difficult for a doctor who explores the boundaries of the soul with his patients. Not difficult at all for a scientist in human development. Only now he is his own guinea pig. He can study himself from inside and out. He constructs the transformation story of My Time as doctor and as patient.

To go forward, he goes back. In college he had dreams of becoming a sculptor. He loved the feel of the clay. But how would he live? Feed a family? He became a doctor but he didn't exactly forget art, either. He's always had a wood-working shop in the garage. Typing out his reveries under the threat of blindness awakens him. This time, his creative drive finds expression—not in clay or wood, but in words.

Everything in his life begins to change. "I found myself getting restless working with patients. Something was happening inside me that was quiet too long." But throw over a lucrative practice to do what—write? Are you crazy? Tap, tap, tap go his fingers on the keyboard, searching for a word, searching for a voice. "I found myself developing skills that made me an artist again," he says. "Suddenly this new persona began to emerge." He keeps typing, keeps dreaming of the future, and comes to an epiphany. "No, I don't want to see patients. I want to write," he explains.

He sets out across the Atlantic to France—the first time he's lived out of the country. "I had to cut ties with my old identity," he says.

The transition process takes several years. One son thinks it's cool. Here's dad dropping out of safe suburban success to become an ex-pat Camus kinda guy in Paris. Me too, dad. The other son is furious—at first. This is not what dads are supposed to do. The boy feels abandoned until he's reassured that his father is not leaving him—he's just leaving his old way of life. His wife gives him space—and grace. Theirs is a close marriage of three decades. "We got engaged three weeks after we met," he recalls. "From the first day, I did not have to take care of her. This is a person with whom I could live." And each of them could explore their individual destinies as they grew closer together.

Still, there is a lot of sorting out to do as he puts his exit plan in place: cutting back his practice, scribbling every day on the computer. Then he takes some big risks. He and his wife sell their house and move to an apartment. He goes to Paris—alone at first. "I was nobody's doctor. I was nobody's husband. No one knew I was a writer."

For Harvey, the long, distinguished period of being the Doctor Fix-It who mends other people's lives is coming to an end. This is going to be Harvey Rich Time.

He gets lucky. Surgeons are able to save some vision in one eye, so he does not go completely blind. And a publisher shows some interest in his writing. He leaves the country to find the solitude he needs to start over. He moves to a new culture, a new language, a new cuisine to emphasize the magnitude of the break with his own past—and the magnitude of his break with tradition. New life after 60?

"It takes courage—the courage to invent yourself anew, the courage to break the old molds and not do what your parents did," he says.

The old mold: Work steadily until a certain age, retire, and die shortly afterward. Or hang on until you drop. There was no My Time. There was no inventing yourself anew, no risk-taking. "You're looking to the future," says Rich. "You're saying to your father's generation: *No, I'm not going to do it your way! It doesn't fit my next lifestyle.* That's like smashing an old piece of furniture that's been handed down in the family for generations."

But that is what My Time is about: smashing old rules of aging to create a new standard of development in late life. "It's absolutely surprising to me," says Rich. "Life was not supposed to be so surprising. This was not on the charts a short time ago." And then he adds: "It's high-anxiety time."

✦

Everywhere you turn you see all this yearning and churning. People moving to North Carolina, taking up pottery, joining a new church, tutoring in schools, doing push-ups, trying to do push-ups, going to the doctor, going to law school, going to visit grandchildren, taking a new job, taking the old job and shoving it, keeping the job, keeping the paycheck, keeping the family together, tending an aged parent, moving back from North Carolina, going to the doctor, *going on and on and on and on.*

These are the outside changes that occur in My Time. The details differ with each individual. Some people seem to change very little. They stay in the same field of work. They live in the same house. Others change almost every aspect of their life—what they do, where they live, who they live with.

More fundamental are the changes that occur inside. Researchers now have a much better understanding of how people change—and how they should change—over the course of a lifetime. In this burgeoning field of human development, social scientists have broken down a person's life into distinct stages—each with its own psychosocial agenda. What's new is the recent attention focused on late adulthood.

From George E. Vaillant, director of the Harvard Study of Adult Development, to Gene D. Cohen, founder of the Washington D.C. Center on Aging, researchers are revising the psychological dynamics of post-midlife development. Instead of slowly sliding downward, most people broaden out during the added years of the health span. Instead of declining, they expand. Instead of withdrawing from life, they push out their personal radius and blossom, opening up their own untapped potential for creativity and relationships.

Building on the stages defined by pioneer social scientist and psychoanalyst Erik Erikson, Vaillant outlines some of the major developmental tasks for adults. The prime stage in middle adulthood is *career consolidation*. You have accomplished the earlier developmental tasks of *identity* and *intimacy*—and now you're focusing on work and family. A career is not just a job but your defining purpose, the core of your being.

There are four criteria in the career consolidation phase: "contentment, compensation, competence, and commitment," writes Vaillant in *Aging Well: Surprising Guideposts to a Happier Life*. "Obviously such a career can be 'wife and mother'—or in more recent times, 'husband and father,'" he adds. For most young men and women these days, career consolidation is usually a combination of both work and family.

By 50 or 60, you have largely completed this task. You have to move on. You get the fever. What kind of life do you envisage at 70 and 80 and 90? What will be the defining purpose of your day? Where will you find *contentment, compensation, competence,* and *commitment?* Chances are you will have another "career" in relationships and in productive work. But what will it entail? To figure it out, you have to let go a little. Instead of "consolidating," you branch out. Instead of narrowing your focus, you widen it.

You move on to a key developmental task of late life called *Generativity,* the task of giving of yourself to others, of giving back to the community. Vaillant describes this time as one of "empathetic leadership," when the need for achievement is replaced by the need for human connection and making a difference. He adds another task in this period: *Keeper of the Meaning.* You become a steward of the culture, the wise storyteller who preserves the moral narrative to guide future generations. Finally there is *Integrity*—getting it all together and finding your spiritual center.

Gene Cohen also divides the path to maturity into phases. As he explains in *The Creative Age: Awakening Human Potential in the Second Half of Life,* there's the Midlife Reevaluation phase when you question what you're doing (roughly 40s and 50s). There's the Liberation phase when you get the freedom and courage to break out of the box of the past (50s and 60s). There's the Late-Life Summing Up phase when you figure it all out (60-plus). And now many people experience the Encore phase when you experience a burst of creativity.

Trouble is, it's hard to know where you are in real time. These tasks and phases are not like stops on a train track where you can buy a ticket and get off in the Liberation phase and then rent a car to drive to *Generativity.* Usually, it's only after you get there that you can follow your journey on a map. While you're living it, you're just making your own way. Still, there's a developmental agenda here and you can't ignore it. Reinventing yourself is about exploring new psychosocial dimensions as you discover what you really want to do in your bonus decades.

◆

Farmers know you can't plow the same field year after year. The jolts keep occurring; your attention shifts, and so does your compass of desire.

"You have an inspiration to give up the things that used to be so pivotal to your emotional and business life," says Constance Messerly Kehoe of Irvington, New York. "You've achieved the things you wanted to do."

At 55, Connie owns a successful company. Her 20-something children are on their own—one is working in the Peace Corps, the other is training to be a counselor. Her husband is a kindred spirit—he works in the company, writes poetry to her, and loves to cook. The business keeps growing—last year Kehoe sold three million dollars' worth of educational materials to schools. "It's my own business. There is no time off," she says.

All in all, she has flourished in the zoom zone of *career consolidation.* "I felt like a pioneer," she says. "The business got very interesting. It was a fun game to see how you could build it up." Back when she was juggling work, children, and her own ambition in the *career consolidation* phase, she says, "If I sold a million dollars' worth of school materials, I'd think—okay, I'm a good sales rep. That's a good achievement."

But now she says: "I showed myself that I could do that. I'm happy to do something else."

Something else. It starts out at a family gathering for Thanksgiving. She is sitting at the dinner table in her cousin's house and staring at the portrait of her great-grandfather, David C. Pursley, who fought in the Civil War. He had lied about his age and joined the Union Army in 1864 at age 16. By the time he was 18, he'd survived the Battle of Wilderness, the Battle of Cold Harbor, and the Siege of Petersburg. He came home to Pennsylvania and prospered in the lumber business. Connie is having turkey and all the trimmings in the large Victorian house he had built for his family. As she stares at his portrait—a successful businessman in his 40s, a stern but not mean face, dark hair, penetrating hazel eyes—she wonders about the teenage boy caught up in war. Why would a kid enlist? The war was going badly—no patriotic glamour in joining up, just the horror of young men dying. He could have stayed home.

The thoughts lead her back to her childhood in South Bend, Indiana. Her mom was a social worker; her father, an aerospace scientist. When Connie graduated from high school in 1965, the civil rights movement was reshaping the political landscape. "That inspired me," she says.

The linkages begin. Civil Rights–Civil War. Slowly this vague interest in the boy-warrior ancestor becomes a passion. Connie gets a history of her great-grandfather's regiment, the 51st Pennsylvania Volunteers, and finds his company. She sees on his enlistment papers that he received a $300 bounty for signing on. Was that it? And a chance to escape small-town Pennsylvania? So much is a mystery. "How did he survive? How much of an issue was slavery to a kid from Pennsylvania?" she wonders.

Instead of clothes, she buys books on the Civil War. Instead of going to the beach on vacation, she goes to week-long seminars on the Civil War.

One day she might turn it all into a book for young adults—the tale of a teenage soldier. Certainly she knows about the book business from running her own company. Certainly as a mother of a son, she knows a lot about the mindset of teenage boys.

But she's not ready to make this project her next career—yet.

Day to day, she's still engaged with her company. She likes going around to schools and selling them educational materials. She needs the *compensation*. The dive in the stock market has postponed any thought of early retirement. "If there wasn't the issue of making money, I could follow this," she says. But in an uncertain economy, she can't stop. Besides, there are people who depend on her. "I'm forced to keep going a few more years," she says.

But all the while, her sights are shifting. She's branching out even as she holds on to her job. She's trying out a new persona—detective historian. And making time for opera and hiking, too. And travel.

She keeps coming back to the mystery of her great-grandfather. "I'm so task-oriented," she says. But the goal is different. "You have a purpose. But there are no stakes. Except that you want to do it well," she says.

Not like purpose in middle adulthood when the stakes are high for making money, raising a family—and meeting other people's standards. With the pursuit of her Civil War ancestor, she is meeting her own standards, fulfilling her own needs. This passion may turn into her next career. Or not. Writing a book on this boy soldier for young adults could be a legacy she would leave to her children—and to future generations of children. Or maybe it's the transitional project to open up possibilities in the bonus decades, like the transitional love affair that sometimes occurs after one relationship and before another.

As Connie works her way through this period of creative uncertainty, she is preparing for *what next?*

✦

Some people can't wait to get to My Time. There's no ambivalence. It's all joy. The transition is usually linked to official retirement. You find it to be a relief, an overdue break from the demands of midlife, an opportunity to be a kid again and hang out and have some fun. You're very happy to leave a job.

When Everett A. Greene, Sr., retired from the D.C. Fire Department, he was glad to put an end to his fire-fighting career. "I thank God I retired from that job without getting killed," he says. He likes the autonomy in his new life, the freedom. "The best part is you don't have to get up in the morning. You get up. But you don't have to. You don't have to punch the clock." He's happy doing things he never had time to do. "I like working in the yard," he says.

But Greene, 63, who's been married for forty-two years and has three grown children, is not doing *nothing*. He has already embarked on another career: public service. He works for various organizations in the community. He belongs to the Masons, and his lodge has an aggressive outreach program. He works at a food bank, giving food away. He helps raise money for scholarships and also mentors elementary school children in a program with Experience Corps, a national organization that provides teachers and mentors in city schools.

In the process, he is closing the circle from where he began to where he finds himself, integrating past and future.

He grew up in poverty in the nation's capital. He proved himself, climbing up the success ladder and out of his past. Helping people— "that has been the focus of my life," he says. It's why he joined the Fire Department and worked there for more than thirty years. It's why he works in the school today. "As a poor boy, I know, if I can save just one body, that would be good." He smiles at the memories. "I think about a lot of things. Somebody had to help me."

Now it's his turn to guide the next generation. That's his new life in My Time.

Each trajectory is different. It's getting there that's important. There's no "right" path. Maybe you don't have to retire, but you want a change. There's nothing really wrong with the status quo. You could keep on doing what you're doing, but you're restless.

There is a deadening of spirit, a chafing of ambition and desire. Successful book editor Herman Gollob describes it this way in his memoir: "A certain wariness had begun to overtake me. In fact, I'd begun to resemble my briefcase: outside, battered and worn; inside, musty and cluttered."

Over the next few years he transforms himself from hyper-hot editor to passionate Shakespeare professor. First, he cast off from the New York glitzy-lit scene that had served him so well for thirty-five years.

That stage of *career consolidation* had run aground. "For some time the fun had gone out of publishing. My competitive fires were banked," he writes in *Me and Shakespeare*. "My career was no longer an adventure," he continues, "but a recurring cycle of the predictable and familiar."

At 65 he quit the publishing world and fell in love with Shakespeare. He went to all the plays and traveled to England. Ultimately Shakespeare led him to a new life. The former editor now teaches students about the life and works of the great bard in English literature. "At the age of sixty-seven, I was embarking on what might turn out to be a new career, a reinvention of myself," he writes.

There can be exhilaration in getting to the bonus decades. You have a sense of power. My Timers are Gray Turks—like Young Turks who want to shake up the world, except that their hair is gray (or newly blond). Their boldness is rooted in experience. They take risks because what have they got to lose? So they start a company, make jewelry, build a school, raise grandchildren, fall in love, change a community, influence the course of history. "There is this new freedom to do the right thing. "It's the *if not now, when?* phenomenon," says researcher Gene Cohen. "It allows people to step out of the box and do sometime very different."

My Timers sit in high places: In the initial cabinet of President George Bush, most of the members were over 60 with successful careers behind them.

They're not keeping an eye out for the next assignment. That gives them freedom to do what they really want to do, what they really believe in. (You might not agree with their politics, but you can see their clarity of purpose.) It's not partisan. Look at Vermont Senator Jim Jeffords who left the Republican Party at age 67 because he could no longer follow its direction. *What does he have to lose?*

It's not about gender. Look at Bonnie Raitt at 52 who put it this way in a news interview after a successful tour: "I feel funnier and sexier. I'm playing guitar better. It's like I finally know what I'm doing. I don't mean to boast, but I feel like I'm on top of my game." Look at Hillary Clinton—a new career as a U.S. senator and *what next?* Running for president in 2008 at age 61?

On top of my game. At a certain age, you get survivors' confidence. After all, you've piled up a lifetime quota of slings and arrows. You know a thing or two about starting over. You're no stranger to change.

And you're life-smart. At 64, New York psychotherapist and author Myrna Lewis is in prime My Time. She has an activist partnership with her like-minded husband Robert N. Butler, who heads the International Longevity Center. As part of the counseling team at Ground Zero in Manhattan, Myrna helped people recover from the 9/11 terror attacks—the most exhaustive and meaningful work she has ever done, she says.

She didn't earn her Ph.D. until she was 62. Never too late and just in time. Myrna is part of the education boom for people in the bonus decades. And she's being very practical in preparation for *what next?* As Myrna explains: "A Ph.D. would help against the natural discrimination that occurs when you think of a 60-year-old woman."

Or a 60-year-old man. Or an 80-year-old man, a 90-year-old woman. *Jolt!*

Getting to My Time is the hard part. Once there, you have every chance to flourish. You're not just reinventing a new stage of life for yourself—you're also helping to shape the culture and overturn obsolete barriers against making the most of these bonus decades. You get used to the drumbeat of anxiety.

2

Breaking Away

*Man cannot discover new oceans unless he
has the courage to lose sight of the shore.*

ANDRÉ GIDE

"IT NEEDS A NAME," says epidemiologist Lisa Berkman of the
Harvard School of Public Health. "We need a name that con-
notes the dynamics of adolescence for 50- to 75-year-olds."

It's Second Adolescence. This is the mercurial transition period between middle and old age. As in "He's going through Second Adolescence" as a way to explain mood swings, shifts in work, relationship
changes. You can almost hear adult children rolling their eyes and saying: *Everything was fine until my parents hit Second Adolescence!*

A primary task in this period is to break away from middle adulthood
and turn to the future. Just as adolescence describes the child in transition, Second Adolescence chronicles the adult in transition. The par-
allels are obvious: significant body changes, significant psychological/
attitude changes, significant external changes in work and relationships. Like a teenager, you can switch from manic energy to listless despair. You may change where you live—leaving home and moving to a re-

tirement community or jumping in the RV the way kids go away to college or take off for San Francisco. You become preoccupied with your body—that wayward or absent hair, that achy heart, that wrinkle. You seem more self-absorbed and spend more time wondering about the meaning of life.

There are obvious differences, too. You're not going to dye your hair green and suddenly follow the Grateful Dead; and you're a lot wiser and more stable than a teenager. But you may dye your hair and follow an Elderhostel tour in Mexico. Just as kids leave their childhood behind and proceed to "starter" adulthood, you are leaving that long stretch of middle adulthood behind and proceeding to My Time.

Many teenagers sail through adolescence with little difficulty. The same is true in Second Adolescence. You may not experience a lot of turmoil. But all the while, you're undergoing internal and external changes that signal normal passages in human development.

Sociologist Phyllis Moen refers to this emerging new life stage for people in their 50s, 60s, and 70s as *midcourse.* "As in adolescence," she writes in the *Handbook of the Life Course,* "people in the midcourse years are thinking about and enacting role shifts that are both products of their past, and precursors of their future, life course."

The temptation is to deny, deny, deny. Between Botox and cardio kick-boxing, you can hold on to your physical exterior for a long time—and enjoy it. But a transition is taking place within. That can't be avoided with a chemical peel or a knee replacement. It churns slowly in the unconscious. The first step is awareness.

"I see it in my dreams," says Washington psychiatrist Lisa Van Susteren, 52. "There are signs of decay." Just a flicker of a thought, triggered by a smell or a painting that becomes an image in a dream. In one scene, she is coming up through the water from the bottom of a river. The water is clear. But on her body are leaves and mud. Clear water, encrusted body. Not a bad dream, she says. But the image of dead, fallen leaves herald the end of her long hot summer of middle age. It is a dying process, the first phase of Mother Nature's annual ritual of winter-spring, death-rebirth. Recognizing that one part of life is coming to an end is also the first phase in personal regeneration.

Lisa, who grew up in Wisconsin, has a pretty chiseled face from her Dutch-Irish background. She is expanding her practice as a therapist. She is married to a high-powered real-estate executive. The oldest of their three children is 15. She and her husband are still in Vaillant's phase of *career consolidation*—still focused on raising their children, fleshing out their résumés and cementing their place in the community. In this dream image, the water is clear in the mainstream pool of adulthood where she swims. But a transition has quietly begun. "I feel it. I know it's coming," she says.

In Second Adolescence, like first adolescence, endings are also beginnings. But unlike first adolescence, there's no cultural timetable for making the transition, no standard that says you're 14 so you should be in the ninth grade. You set your own schedule—or it's set for you by circumstance. The main thing is to get started.

✦

Once you get into your 50s, you can't escape it. You're hit with physical changes the way kids suddenly shoot up in height and start puberty. Women go through menopause. Men go through their own kind of menopause; the technical term is andropause. You can't ignore the medical landmarks: regular mammograms, regular PSA tests. "By the mid-fifties, everybody has got something—some health problem," says Berkman, who worked on the MacArthur Foundation Aging Project. "It may not interfere with function in any way, but it has to be managed."

Physical changes echo emotional changes. "Teenagers struggle with how to be your own person and how to stay connected. That's very much the task of people in their 60s," says psychologist Philip A. Cowan at the University of California, Berkeley.

But unlike the teenager stereotype, you may get nicer. You learn some things when you can't read the menu anymore without glasses, when your knee aches as you climb upstairs. "Humility and kindness?" suggests Berkman with a smile. In research by Harvard's George Vaillant, people who age well become more grateful rather than envious, more generous rather than competitive.

Your role in the outside world changes, too. Just as adolescents face college entrance exams and first-job hurdles, you also get tested in the workplace. It used to be you had to make it in a career by age 40. That has slipped a decade. Now you have to have made a place for yourself by age 50. Then the pyramid narrows. Unfair, but it narrows. "A few become chiefs. The rest aren't even Indians any more. They get run off the reservation," says Berkman.

Meanwhile, you may hit some turbulence in your personal life. Marriages get stressed as the focus shifts from the nuclear family to a wider and more diverse circle of people you care about. It's not such a paired world and being single is more the norm, especially for women. In this socially fluid period, friendship and romance flourish. Fortunately at 60 you are much better at pursuing relationships and making the most of these opportunities than you were at 16.

It all adds up to a very dynamic period in your life. Moen, who directed the Cornell Employment and Family Careers Institute and is now at the University of Minnesota, lays out the changes. Second adolescence, she writes in the *Handbook*, is when people "begin to think about, plan for, and actually disengage from their primary career occupations and the raising of children; launch second or third careers; develop new identities and new ways to be productively engaged; establish new patterns of relating to spouses, children, siblings, parents, friends; leave some existing relationships and begin new ones."

Are you ready for all this?

The changes you are likely to face in this period are overwhelming. It's also a time of urgency. "That's what we have and adolescents lack," says Berkman. "Young people can't see their way to the future. We know what the future holds. Postponement is not a viable option."

Gro Harlem Brundtland, former prime minister of Norway and di-
rector-general of the World Health Organization, shocked her colleagues when she announced that she would not seek a second term as
head of the international body based in Geneva. At 64, wasn't she lucky
to have another chance to hold on to the brass ring? Wasn't she lucky
not to be pushed out? It's not that she didn't like her job. She did. But
she felt she had accomplished most of what she'd set out to do. More
important, she looked ahead, calculated the time she thought she had
left, and decided she wanted to do something else.

"I want to go back and be part of my grandchildren's lives," she says.
Five years is a lifetime for a child. If she went out for another five-year
term at WHO, she'd miss out on her grandchildren—she wouldn't get
to know them before they grew up. A pioneer woman in medicine and
politics, she has filled her adulthood with public achievement, all the
while receiving support from her family. Now it is time for her to make
family the priority. "I need to be home," she says.

Postponement is not an option.

✦

How do you know when it's time to make the break? Most men and
women go through a slushy DMZ period with one foot in the past, one
foot in the future. You venture out. You get pushed out. You hang back.
All the while the drumbeat of restlessness gets louder.

Some people are initiators in this transition. That's one way to get to
My Time. You want to make a clean break and go out in a blaze of glory.
That's your style. You plan, you execute, you go! This doesn't solve the
problem of *what next?* That question comes later. For the moment, all
your attention is focused on making the break. You cut loose with a bang.

Pat Mattingly of Dallas is an initiator. A soft-spoken woman with a
warm smile, she looks like a schoolteacher. She is a schoolteacher. If
you were 5 years old, she is the kind of person you'd feel safe with.

And you would be safe. There's a rock-solid *trustworthiness* about Pat. She is all Texas—grew up in Texas and never left. "I'm a long-time educator," she says demurely. For twenty-six years, she was the head-mistress of a private elementary day school. She devoted her life to making the school a success and tending to the needs of everyone involved. She's a pleaser. *The good girl.* "Compliant," she says with a playful smile. A nice, pleasing woman, you'd think.

You'd be wrong. Indeed, Pat is nice. She is pleasing. But she's also a rule-breaker. Beneath the outward persona of establishment good girl is a determined Texas rebel—the "outsider" who is "going to show 'em." As a woman in a male-dominated state. As a woman in a male-dominated field of independent private schools. As a Texan in a field dominated by the East Coast. She showed 'em.

"It was a total job," says Pat, 66, who never married. "Along the way I found out I did know how to run the ship better than I thought. The emphasis was on the child. I wanted to make the school outstanding. I was a lone woman with the old boys."

She was on the board of directors of the National Association of Independent Schools. "At that point I was representing women, the Southwest and early childhood," she says. Most of the others were men who ran secondary schools in the Northeast. "I had a very exciting time. I loved it. My network expanded. My skills expanded. I learned a lot. I was not just running a school. I was a leader in education."

The U.S. Department of Education awarded her school a blue ribbon for excellence. "That said to me—Okay, we've been validated. Something is going right. I must have accomplished something!"

Pat smiles. Demurely. With the single-minded focus that she applied to her career, she examined the future. She wanted to master it the way she had mastered the past. She looked around at her colleagues—so much upheaval in the world of private schools. Most heads don't last ten years. She was getting close to thirty. "I said to myself: I don't want to do this forever. I started winding down." She saw the people who can't leave—who hang around, jeopardizing the chances of the new head and destroying themselves as they sink deeper into has-been land and depression. "I wanted to get out while the getting was good. We were on top," she says. "I went about it methodically."

She planned her retirement over several years. By the time it happened, she and the school were ready. "I went out in a blaze of glory."

And she was determined not to look back. She marked the calendar for the next school year. Whenever there were major school events, "I planned trips to be away during those times . . . to change the routine," she says. Even driving around Dallas, she would avoid taking the route that led to the school. "I never went down the same road I had driven all those years," she says. She hasn't set foot in the school for two years. "It doesn't mean that I didn't care," she says. It's something of a surprise that she could devote so much of her life to the school and, now, "it doesn't matter to me."

A complete break.

Now, what? *Jolt!*

Making the break on the external level is only part of the transition. There's also the internal transition, which is usually slower and less controllable. And there's the unanswered question of the future. What are you going to do?

"The first week I thought: I'm going to be depressed. I'm going to be bored now that it's happened," she says. "The first three days, I slept late, I moped around. I didn't get dressed. I was reading. After three days, that was enough." She says, "Well, so much for this. I've got to get up and get moving."

And so she does. She travels. She goes to the opera. She joins a fitness center—she has no major health problems. People come up and ask: *What's happened to you? You look so much better!* Then she wonders: *What did I look like before?*

She does some reckoning: "I know I was sleep deprived. I never let go. I was under considerable stress that I would acknowledge only occasionally. This was a weight on me. I felt responsible for so many people. I was keeping everybody happy. The board of trustees. The parents. The teachers. The students. All of it was stressful. I took it more seriously that I needed to."

Now she's lighter. She's seeing more of her friends. She works on the opera guild. She travels to Russia. She has a romance. "I'm looking for hundreds of things to do. It's like I'm making up for lost time," she says. "I don't want to miss something."

Pat is playing. She's enjoying this rush of freedom. She also has a sense of urgency. "I'm afraid—if I don't do something I always wanted to do, I might not be able to do it. Healthwise. You know: I'm finally at the Taj Mahal and not able to walk up the steps!"

Pat has plunged into Second Adolescence. She's broken away from the past—externally with her decision never to go back to the school. And now she is breaking away internally. She is putting the past into perspective and turning to the future. Like a college freshman who has lots of interests but hasn't settled on a major, she's trying out different scenarios. Meanwhile she's having a lot of fun.

◆

When Queen Elizabeth I ruled England, there was no adolescence. Until 1900, life was too short. You went from childhood right to adulthood without any extended maturation process in between. You didn't even have much of a youth either, with high death rates in infancy and childhood. If you survived, you went to work as soon as you could be useful. Child labor was the norm. So was teenage motherhood. Children were perceived—if they were perceived at all—as little adults.

The concept of adolescence is recent. The term didn't come into the culture until 1904, when American educator G. Stanley Hall published *Adolescence*, a scholarly tome describing the teenage years as a separate and stormy phase in development. By then, life expectancy had increased to about 50. Adolescence, as a transition phase, emerged only as people lived long enough to stretch out the life cycle and allow some time to grow between childhood and adulthood.

A similar evolution is taking place today. With longevity, the life cycle is stretched out even further. More stages have been added to the psychological course in personal development. The result is My Time.

As psychologist Philip Cowan says: "It is a new stage in the life cycle." Cowan and his wife, psychologist Carolyn Pape Cowan, have studied how families and couples respond to change throughout the life span. Now in their 60s, they are personally going through this new period, which is like adolescence. "It is a transition," says Philip Cowan. "It's an opening up. In my parents' generation, it was a closing down."

Second Adolescence shares two important features with the teenage years. The first is *Empowerment*. For teenagers, this is physical empowerment. They are suddenly as big and strong as their parents. For people at 50 and 60, it is *life empowerment,* "which comes from wisdom and experience rather than hormones and physical growth," explains psychoanalyst Harvey Rich, who switched careers in Second Adolescence.

The second common feature is *Dreaming,* he continues. This is the opportunity to try out different destinies—what psychiatrists call "omnipotential." One day a teenager wants to be an astronaut, the next day a spy. One day a girl may want to have a baby, the next, play the guitar, and what she may actually do is stay in bed until noon. In school, teenagers are exposed to a smorgasbord of subjects from DNA to Chaucer. The sign of getting out of adolescence is when young people settle on what they want to do. They major in biology and that leads to a job in a drug company.

In Second Adolescence, you need to dream again. You need to open up and experiment with different scenarios the way you did as a teenager. One day you take piano lessons, the next day you visit Civil War battlefields. Another day you sign up to study the classics, or baby-sit the grandchildren, or volunteer for your local hospice. Or just sit in the garden. You don't know which scenario will become your next "career." You don't care. It's nice just to hang out for a while. School's out, midlife is done. Get in the RV and go.

The sign that you're getting out of Second Adolescence is when you settle down and figure out your priorities for the bonus decades. Life empowerment gives you the strength to break away and the talents to build anew. Dreaming wakes you up to a future and shakes you out of the rut of middle age. You need both in order to get a life in My Time.

✦

Sometimes you can't move forward. You're stuck. Nothing seems to work out.

The Garden of Eden scenario is familiar in love. You try to repeat the ecstasy of perfect parent-child love in present relationships. Fantasy and reality clash. You are inevitably disappointed. The Garden of Eden story carries a stern warning in both love and work: You can't get back in. The entrance is guarded by angels with flaming swords.

Some people concoct a Garden of Eden scenario of the past, a freeze-frame memory that retains only moments of glory: Captain on the police force. First-grade Teacher of the Year. Foreign service officer when Saigon fell. Helpful wife of the rising star at the bank (he's been dead for ten years). Engineer in Mission Control on Apollo 13. You can get trapped in the high point of the past.

But there is life after the high point. Jimmy Carter is the poster child of regeneration. He achieved the ultimate public high point— the presidency. And then the ultimate public low point when he lost the election. It took a long time for Jimmy and his wife Rosalynn to mourn their moment in the White House. They chronicle those years in their memoir, *Everything to Gain:* "It was deeply discouraging for me to contemplate the unpredictable years ahead," writes Jimmy. They were facing what many people in their 50s face: "the involuntary end of a career and an uncertain future, the realization that 'retirement' age is approaching; the return to home without the children we had raised there, new family relationships, for which there had been no preparation." And there was no place to hide to nurse their wounds. As Jimmy continues: "All this was exacerbated by the embarrassment about what was to us an incomprehensible political defeat and also by some serious financial problems that we had been reluctant to face."

But they did move forward, creating The Carter Center in Atlanta. "It had taken a long time. We had to work our way through various stages—self-pity, anger, discouragement, anxiety," writes Rosalynn. Finally they came to "the exciting discovery that our lives do not need to be limited by past experiences," she continues. Quite the opposite. In their bonus decades, they have had an enormous impact on international politics, health, and social change. And on to another high point: Jimmy's acceptance of the Nobel Peace Prize in 2002.

Give yourself plenty of time. The transition isn't just rationally made. You have to do it emotionally and through new experience. In this way, you transform your high points into the muscle of life empowerment— and then you can go on to other high points.

The process may take years. People have their own rhythm. There's no rushing it.

C. Boyden Gray, 60, the craggy-faced wunderkind lawyer of the Reagan-Bush years, knows what he wants to do in My Time: "To be engaged in making a contribution," he says. But he doesn't know what shape that contribution will take. He's casting about, drifting, searching. He's ready to make the leap—if the right thing comes up. That's his style—to let the big chance come his way, and it usually has.

For twelve years Boyden served George Bush senior—eight years in the vice presidency, four years in the presidency. He knew he was making a difference, but it was something more—a real friendship with the Bush family.

He remembers going to the Christmas party at the White House. At the time, his marriage was breaking up and he sought out the First Lady. *"Barbara,"* he said. *"I have some bad news."* She turned to him and clutched his arm. *"You're not going to leave George, are you?"*

"Oh no," he said. *"I'm leaving [my wife]."*

"Oh okay," said Barbara, much relieved. They were that close—a special bond with George and Barbara, beyond just working together, apart from grabbing the brass ring of history together.

"I've had the best," he says. "You couldn't duplicate that." So many great moments. The familiar cackling voice of the president on the telephone telling him: *Not bad, old boy!* All the things he did. Laying down the framework for deregulation. Protecting his boss against the fallout from the Iran-Contra scandal that had tarnished the Reagan administration. The time he let a newspaper have a critical arms-for-hostages memo from the Reagan years, neutralizing the issue in the presidential campaign. *Not bad, old boy!*

Things like that.

He's been putting things like that in the memory box. Several years ago, he wrote an account of Iran-Contra that he titled "The Death of an Avocado Salesman" because one of the characters was an Israeli spy posing as an avocado salesman in Mexico. (He couldn't get it published.) But stories like that are the coin of the political realm in Washington circles. Boyden will always have a role as raconteur of behind-the-scenes history.

It's just that for him; the past is now past. "It was central to my life for a time," he says. "I don't think it is anymore."

For the last decade, Boyden has been back at the law firm. He keeps testing the waters. Education? Politics again? What's the right thing? He doesn't know. "I still don't know what I want to do when I grow up," he jokes. To be sure, he's trying out different scenarios. He taught a course at Georgetown University on the media and politics. That was good. "The students get it," he says. "They see the bias in the press," he adds, and then he grins.

Slowly he shifts to the future. He might go back into the government again, but he's not salivating. He knows he's got another decade or so to make a difference—and he has to figure out what that will be pretty quick. He makes a joke of it. If he doesn't find a way to make a contribution very soon, that would mean he's flunked Second Adolescence, he quips. And he's never flunked anything. Magna cum laude from Harvard University, Law Review at the University of North Carolina Law School, Supreme Court Clerkship for Chief Justice Earl Warren, special counsel to the senior George Bush.

"A lot of it is plain dumb luck," he says. "I've had a lot of good luck—a lot of opportunities came my way. I don't think I blew them, so maybe I'll be lucky enough for them to come again."

At 60, he's healthy, energetic, plugged in. His priority is his daughter. He has to see her safely into college. He's remained a bachelor. There's been love, and love lost. What's the old saying—lucky at cards, unlucky in love? He grins. Humor is key, he says. He can always find a parking place, but not the right woman. He laughs again.

There's a future out there. He's going to find it. You can't just retire and do nothing. "You'd die," he says. "The boredom!"

Boyden is cautious. He wants the right thing—in work and in love. Boredom is not an option.

✦

What do you do if you feel stuck? You're losing momentum. You can't translate the unformed dream in your head into some shape in reality. It's as though you have a kind of Writer's Block in life. The poet William Stafford had a famous piece of advice for young writers: *Lower your standards*. Writing is a process, not a product. So is your life.

You have to examine what is holding you back. An image of yourself in the past? You don't have to work in the White House to have a high point. Think back to your *a-ha, this is it* periods—in love and work. Was it when you joined the Peace Corps and lived in Morocco? You remember the one-room school where you taught, the pink walls of Marrakech, the Humphrey Bogart jokes about Casablanca.

Or was it the last big job? You headed the department that changed the formula, improved the bottom line, raised the standard, reduced the crime rate. . . . Or is it your current job—or relationship—because that is where you get your status and identity as a person?

A lot depends on the rumble of anxiety in your chest. How much is the status quo taking out of you?

Sometimes it's a blessing in disguise when a high point goes sour on you. That makes it easier to make the break.

Bernard Tresnowski is the kind of guy who listens to tapes of Great Minds—St. Augustine and the like—when he's working out on the treadmill. "When you get older, you contemplate your own mortality," says Barney, 69. "Death is a huge barrier to satisfying your curiosity," he quips. Barney has always been curious: Ever since he was growing up in the steel-mill town of Gary, Indiana, where his dad was a policeman, his mom a secretary, and he got a football scholarship to the University of Michigan. Ever since he retired from Blue Cross–Blue Shield Association (BCBS) and went to law school at age 62. "You look ahead. One of these days, it's going to be all over with. I've got so much curiosity. That drives you. That drives you to listen to tapes to exercise," he says.

Curious, determined, driven. In between Gary and law school, he rose through the ranks of BCBS and hit the high point when he became president of the association. Then came the low point when the giant not-for-profit health insurer was shattered with scandal. There was Barney in front of the television cameras, answering to charges of corruption from a U.S. Senate investigating committee. "It caught us all up short in terms of our failings. It uncovered things that were very troublesome—that I didn't know about," he says. "The media was on my back. I said: *We made a lot of mistakes. We're going to fix it all.*" The criticism hurt the rank and file. "A lot of people felt it was unfair. Because of a few bad apples, why should we all suffer?" He pauses and answers his own question. "That's the story of life," he says.

No formal charges were brought against the association, but the do-good public-service image of the health care organization was badly shaken. And so was Barney.

He decided to retire. He had been CEO for thirteen years. "I burned out. The last three years of the Senate investigation—it drained me so badly. I lost all my energy, my drive." He says. "It was time to go. I wanted to do something else."

He was lucky that he could retire with a comfortable pension. Some people are caught in the burnout bind. You know it's time to go, but you can't afford to leave the job—or a burned-out marriage. You don't see what you could go *to*. You can't envision a future.

Barney held on to his curious self that loved to learn and saw a future in going back to school. As he says: "Law school was refreshing. It was a catharsis. When I finished, I said to myself: *I'm still learning.*"

Now he works for free at the Legal Assistance Foundation of Metropolitan Chicago. He wants to help people. "The bonus years—it's a time to give back. I'm not uncomfortable. I've got a nice pension. Why not give some of it back?"

He remembers a client who came to him to get a divorce. She was charged with shooting her husband and *his* girlfriend—not fatally. "She didn't intend to kill him. She intended to scare him," he says. "I got her a divorce. I got her sole custody. I got her maintenance. I got her child support. She's out of a bad situation. That's the way we help."

His client looked him in the eye, tears rolling down her cheek, and said: *I just want to thank you so much.* "That was such a sense of satisfaction. I helped a human being in a terrible situation," Barney says. "We don't get paid. We get thanks."

Helping people—that's why he got into the health-care field in the first place. That's why he's doing pro-bono law today. Just because you break away from the past doesn't mean you don't hold on to your life themes. Learning and helping are constants for Barney—but with important differences.

When Barney travels and he comes back to the hotel room, "the red light isn't flashing. Nobody is pounding on me," he says. Back then, "everybody was after me, nipping at my heels. You're constantly on the move. You can only do that so long. Then you burn out."

Now this husband and father of seven and grandfather of ten is having a ball. "I'm a better person now. I'm more relaxed. When I was stressed, I was probably impatient and less considerate of other human beings," he says. At the law office, he has time to make friends and get to know his clients. Everybody else is stressed. "I'm sitting there thinking—Gee, this is fun."

◆

You soon find out that a high point in the past is not the "last act." You have a future. An important element in first and Second Adolescence is the sense of possibility. Teenagers have always looked ahead. For those over 50, this attitude is relatively new. It is also the key to making the most of the bonus years.

To be sure, your vision of tomorrow is different. For teenagers, the future is distant, something to aim for like the North Star. In My Time, you look for potential in the daisy by your doorstep. The main point is that you glimpse a future.

Mary Woolley, 55, gets such a glimpse quite unexpectedly when she is asked to bring in her old Girl Scout memorabilia for an office party. The party has an outdoors theme, and Girl Scouts go camping, right? *Do you still have your Girl Scout stuff? We could use it in the decorations,* says a colleague.

That leads Mary to a chest of drawers in a spare bedroom. She pulls out a box in the back of the drawer and opens it. There are her Girl Scout pins—and also her grandmother's jewelry—not real jewelry, decorative pieces. As she pulls out the necklaces and bracelets, she is struck by an overwhelming thought: "When my grandmother was 55, she was an old woman," says Mary. "She wore old-lady black shoes. She had false teeth. Her hair was gray."

Mary is the same age as her grandmother. Her hair is auburn; she wears a designer suit and carries a brown alligator power briefcase. She is wife and working woman. Her four children are grown; one is married. As president of Research!America in Washington, she is a rainmaker in medical science. During her twelve-year tenure, the organization's membership has tripled.

She looks over her grandmother's jewelry and is startled by the difference in their lives. After her grandfather lost his job at the Elgin Watch factory in Illinois, her grandparents moved to the country. Her grandmother, who had once played the piano in a music store so customers could decide if they wanted to buy the sheet music, missed the city. "They were old for a long time," she says.

Her mother was in between—not as confined as her grandmother, but not free the way Mary herself is. Awakened by the war, her mother served in the WACs, went overseas, and got married. And then *oops*. The war was over. Women went back into the kitchen. How did women deal with going off and fighting the war and then coming home and making dinner? "They became alcoholics. That's what my mother told me, " says Mary. In the days of manhattans and martinis, her mother missed out on midlife as well as the bonus years.

Mary sees in the jewelry the potential she's been given by history. She has a sense of possibility that her grandmother and mother never had at this age.

The Girl Scout pins also remind Mary of who she was. The smart one. She was a troop leader. She had gone to national Girl Scout conferences. She remembers in school when she got the highest score in math on a national test, and the teacher said it must have been a mistake because no girl could score that well in math. "I accepted it," she says with a smile. "That was the way it was."

Now she doesn't accept the way things were. Not in her work, not in her personal life. She has rejected the old rules that constricted her mother and grandmother. That's what she thinks as she puts the jewelry back in the box.

In breaking away from the past, you also go back to it. With all this mulling over the past, Mary feels the rumble in her chest. She's aware of a new restlessness. Is she ready for a change? She doesn't know what. She's getting impatient. She'd like to have grandchildren. And, if she goes on to do something else, she wants it to be something big. She has a future in mind. And she knows she has at least thirty more years of vitality to go.

Mary is thinking—New stage. Not old age.

3

Transforming Loss

In the depths of winter I finally learned that
within me there lay an invincible summer.

ALBERT CAMUS

M Y FRIEND AND I SIT in the garden on a long sweltering August night and divide the world into "drifters" and "doers." The
drifters are those who follow the predictable track and don't experience
major difficulties along the way. The doers are those who are tested by
catastrophic loss and forced into action. "You have to act fast. You don't
know how to do it. There is no road map. You're just forced into it.
Some rise to it and some sink," she says. "Nothing frightens me now. I
see people who are afraid. I say to them: you can deal with it."

This woman is riding high in My Time. At 64, she has come into her
beauty—a combination of regal true-blue, whimsy, and good bone
structure. She is a professional photographer, with several books on her
résumé and a heavy schedule of lectures and exhibits. Her daughters
are established; one is married, the other is engaged. "I feel free," she
says. "You have to prepare to enjoy this time in life. The fact that my

life is good now—that I'm enjoying it—I'm sort of stunned. And I don't even feel guilty. I'm actually enjoying my life. The truth is I am."

Is suffering the kiln of creativity, she wonders? Is it through the transcendent process of grief that consciousness is deepened and the capacity for renewal is forged? If not tested, do you drift along and miss out on this bonus period? "This is all about resurrection, right?" But first something has to die. How can you regenerate if you don't have to—if you can still hold on to everything you had? She leans back in the wrought-iron chair. The citronella candles are flickering, a half-moon has risen above the trees. The challenge, she says, is to transmute pain into art, to take unhappiness and transform it into the art of photography, the art of loving—her family, her friends, the art of living—tending to her needs and laughing again. But first comes the pain. Then, out of suffering's ashes come the freedom and energy to be a doer, not a drifter.

If she's learned one thing, it is this: "Urgency is huge and the sense of the shortness of time you have," she says. "You need to make the best of these wonderful years. Anything you really want to do—now's the time to do it. Do it now! Not next year. Now. Stop everything. Do it now."

Alexandra Korff Scott has an important message for those on the cusp of My Time. For the long stretch of middle adulthood, she has been a woman of quiet privilege and contentment. A successful husband at the World Bank. Three healthy children who do well in school. A Christmas card list of several hundred names.

And then, sorrow shatters the quiet.

It begins ten years ago in a hotel restaurant in upstate New York. Sandy's with her husband and college-bound younger daughter who has been looking at universities. Her older daughter has just left to drive to Long Island. Her son is on a fishing trip in Alaska with his best friend from college. The announcement comes over the loud speaker: *"There's an emergency call for Mr. or Mrs. Scott."* She goes to the front desk to take the call from her sister: *"I have bad news. The state troopers are here.*" She thinks, oh God, her daughter's had an accident. No, her sister is saying that her son's been involved in a plane crash. Whew, goes her mind in slow motion. It's not her daughter. A plane crash? Her mind stalls. The glad, handsome son who's just graduated from Princeton University. He'll have a great time telling his friends about that, she quips to herself. No, the voice on the phone is saying something else: Her son has been killed. Killed. Killed. Killedkilledkilled.

She remembers handing the phone to her husband. She remembers telling the maitre d' that they were not going to finish dinner, they were going upstairs to their room, to put the charges on the room bill. She remembers the three of them, stunned, crying, holding on to each other in the hotel room. Killed. Everyone in the small plane that crashed into the side of a mountain in Alaska, killed. Beloved son and brother—killed.

"We were all crying. I stopped and said: 'Listen. We are not going to let this destroy us.' I felt a determination that we as a family would survive this. We would not allow it to destroy us. I imagined myself trying to drive a small boat through rocky water. I felt I was captain of the boat. I could see myself going up and down in the boat. I was determined to get to safety. That's the way I remember dealing with it."

Five years go by. Sandy Scott's husband is in the intensive care unit at Memorial Sloan Kettering hospital in New York. He has lung cancer. The doctors say he can beat it. Two surgeries. At 7:30 in the morning the phone rings in the apartment where she is staying. *"Uh, Mrs. Scott,"* the male voice says. *"You know how your husband had difficulty breathing?"* Well, yea, she thinks. He has difficulty breathing. That's why he's in the hospital. Why is this guy telling me this? "He had a problem with the breathing last night," continues the voice of the physician who was on duty, "and he expired."

Expired? What's that? Her mind stalls. All the medical terms she'd had to learn in the last few months. Expired? *Expired.* "You mean he's dead?"

"Yes. He expired," says the voice. Expiredexpired. Killedkilled. Killed-expired.

"No one thought he was going to die," she says. "No one suggested this might be a possibility."

The same combination of numbing and competence takes over as she reels from the double shocks of loss. "It happened in a second. Somebody just drew a shade down in my life. My life, which was light-bright, went dark. I didn't think it would ever come up again," she says. "This is the house of death. I felt, omigod, I'm losing the whole thing. I'm losing the whole family that had been so incredibly happy."

As she lies awake in bed, she can still hear, burned into her brain, the tick-tock of the clock in the hotel room in upstate New York the night when sorrow invaded her family and thrust her into the roiling dark space of grief. "I have to. I don't know how. I have to find the way. There's no other choice. You can't let the boat sink," she says.

You rise to it, she says. You grieve and you grow. It's your own September 11, she says—a clear, unambiguous tragedy that is not supposed to happen. Parents don't lose their children in this era of longevity—after all, 98 percent of children in the United States reach their 25th birthday. Losing her son is the unexpected life-crushing assault. Yet, like 9/11, there is another truth in loss, she says. Tragedy is also galvanizing for survivors who are taken out of the ordinary dullness of their daily lives. Suddenly you have the opportunity to be heroic like the firefighters at Ground Zero. Crisis brings out hidden strengths, latent gallantry, and generosity. Catastrophe is the closing-off of dreams, she says; yet it can be liberating for those who must carry on.

"The time my son died was a nightmare for me. But at the same time, as I look back, I see that I gained a lot of strength and self-confidence from the feeling that I was the captain of the boat and fully in charge of the seemingly impossible task of dealing with our grief and trying to hold us all together as a family. Our boat rocked a lot. But it held," she says.

"When my husband's illness and death came on top of that, it seemed unbearable. The fact I survived all that makes these bonus years an even greater bonus. Those who have suffered and are the stronger for it really appreciate the bonus years."

Confronting loss defines her transition from midlife to My Time. At first, she says, you are consumed in pain, absorbed by the darkness of tragedy. All you do is think about the one you lost, talk about the one you lost. A few months after her son's death, she was having lunch with a close friend who finally said: "Would you mind if we talked about me?" That stopped her. Of course not. For the rest of the lunch they talked about the breakdown of her friend's marriage. For two hours, Sandy listened to someone else's pain. She finds that she is a good listener. Where before she was immune to the private drama of others, now she is attuned to their psychic pulse. She has empathy in her bones and becomes a grief counselor. "When you've been through something very difficult, it enables you to help other people. I do it naturally with people who have lost a child or a spouse. You're able to help them. You have the authority of experience. You don't know what to say unless you've been there. I'm in a much better position to help other people," she says.

It's an old cliché, she says. Before loss, everything is in black and white. After loss, everything is in color. Your senses regenerate and become more powerful—this is the unconscious part of the grieving process. You see and hear and smell and touch differently—with more vigor, more sensitivity, more compassion. "If you are a creative person, when you pass through the grieving process and come out the other side, you will have an amazing amount of pent-up energy," she says. She could feel it start to emerge. "There is that energy thing," she says, a new vitality to apply to her relationships, to put into her art.

Sandy breaks with her past, cutting ties to her old identity. After her husband's death, she clears out the clutter of her old life. In a symbolic cleansing, she overhauls her house. She throws out the accumulated mess of records, books, pillows, extension cords—and guts the interior. Three years later, she oversees a major renovation—new paint, new bathrooms, a new kitchen, a new office overlooking the trees on the corner of her street. "It's a bug that gets into you," she says. "Other people's clutter has been cluttering up my life. You want to trim down and get to basics. You want to live with the things you really love."

She redefines her family with new rituals for the holidays. One Thanksgiving she takes her daughters on vacation in Arizona. "We were going to have fun," she says. "We could be a family even with two people missing. It was important to get out of the family rut." In time, the family expands with the two fine men her daughters bring into the clan. She thinks about her role as matriarch. "We are a family, " she says.

All the while, Sandy reconfigures and cements her intimate circle—friends from her childhood, friends in the neighborhood, friends who share sorrow. "It's extremely important," she says. In the "busy years," as she calls them, "I put my friendships on hold. I didn't like them any less. I didn't have time, except to get through the day. Now it's wonderful. I can reach out to them on a deeper level and we can connect again."

She throws herself into photography. "When the kids were little, I was dying to do photography," she says. They would go off to day camp. "It was only an hour and a half. I ran out and took pictures. I thought, oh, if only I had more time." And now she has the time to do what she loves to do.

Her attitude shifts. She used to concentrate on getting ahead in her field—producing books, giving lectures, teaching photography. "That's the wrong way to look at it," she says. "That's recognition. That's not what these years are about. I don't give a shit about my résumé now. I just care about doing it and getting better at it. That's the freedom you get."

In the process, she transforms her pain into art with a special book, *The Soul in Balance,* that features her photographs of the gardens of Washington National Cathedral. The book is a collaborative effort with another woman and poet Heddy Reid, who chose most of the texts to go with the photographs. Heddy, our mutual friend, had also lost a child. The book is dedicated to their sons who died.

Meanwhile, Sandy finds herself becoming more adventurous. Not just in photography but with people. Once a reserved matronly type, she begins to walk on the wilder side. She goes to work out at the gym and learns slang. *You go girl,* says one of the trainers. "That brightens my whole day." She hangs out with the Dog Park Group—an eclectic group of dog owners who meet every morning in a park near her house. When a rug merchant stole her rugs on the pretense of cleaning them, a feisty young lawyer in the Dog Park Group came to her rescue and together they confronted the store owner and got her rugs back. "I never would have done that before," she says. "I'm being more wild. I'd never been wild. I'd been pretty staid. I feel totally more at ease and free with people," she says. "A lot of it is a matter of self-confidence." In the busy years you are building up your reputation, trying to put your best foot forward, she says. "Now we don't care. I don't worry if someone doesn't like me. That gives you a freedom to be more outgoing."

All in all, Sandy Scott is valedictorian of Second Adolescence. She leaves midlife behind. She stretches her mind and her heart, experimenting in her work as well as in relationships. She finds purpose in photography. She gains fulfillment in helping others. She learns to take care of her body – with exercise; she's even more adventuresome in what she eats. "It will be expensive. It will be fattening," she poses, "I just do it. Now I'm the boss."

She finds joy. The glorious wedding of her older daughter! Her son's girlfriend from college is a bridesmaid. "I think of her as the person she is. She's a friend of ours. We share this cataclysmic loss," she says. But they are not frozen in it. All of her son's friends come to the wedding and do a special spoof nude calendar of the festivities. She shows me the scenes and bursts out laughing.

As Sandy gains a fuller consciousness of her own self—both her aloneness and her connectedness—everything starts to crescendo in her life: Her family expands with her sons-in-law, her photography takes off, her extended family of friends, gym pals, and dog walkers widens. There's some romance, though she notes: "I feel perfectly content with thirty-five years of a happy marriage. I'm not hitching my happiness on having another one."

She is a woman of a certain triumph—there's this flush of exuberance in having achieved her place in the bonus decades. "I feel free. Financially I'm free—educating the children, paying the mortgage—we've done that. I feel free from the responsibility always to be thinking of what is best for the kids. I am free of the responsibility of thinking what's best for my husband. I loved him. He decided what we would do. Now I decide. I'm in the driver's seat. I can start afresh. I feel liberated in a lot of senses."

What makes the difference between doers and drifters? Tragedy is only part of it. How you respond is the other part. Sandy believes it hinges on taking risks—big risks that change your course and little risks that define your daily life. Do you dare to be bold?

Here's a small thing, she says: She is living temporarily in a downtown residential hotel. The attendants at the desk all go home at 8 P.M. The garage is locked and she has a card that sometimes works and sometimes doesn't. After our supper, she drives back to the motel, gets out her card (it works) and enters the underground garage. The iron doors clang shut. Everything is empty and black. She parks and starts walking, listening to her footsteps echo across the dark vastness of the concrete floor. Who would know if something happens to her? She is completely on her own. She just has to suck up the fear and do it.

"That's part of My Time," she says to me on the phone after she gets safely in her bed. "You have to take risks. You have to be bold."

Parking the car alone in an empty garage at night is a metaphor for living with necessary risks so that you can make the most of the bonus years. It is not all Mary Poppins–Morning in America. My Time takes work. My Time takes courage. My Time takes wisdom. "That's what you gain when you get older," she says. "What you lose is you can't run as fast. But you gain wisdom."

She tells me that in a few weeks there is to be a gala program to honor *The Soul in Balance* and open an exhibition of her photography; she invites me to attend.

But we do not meet again.

Over a weekend, Sandy comes down with strange stomach pains. Her daughter takes her to the hospital: suspected hepatitis. Three days later, Sandy Scott is dead. An autopsy reveals that the cause was advanced liver cancer—the tumor had burst and she succumbed quickly. She never knew she was sick.

At her memorial service in the spare Presbyterian Church, all of us are numb—too stunned by her sudden death to comprehend its finality. Yet we grasp her gift. Her daughters speak of love and laughter in her life. Her friends, old and new, celebrate her talent to create lasting images, her capacity to care in lasting relationships. Her legacy is profound for those who follow. Although her bonus years were cut short, she has provided a road map for realizing the potential of late life—marking the highways of courage and urgency, the overpass of faith in possibility.

The sign posts are in *The Soul in Balance*. In one photo of a still, snowy scene of winter stands the twelfth-century Norman arch at the entrance to the Bishop's Garden at the National Cathedral. It is a gateway that beckons. Next to Sandy's haunting photograph of the arch are the words of Henri-Frederic Amiel: *"Life is short and we do not have too much time to gladden the hearts of those who travel with us, so be swift to love and make haste to be kind."*

✦

Most of us do not experience this kind of catastrophic loss. The personal 9/11 tragedy that rushes in unexpectedly and changes everything is relatively rare. And not everybody can regenerate out of such sorrow. Trauma claims many victims among its survivors. Studies suggest that about 30 percent of combat soldiers develop depression or posttraumatic stress disorder. The toll is similar for those who are traumatized on the domestic front. But these mental conditions can be treated, and many people are able to recover from a traumatic loss.

Those who regenerate like Sandy Scott are role models in resilience. Just as the resilient child in a crisis-ridden upbringing grows *up* fast, the resilient adult who experiences trauma grows *out* of midlife fast. Those struck by sorrow seem to get on to a fuller, more mature stage of development more quickly than others with smoother trajectories. In the process, they become mentors on how to transform loss into new life—how to get through the transitional passage of Second Adolescence and on to My Time.

Everyone has a story. Losses are part of life, like rain and root canals. Many mental health researchers believe that loss is the crucible of psychological growth. Author Judith Viorst puts it this way in her seminal work, *Necessary Losses:* "When we think of loss we think of the loss, through death, of people we love. But loss is a far more encompassing theme in our life. For we lose not only through death, but also by leaving and being left, by changing and letting go and moving on. And our losses include not only our separations and departures from those we love, but our conscious and unconscious losses of romantic dreams, impossible expectations, illusions of freedom and power, illusions of safety—and the loss of our own younger self, the self that thought it always would be unwrinkled and invulnerable and immortal." She proposes "the view that it is only through our losses that we become fully developed human beings."

Not all losses in this broad definition are experienced as painful or tumultuous. Some are welcome events like sending children off to college. Some are expected: the death of a parent. Some are trivial—a freckled age spot on the back of the hand. Researcher Paul T. Costa, Jr., at the National Institute on Aging, prefers to talk about stress as the common denominator in human development. Stress can be caused by a variety of negative and positive events. Stress includes loss—the loss of life, the loss of health, the loss of a job, the loss of a relationship. It also involves threats—uncertain danger where the outcome is unknown. Your new boss wants to shake up the company and you don't know where you'll fit in, for example. In addition, stress is caused by challenges—a new job, a new marriage.

At 50 you are much better able to handle stress whatever the cause—negative or positive. Life experience allows you to compare a current stress with what's happened in the past and with what's happened to others. You put it in perspective. "There is a thing called wisdom," says Costa. "Older people make social and philosophical comparisons and find meaning in events. They see events more as challenges."

You are able to evaluate threats more accurately than a younger person. You've been through this before. You have a better awareness of when things are going wrong and how to make them go right. You are also sharper in appraising challenges—what's needed to succeed and why you should jump at the chance, or not. And you are in a better position to confront loss. As Costa says, older people are more likely to see opportunity in negative events. "They also respond with direct action rather than emotion. They take steps to deal with the situation."

All in all, people over 50 are remarkably stable as they weather the usual lifelong patterns of losses, threats, and challenges.

Major losses—what researchers call "negative life events" such as loss of a loved one or diagnosis of a serious, incapacitating illness—are uncommon on an annual statistical basis. Most people heading into the bonus years are not suddenly struck down by a catastrophic illness. For example, only 12 percent of people over 65 say poor health is a "very serious" problem for them, according to a survey of more than 3,000 Americans by the National Council on Aging (NCOA). That's about the same rate of poor health among adults 18–64.

What's more, lifelong happiness depends less on outside events and circumstances than on an individual's disposition. As researchers from the Baltimore Longitudinal Study of Aging note: "People quickly adapt to both good and bad circumstances, so the impact of special events can be fleeting; but people who are sociable, generous, goal-oriented, and emotionally stable consistently report higher levels of happiness and lower levels of depression than others."

This is not pop-psych blather about the importance of thinking positively and all your troubles will wash away. This is about who you are and how you respond to stress of all kinds. Over a lifetime, your wheel of positive and negative jolts goes up and down.

When a big one hits, you have to respond. There is no room for drift. You are blasted out of your status quo.

Peter Barnes of Baltimore is the typical workaholic lawyer at a big-league corporate law firm. A handsome man who always got good marks in school, he retains a boyish laugh and underlying sweetness unspoiled by success, even though he's a top-flight litigator. He's never been sick a day in his life; he doesn't even go to the doctor. When he gets ready to attend the fortieth reunion of his high school class at a rigid school for boys, his wife notices that he looks a little peaked. That Gray Lawyer look, he says.

"For the first time, I was aware I'm not feeling so great. For some reason, I can't tell you why, I went to the doctor. I had abdominal pains. My skin was gray. I was getting ready for a trial. I was going nuts."

After a series of tests over the next couple of months, he ends up having a colonoscopy. "I wake up in the recovery room. The doctor said: *We're glad you came in today because you've got a problem. We're sorry to tell you but you're going to have to have an operation right away.*"

Diagnosis: Stage III colon cancer. He is 58.

"I couldn't believe it. What happened was I went in there in control of my life. When I woke up, people took my life over."

Everything happens very fast. He tells his two grown children not to worry. His wife, Jan, drives him to the hospital in the early morning for surgery. "It was dark out. Cold as hell. I remember walking down this linoleum corridor—a scary corridor from an alien movie—and turning the corner to the operating room. A lot of people. The last thing I heard was 'Don't worry, Mr. Burns.' I wanted to yell. I'm Mr. Barnes. You better check! Have you got the right body? I couldn't say anything. I was out."

Have you got the right body? Yo, fate! Don't you think you'd better check? Have you got the right person?

Fate nods, affirmative. It's his body. There's been no mistake. Five days in the hospital. Fluids in, fluids out. "I was walking around, attached to all kinds of crap." Over the next year, he undergoes an "aggressive course of treatment," as the doctors put it—radiation and chemotherapy. He is never in great agony or pain, he says.

He doesn't think about the office. "It just went off the radar screen. It was amazing. It just disappeared in terms of what I was thinking about. I didn't give a shit what was happening at the office. It was like a light went out. Work went from having been all consuming to being not there."

Instead he enters the strange nation of Sickland, taking up residence in a foreign territory reserved for the very sick. His job is to get treated. It's very hard work, consuming 24/7 work—and he's not the one with the billable hours anymore. He has no control. He's just there. First stop is the basement dungeon at the Greater Baltimore Medical Center, a scene out of *Macbeth*, he says, with a couple of crones surrounded by boiling cauldrons, doing their magic rituals with a radiation beam. There's no dignity in this: He lies face-down so that the devil's handmaidens can determine where to aim the radiation. "It was like they shoved a 50-pound beach ball up my ass. Then they would say: 'Relax.' I'd think: *Lady, if I relax, this beach ball is going right up through to the fourth floor.* I'd say: 'Don't you think it's time to take it out?' They'd say: 'Relax.' They weren't very concerned. They'd talk to each other about the weather, about their children. *Relax?*"

He moves on to somewhat gentler rituals of treatment and bonds with the other denizens in Sickland. "You see the same people. You see how really brave human beings can be. Some types of cancer are disfiguring and painful," he says. "One man, small thin guy. He had cancer of the head and jaw. The left, lower side of his face looked like it had been kicked in. He was in a lot of pain. He didn't complain. We'd talk—how much longer? What's your prognosis? Yeah . . . they're going to keep treating it." Most of his fellow citizens were upbeat. "They were optimistic. Things were going to be okay," he recalls.

There are moments of triumph. "On my last day, all the technicians came out and cheered. They gave me a big hug. For what? Getting zapped! Congratulations, they said. You're through!" He'd finished one assignment, but the job is far from done. Next come eight months of chemotherapy. This kind of work is hazardous, he quips. As an occupation, getting treatment would never pass federal health and safety regulations. There are consequences—numbness in the toes, some sudden brain blurring—Where am I? Who am I? Who are you? And the damn "tourista," like having chronic dysentery.

Peter takes a break from his treatment job to get a haircut. "Getting up from the chair I looked at this thing in the mirror. I weighed a good bit less than I did in high school. I looked like some sort of eel."

He gets better. It takes a year. "I certainly didn't think about work. I'd think about what I'd like to do. Then I'd run for the can. I wondered what the hell could I do if I have to crap all the time? Will this ever stop? This period went by very fast. At the time, it felt like it was dragging. Looking back, it was a blur," he says. "The thing I thought about most was—What do I want to do?"

What do I want to do? He doesn't really want to go back to work, but he doesn't know what else to do. His firm has been very supportive, covering him throughout his illness with comprehensive health insurance and disability payments. He tells the firm's managing partner, who is also a friend: "I'm not sure I want to come back," but he agrees to return—not as a partner but as a part-time counselor. He takes on a pro-bono case that lasts a year—a departure from the high-dollar-stakes litigation of his past. After that he wrestles with the question: Can I leave or not?"

He works through his finances, he works through his psyche, he works it out with his wife—and decides to leave the firm. "I'm glad I practiced law for thirty-six years. I don't want to do it for another thirty-six," he says.

His health crisis is the triggering event. "It came out of the blue and blasted me out of the rut. I always thought I'd get out of the rut. Suddenly I was out. Once I got out, I was out," he says. "It gave me a requirement and an ability to start thinking about what I want to do."

The process of breaking with the past takes about three years—one year of treatment, another two years at the firm ("three years of decompression," he says)—much more fortunate than those who are suddenly laid off or retired without a cushion period.

Now he's dreaming. "At the moment, it's like being in heaven," he says. In the long lush months of warm weather, he sits out on his deck, surrounded by giant pine trees, and listens to the song of a cardinal, the squawk of a blue jay. He has more time to think about his wife, instead of being caught up with "I'll see you tonight, dear." He plays around on the computer. He reads. He answers an advertisement in a business magazine for ad copy writers—maybe that will be his next career! Maybe he'll be a poet! He volunteers at an animal shelter on Fridays.

He visits friends. "I realized that time is the most precious thing," he says. "Friendship is more important than ever." Once he regains his strength, he goes on a bicycle trip to New Zealand with a close friend from childhood. Back home, he takes long walks with Magnum, his black poodle companion. He keeps going to the gym three times a week. He looks and feels better than he has in decades.

"I'm now in a wonderful no-man's land," he says. "Doing nothing all that much—and assuming that at some point, I'll do something else. I'm not too worried what or when."

"I think you're finding yourself, my dear," says his wife. "And anyway, you're having fun."

One of the biggest lessons he's learned through his sojourn in Sickland is to . . . *relax*. And enjoy. "It made me realize, it's not bad—just to be," he says. "I used to be so concerned about being seen as not being busy. A lot of people are concerned about that even if they hate the something they're busy at," he continues. "I'm not uptight about what I'm doing or not doing. That's one of the best things to come out of this."

He grins. It's good to be out of the rut. Not that he was in a bad rut. That's the subtle but important shift in Second Adolescence. Urgency changes the existential question from: *I like what I'm doing so why not keep on doing it as long as I can?* to: "I was conscious of the fact that I may not have much longer to go," as Peter puts it. "Today may be my best day. I have a finite number of days. Do I want to spend this period on what I've been doing?"

So how do you answer that question? *I have a finite number of days. Do I want to spend them doing what I've been doing?* That is *the* conundrum for those on the fault line of My Time. Do you look forward from the present and see no boundary on the horizon? Or do you look backward from the endpoint? Do you evaluate what you're doing—and who you're doing it with—and think. This works. Why change course? Or is something gnawing at you? With a finite future, do you want to spend the bonus years like this?

The role of crisis is to clarify the existential question of the bonus decades and demand an answer. Sometimes the circumstances of loss define how you change: You simply cannot keep on doing what you are doing—whether it's in a marriage or on the job. Your spouse seeks a divorce. Your company goes bankrupt. You don't have the option to stay in the status quo.

The danger is that you become paralyzed by loss and shut down. You don't even drift; you sleepwalk. But that's not the norm. Study after study shows that you're much more resilient in the face of crisis compared to young adults. Peter Barnes, with his health crisis, illustrates the psychological alchemy of Second Adolescence. He takes a major loss and turns it into a threat. Then, he takes the threat and makes it a challenge—a challenge he now cherishes and enjoys. If the surveyors of the National Council on Aging were to ask him to rate his health status today, he'd say: excellent.

✦

For most people, there is no one huge loss. But there are a lot of little losses. You lose parts of your self. Usually these are surface losses, predictable losses. You probably can't run as fast or see as well as before, for example. And these kinds of losses don't interfere significantly with your life.

But you learn an important lesson in these little losses: You may find relief after loss.

Neuropsychologist Margery H. Silver at Boston Medical Center explains it this way: "With any change, there is a saying good bye. You are mourning certain things you can't do anymore." Then she adds: "In a way that's a relief."

She gives a small example: She had never learned to play tennis. "I was one of these kids who could never do anything in sports. I wasn't good at it," she says. In youth, this was experienced as a blow, a loss. Then in midlife, she took up tennis—with a different attitude. "It's too late to be really good at it," she says, so she changed her goals. "I might as well just have fun," she says.

She got over that old loss of not being able to "do anything in sports" and turned it into the gain of being able to do *something* in sports and enjoy it. Obviously playing tennis is not an essential passage in personal development—but the shift in her approach to tennis illustrates what can happen when you confront loss. "It's letting go of something. It's freeing," she says.

It's letting go of the "have to be good" standard of previous decades, the "have to be a certain way" measure of success, the "have to do this" sense of obligation. You are freed from the burden of "shoulds" and "oughts." You start doing what you want to do—what you enjoy doing—and after a while, that mindset can lead you to a new life.

Loss can free you from the past.

Sometimes loss is hard to grasp. It's not outside, but inside you. You have lost your way. There's a generalized loss of passion for life. This is burnout. You are suffering from a loss of self. A voice inside is calling on you to stop the status quo. But how do you confront this loss of self? Especially if you don't have to? On the outside, everything seems to be going along pretty well. But inside, the drumbeat is too loud to ignore.

A common scenario is to make your own crisis. You create a loss that will free you from the past. Many people do this unconsciously and wait for the crisis to explode—in work and in relationships.

Some do it consciously—and deliberately. You know you have to stop and make a change. You confront the loss before it confronts you.

Bliss Browne, 53, knows she is heading into transition. She is drawing on a whirlwind resume—priest, banker, community leader, mother, wife—and getting to a place where she can just think.

But first, she had to go through a loss of her own making—a very public loss.

For more than a decade, Bliss has run Imagine Chicago, an innovative program that imagines ways to improve city life—and then sets up specific projects to turn imagination into reality. The nonprofit organization has launched community programs to bring ages and races together and bridge social and economic differences. The concept has spread to 18 countries on six continents.

Bliss is consumed with her mission to help people and whole communities. But after years of working 24/7, she was beginning to lose her compass. She saw the signs. One time she came home from an overseas trip, flying 36 hours straight. She felt she had to be in the office the next day at 8:30 to set an example for the staff. Then she thought again. As she says: "Having to work to the point of exhaustion to be a good boss? This is silly!" *Jolt!*

Another jolt came when she was invited to submit an application for a big grant that would have paid her salary for the next three years. The message in that was: *Keep doing what you do so well.* That was the problem. "I could not bring myself to do it," she says. "I didn't want to be doing things just because I could."

But how could she stop in the midst of so much success? Her organization is a model for community activism. Many people count on her. The office in downtown chicago is a magnet for people seeking new connections for their lives and communities. On the walls are paintings, quilts, and posters created by those who participated in projects over the past ten years.

In one of the first initiatives, teenagers were sent out to interview community leaders. They painted a "dream tree" of the visions and commitments needed to make a better city. The images tug at her from the office walls. All the participants in Imagine Chicago projects are part of her extended family. Will she be abandoning them? What will be lost by giving up the office; Imagine Chicago's institutional 'home'? Will she destroy the institution she worked so hard to create?

As she wrestles with her decision, a friend drops by the office for a visit. He suggests: *Do an experiment—take all the pictures off the wall.*

So she takes down all the treasured objects.

Then he asks her: *How do you feel?*

She replies: *I feel relieved. I feel very relieved.*

That was the turning point. She realized that the paintings were symbols of stories inside her. She did not need to keep them on those walls to preserve their memory. To pack up was to let go of a burden. "I expected to feel a deep grief. I didn't feel that way. I felt someone had taken a great weight off me," she says. *Jolt!*

"I take on responsibility for more than my share. I don't always know how to set it down."

In December 2002, Bliss set it down. She closed the office and let the staff go. Imagine Chicago will continue, she says, as a source of vision and ideas. She will serve as consultant to the international Imagine movement, but not as the initiator and manager of new programs. She's leaving that to the next generation of community leaders.

Closing the office is a loss—the loss of a place, the loss of a role, the loss of a daily schedule—but it is a "good" loss. With this decision, she takes the first step in recovering the loss of her self.

Bliss moves her office into her house. This allows her to shift focus. For years she submerged her personal needs into her public role. "My marriage has not been on my active radar for most of my married life," she says. "I made a home mostly for my children. It hasn't felt like home for me. Imagine Chicago was my home base."

Now her home is home base. The Imagine Chicago dream tree hangs in her living room. The teacher quilt hangs in her home office. She has spent weeks tending her garden, which is now flourishing.

Weeks fixing up the house and getting it repainted. "I'm loving being here," she says. The children are away at school. She has a chance to clean out the closets of the past; a daily ritual of filling up 30-gallon bags of clutter and boxes of books to give away. And she has a chance to think.

She wants to know the truth in her marriage. She and her husband had lived such separate lives. Could they come together at this stage? There were times when she had thought they were headed for divorce. Now as she focuses on the daily rituals of the relationship, she probes deeper. After months at home, Bliss finds her truth: Divorce seems inevitable. "I need to either be on my own or with a real partner with whom to share a common life and set of commitments," she says.

Breaking up a marriage is painful—another public loss. But for Bliss, it is also another *settling down*. "These necessary losses have catalyzed a deep process of renewal," she says. "I am looking at the loss process as a purification process."

When Bliss was a teenager, she and her best friend used to get up at 6:00 A.M. and go down to the beach at Lake Michigan. They'd talk about what kind of life they would lead, and how they'd search for the truth. They prayed together and wrote in their journals. Bliss always wanted to make a difference. After college, she went to divinity school and earned a master's degree in theology. She was ordained in the Episcopal church. Since the church limited opportunities for women, she went to work in a bank and earned an MBA. While on assignment for the bank in England, she became the first woman priest to preach in Westminster Abbey.

Back in Chicago, she got involved in community issues—all the while working at the bank, assisting at a parish and raising three young children. She could have ended her resume there. But she turned her busy life upside down and changed course. At 41, she put the threads of spirituality, leadership, economics, and motherhood together and started Imagine Chicago.

Now she is reinventing herself again. She could have stopped with Imagine Chicago (and her marriage) and coasted — on the outside, anyway. But on the inside, she needed to lose that former life to find a new one.

A charismatic woman with blue eyes and short fluffy hair, Bliss is tending to her own needs – perhaps for the first time. She is working on her body, gaining strength and shedding pounds, similarly to the way she is getting her home restored and shedding its clutter.

She ponders the transition from mother to grandmother. She looks forward to the birth of grandchildren, although that's a ways off. And she wonders about "how to become a grandmother in community development," she says. "Imagine Chicago has been mother's work." "I've really started thinking about how a grandmother would approach public life."

Grandmothers can encourage the potential that exists in every child without the distractions of daily chores. "There's a givenness of grandparents—an ability to see with more creative detachment. They hold on to the promise without all the clutter." Grandparents, she points out, can be attentive and wise, without being controlling. How might that translate into a new public role for Bliss? "How do you stand alongside communities in a way that's encouraging? That listens carefully? That shares wisdom without being prescriptive?"

"With programs that are hands-on, you have less time to think," she says.

For Bliss, the hands-on days are over. In My Time, she is going to think. She can see the outlines of new destiny. It involves "making a home for me" and once that's been accomplished, she can turn to "offering a home to the world," she says. The woman who created the Imagine movement in the public arena is now where she knows she needs to be ... imagining the next chapter for herself.

4

Dreaming

It is not because things are difficult that we do not dare;
it is because we do not dare that they are difficult.

SENECA

YOU LET LOOSE. You're a kid again. You take off from the mainland of your life and have an adventure.

"I am dreaming and having a wonderful time being a student," says
Mary Kunze of Elm Grove, Wisconsin. At 64, she's spending a semester in Rome to get a Ph.D. in institutional bioethics. "So many things
happening here—just finished a three-week course on Moral Democ-
racy, de Tocqueville stuff, fascinating." She lives in an apartment on the
via degli Andosilla, attends classes at the Pontifical University. Like
every student who has journeyed to Rome over the millennia, she is
discovering the wondrous mystery of an ancient capital—and discovering her self. "Rome is not an easy city. When I leave I feel that I will be
on my way to being a citizen of the world," she continues. On her way
by learning, growing, wondering, and having fun. "Must run, Plato's
Crito is calling me."

Rome is a long way from the American heartland where she lived in a town of about seven thousand people and worked in hospital administration. A long way from her four grown children and an ex-husband, the man she met at 21 and married six months later. A long way from the convent school stuff of her girlhood that she is turning into a stronger commitment to Catholicism and a more adventurous confidence in herself.

She doesn't know what she will do with a Ph.D. in institutional bioethics. Certainly after the scandals on Wall Street and in the church, institutions could do with some ethical expertise. Meanwhile, she is opening herself up to new geography, new experience, new skills. It's as though she's her own research project. Studying in Rome is her experiment in personal development. She's eager to see what happens.

As she explains before her departure: "I'm going to Rome for six months. I'll be studying in a foreign language. It doesn't frighten me. Finding nice pantyhose worries me more," she quips.

Mary relishes the new lightness in her life, the freedom just to be and enjoy. She looks like a Viking goddess—pale skin, soft eyes, blond hair, big bones well padded—a plus-size goddess. She's struggled hard to get to this point.

About seven years ago, her midlife collapsed. Her marriage broke up. Her mother died. She developed heart disease. But looking back, she sees her losses in a different light. "Losing my mother, losing my husband, losing my health—it freed me," she says. "It's true. All these losses freed me." They freed her to dream and figure out her *what next?*

Dreaming is an essential feature of Second Adolescence. It is part freedom to roam in new territories of experience and emotion. It is part education to expand the mind and learn new skills. It is part journey, a passage of discovery and resetting of your internal compass.

. The challenge is to grow *out* of midlife and search for a new destiny. Teenagers are expected to dream. They go to school and camp, they have internships and summer jobs—all to spark imagination and provide them with the skills and experience they need as adults.

The same is true for people who have completed the agenda of adulthood. You need to dream. It's okay not to know what you want to do—or to want to do too many things. Teenagers aren't supposed to know what their career will be when they start college or take their first job. That's the task of growing up.

In Second Adolescence, you face a similar task. You have to loosen up your psyche to invite new stimuli. You may need the equivalent of school and internships and temporary jobs to help you explore your way to the future. You can't be expected to settle on your next life right away. After all, the notion is just sinking in that you have these bonus decades ahead of you.

There is no formal training or institutional structure to help people through this transition stage the way there is a whole education system to ease the passage of adolescence. Society is lagging far behind the demographic explosion of My Time. Where can you go to get an advanced degree in maturity?

You're on your own. You do it by instinct. You put together your own curriculum to gain new skills and experience. You make your own rules for socializing and contentment.

In this culture of do-it-yourself human development, older men and women are flooding back to college and attending life-learning centers. They are taking temporary jobs and part-time assignments. They are traveling extensively, the way college kids spend a year studying abroad. They are joining AmeriCorps or the Peace Corps—to get a change of scene and "give back" in public service. They are finding new ways to have fun—the "what you've always wanted to do" trip to Las Vegas or Key West. They are hooking up with old friends and rereading the bible.

All this dreaming gives you the chance to experiment with yourself and with others. Sometimes, that course you took at a community college or that volunteer job you pursued at the hospital will lead directly to your main goal in the bonus decades. Other times, these pursuits go into the memory box as an interesting learning experience or fun adventure that expanded your horizons.

As you dream of the future, you reckon with the past. You sort out the different lives you've led as child and adult; you identify what is most important and move on. Out of the reckoning comes renewal. Out of the dreaming comes purpose. You envision a future. Dreaming is the transforming activity that forces you to grow, inside and out.

Mary Kunze has no choice. Dreaming is her pathway out of crisis.

The marriage came apart in July 1995. The next month, when she went swimming in Lake Michigan with a group of friends, a woman asked her: "What are you going to do with your life?"

Mary didn't know what to say. "I thought—'do?' I've got to 'do'?" she recalls. The friend persisted.

"What made you the happiest?"

"When I was at Northwestern going to school," Mary replied.

"Well, then, go back to school."

Mary is forced to address the question: *What are you going to do with the rest of your life?* One way to start is to identify *what made you the happiest?*

Mary was 40 when she went to Northwestern University. She had always worked, starting out as a clerk typist at the Medical College of Wisconsin. She worked her way up to be hospital vice president. In 1984, at the age of 46, she completed her college equivalency and graduated from Northwestern University's Executive MBA program.

At this point she had become the super-successful, trail-blazing executive mom with four kids in school, a good housekeeper to keep things running smoothly at home—and a ho-hum marriage.

But when the marriage ended in the summer of 1995, she was 58, a suddenly single empty-nester. *"'Do?' I've got to 'do'?"*

The friend's question turned her around. "I dried myself off and got to work to get into school," she recalls. She had to scramble to pull together her record and get recommendations. But the next day, she delivered her application to the Medical College of Wisconsin—and was accepted in the program for a master's of arts degree in bioethics. "I went to court to get the legal separation the same day that I went to orientation for class."

The upheaval continued. Six months after starting school, she suffered an attack of angina. Pain shooting up from the chest into the neck. She was rushed to the hospital and had quadruple bypass surgery the next day. That knocked her out for a semester.

"It was a blip," she says now. She points out that she never had a heart attack. Her vessels were clogged; now they're cleared out. "I caught it in time," she explains. "The doctor said to me: 'Your greatest enemy is stress.'"

For many years, Mary had taken on the stresses of being the family caretaker. She nursed her mother who had suffered a massive stroke. She was at the bedside when her mother died. Her children married and were starting families. She was at the bedside for the births, too.

Now Mary is looking after herself. She graduated in 1999 with a master's degree in science. Then she was accepted into the Ph.D. program in Rome. *What made you the happiest?* Going to school. For Mary, the Rome semester is the grand finale of her dreaming period.

"I'm on the brink," she says. "I can do just about anything. I really know who I am. I know my strengths now. I'm on the precipice of a new adventure. I feel so whole. I wish I could have felt this way in my 20s. You have much more energy at this age. You have a hard time holding back."

Mary sizes up the competitive edge for women in My Time. "We have hair color. We have cosmetics. We have confidence. We know our style. We can put together a good package. We don't have PMS or children to go home to. We don't have anything to worry about but doing that job," she says.

She speaks for both men and women in My Time when she says: "We have stability, wisdom, experience. We are going to be competition."

For people like Mary, dreaming is preparation for major public roles in academia or in an institution such as the church. For others, dreaming is the prelude to a creative pursuit such as performing in the theater or playing music. Dreaming also opens up the way to reframing relationships. Once you learn how to dream, you make it a habit. Dreaming allows you to keep learning, growing, discovering; you keep having adventures and taking risks.

Mary's adult children don't quite get it. They are settled with youngsters—and a little hurt that she's not around to do the traditional grandmothering. But there's time for that. "I can put a little pepper into the lives of my grandchildren," says Mary. And now, Mom's gone off to Rome. The children worry about her. Can she handle it? Mary laughs. There's some role reversal going on here. Who's the kid going off to college?

As her son said to her before she left for Rome: "If you don't like it, Mom, you can come home."

✦

Dreaming is also the antidote to uncertainty. You feel anxious because the future is unknown and the bonus decades are stretching out in front of you. Ask yourself: *what made you happiest?*

"The big decision is what are you going to do? Continue working? Do volunteer work? Pursue something you've always wanted to do? Work on painting when you've been an engineer? Go back to school and train for a new career? Just be retired and play golf? People have those choices. In that way, this period is like adolescence. You're kind of overwhelmed," says Boston psychologist, Margery Silver, co-author of *Living to 100: Lessons in Living to Your Maximum Potential at Any Age.*

"You also have maturity. In adolescence you make choices of colleges and mates without knowing who you are. At this point you have these years of maturity to do things that are right for you. You have a sense of values to choose what is most fulfilling for you. That's what is exciting about it," she says.

"It's the first time in history we've had adults making these big decisions."

Often it helps to stop. Take a break. Do something completely different.

My cousin is a Boston lawyer—a cousin who is like a brother, whose children grew up with my children. When he officially retired from his firm at age 65, he'd been so busy that he hadn't a moment to plan what he would do next. So he gave himself an interim assignment: build a summer cabin in the Maine woods far away from home—"to change the subject," he explains.

Working with his hands is a way to clear the cobwebs out of his mind. He has no intention of becoming a builder in the bonus decades. But he has to change the subject of his life in order to start anew. He has been so tied to the office, he wouldn't know where to begin to dream. He knows if he stayed in the Boston area, he'd get busy with requests for his time—to work on this committee, to head that community project. He's been busy all his life meeting the needs of others. But he senses the My Time imperative of having to make a bigger change.

The house project is like the dish of sherbet between courses in an Italian dinner. It clears the palate so you can savor the next course. He has to clear his palate before starting a next career—whatever that may be.

He gives himself a year of soffits and shingles, sewer lines and light switches. Alone, he pounds nails and ponders; he's had a straight-H history: Harvard College, Harvard Law School, a stint in the Marines for Hardening, one Happy marriage. And he has something else, a musical talent—an ear for composing and a tenor voice for singing.

As he picks out a soft wash stain for the pine-paneled walls, he ponders some more. His legal career is over. His children are grown—married and starting their own families. His grandmother lived to be 98, so he knows he has the genetic fuel for several more decades. He finishes the roof. He thinks about music. Now he has the time for singing, composing, playing the piano. But there are other things he cares about, too. He installs the sink, puts knobs on the kitchen cabinets. The grandchildren—he wants to leave them something special. A better world, of course. And this little house! A place to gather and sing and keep the family together.

And so, he dreams and reckons, reckons and dreams. By the time the one-room cabin is finished, so is he. He is ready to turn to the *what, next?* question. He doesn't have an answer, but he gets to the question.

Second Adolescence is about changing the subject of your life. You are searching for different scenarios and trying them out—sometimes only in your head, other times in practice. You may need a change of scene to get away from the triggers that kept you in line during all those years in the zoom zone.

It's not about extending the same old, same old midlife on a more relaxed schedule. "It's a huge change," says Gene Cohen, director of the Center on Aging, Health & Humanities at George Washington University.

As you get into these bonus years, you need a purpose—a grand plan. As Cohen says: "It's a job to find a job and it's a job to find the right retirement experience. When you think of the most important things in your life, you don't do them casually. You don't look for a job casually. You don't choose a spouse casually. You don't buy a house casually. Why should you take retirement casually? But you are likely to do that. When you find a spouse or a job or a house casually, you pay the price."

Most people don't have a plan. Even fewer have a strategy to implement a plan. In an ongoing study of more than a hundred people, "a mi-
nority have any retirement planning," says Cohen. "Of those who do,
it's only financial planning." The men and women in the study are over
60. They are retired, partially retired, or within one year of retirement.
They lack what Cohen calls "social portfolio planning." What's the plan
for spending your social portfolio in My Time? For broadening your
perspective on work and relationships and, as Cohen puts it, "tapping
potential"?

✦

Dreaming takes time—at least several years; sometimes a decade or
more. Even when you've prepared for your official retirement, you may
not have a plan for the bonus decades. Yet.

Nancy Carson is a top WAAW: *Washington Attractive Accomplished
Woman*. She has a stellar résumé: She ran a major program at the Office of Technology Assessment. She's worked on Capitol Hill; she's
worked for a lobbying firm. She labored long for the federal government. Along the way she married—twice—and is now single with a
grown daughter from the first marriage.

At 63, she's healthy and active—and out there, searching for her
what next? She guards her attractiveness. Thin with good hair—a bowl
of short, soft, gray-blond curls framing a square jaw. Her eyes light up
when she laughs.

When she took early retirement from the government, she was 55. "I
didn't have the vaguest idea of what to do with myself," she says. "I
thought I could get a senior job in a foundation. I wanted another big
job." Someone pointed out to her that a person who was healthy and
active at 55 would likely be healthy and active at 85. "Good news? I
was horrified," she says. "It dawned on me that I didn't have to figure

out just one more job, I had to figure out two or three—and that might not be good enough."

She did prepare for retirement "with workshops, visualization exercises, financial planning guidelines," she says. "I was never unsure about leaving my job and taking the retirement option. The timing was right. I had earned a life outside the nine-to-five workplace, and I wanted to learn and do new things. So I took the leap."

But about eight months into retirement, things are not going all that great. She had just dropped out of yet another Follow-Your-Bliss seminar, when she confided to a friend: "But I prepared for this, and did all I could to get ready."

Her friend wisely replied: "Just because you prepared for it doesn't mean you don't have to go through it."

"Ah yes, the old mistake," she says. "Surely if I plan for something I can avoid the hard part—in this case, occasional feelings of uselessness, great uncertainty about money, becoming a person the society sees as having an interesting past but probably no future."

This is the dark side of hitting the bonus decades that gets glossed over in those fancy brochures for cruises and leisure condos. Society isn't ready for Nancy. She is confident that she can have a next "career." And she can. But it's not quite like she thought.

With her résumé of accomplishment, she checked in with the head of a foundation, an old colleague. They had been on panels and committees together. So she went to him, *mano a mano*, executive to executive, to talk about the job she was looking for.

"You want another big job?" he asked, incredulously.

"A look of horror came over his face," she continues. Here she was, a woman in her prime years of productivity. "I wanted a real job," she says. "I wanted to get a job in New York." She looks away. "I could not get a job in New York." She kept hurling herself against the wall of ageism—the subtle and not-so-subtle senior cleansing of the workplace.

But in the process, she has allowed herself to dream. To be sure, she's working. She has consulting jobs. She has her pension. She takes on freelance writing assignments to supplement her income base. And now she can play like a student on summer vacation. She slows down a little and enjoys herself. "I can be outside on wonderful days, go to the National Gallery when it's not crowded, walk the river in the early morning, plant trees, read, hop on the train and spend a weekend in New York, take classes and enjoy life." She has more time to spend with her adult daughter. She looks after her mother long-distance. She goes to writing workshops and takes courses. "I can educate myself indefinitely at the community college for nothing."

She understands the challenge of the bonus years. She wants reinvention. Meanwhile, dreaming has become a full-time occupation. Mixed in with dreaming is the important psychological task of reckoning with the past. "I have more time to reflect on my life, to think about what is important and fix things. Long ago I gave up trying to fix other people or the world, but I can still work on myself. I have time to build an even stronger relationship with my daughter and her husband. I have time to work on the still-difficult relationship with my mother. In an odd way, the cultural disinterest in the elderly frees me up to do what is important, even if small. Fame, headlines, or making it to the top of a corporation are no longer options, so I can let go of anything connected to those objectives. I can drive people on errands. I can savor the friendship of neighbors. I can encourage younger women that they do not have to get everything right the first time—and I can reassure them that their children will turn out just fine."

Nancy is changing the subject of her life. You can't hurry the process. It can take years. She hasn't found the *what next*—yet. But she's making the most of this transition period. "Am I still worried about those next three jobs? You bet," she says. That's part of being "in an achieving culture, still thinking you have places to go, people to see, and things to do—but knowing you have no time to waste," she says.

✦

Men and women face the same general tasks in getting to My Time. You get through this transition phase by letting go of your old midlife identity and trying out new scenarios to help you figure out what you want to do with your extra decades. Eventually you find your focus and start framing an organizing principle to bring together the disparate parts of your life and give you a sense of purpose.

The process is universal—but doing it is highly individualistic. Traditionally, men have been more rooted in "the job" and women have been more involved in "the home" and raising children.

Men usually get to My Time with a solid job résumé but not as much experience in personal relationships and community activities— what researchers call "social engagement." Women may hit Second Adolescence with great skills in home-building and social networking, but not as much time logged in "the job." For men, the task in My Time is intimacy. For women, it's autonomy. He wants to bond; she wants to achieve. Both want to make up for lost time.

If you're a baby boomer or pre-boomer, you have probably been juggling dual roles for some time. You may get to this transitional period on different time schedules. A woman who takes "time out" to raise children, and doesn't really get on a career track until 40, is not about to quit at 60 or 70. She got into the zoom zone later and is hitting her career prime later. She's delighted to have the freedom from child-raising responsibilities to throw herself into "the job." Her husband of the same age, who has already spent several decades in the career market, may be more than ready to cut his ties to "the job" and learn piano. Or visit the children at college. Or wish his wife had more time for him.

It gets down to identity. For many, "the job" is a source of identity. When you leave a job, you leave behind a label that you've attached internally to your sense of self. Nancy Carson puts it this way: "People always ask you: What do you do?" Much of Nancy's WAAW identity had been linked to a high-powered job.

"That was hard for me," she says. She pauses and looks away. "But not very hard," she concludes with a smile. Redefining identity is an essential task in second adolescence. As Nancy continues: "I had more career success than I ever thought I would. My identity was not so framed around a particular job. But it is framed around accomplishment."

In her dreaming period, she uncouples her identity from a specific career or title. She is broadening her definition of accomplishment to reflect all aspects of her life. It encompasses work and relationships. It shapes not only what she does but how she feels and who she loves.

This re-calibration of identity is a significant change. You're not changing your basic personality; who you are is pretty stable. But you are undergoing an internal shift in your sense of self.

Dreaming helps you build up this new sense of self for the bonus decades. You need to give yourself plenty of time for this internal shift to take place.

✦

The temptation is to attack the future the way you managed your mainstream career. That way you remain in control—or so it seems. You make a to-do list: Renovate the kitchen, write a book, build a deck, sort through family photographs, visit your mother's cousin in Kansas, e-mail high school classmates, surf the web, volunteer at church, really do the garden this year.

As one "retired" man said to another: I'm so busy now I don't know how I ever had time to work.

There's a difference between constructive chaos and chaotic busy work—between exposing yourself to new scenarios and "scattering" yourself. Like a cable connection trying to take hold, you flop in and out. You have noise in your life, but no narrative.

The danger is that you're not making a transition. You remain stuck in the past. You do a lot of things, but you aren't changing the subject of your life.

Dreaming takes a certain amount of focus. It's a feature of Second Adolescence to jump from one thing to another. That's how you learn. But after a while, you need a plan, an organizing principle, to manage this jumping around. If you are suddenly cut loose from a job—or from a marriage or a full-time parenting role—you may not be used to this kind of freedom. Like a freshman in college, you go out for everything.

You end up in chaos for a while. That's okay—chaos is part of the transition process. As long as it doesn't go on too long. As long as you get to where you want to be for the bonus decades.

Bill Matuszeski has twinkly eyes, gray hair, good Polish peasant genes, he says, a law degree, an Aussie hat, and a quick sense of humor. He retired a few years ago at age 59. He knew it was time. He'd had a great thirty-five-year run shaping environmental policy. He capped his career as director of the Chesapeake Bay Program at the Environmental Protection Agency. With a change in administration, he didn't want to go through it all again.

It's a perfect script. He retires with honors. Now he has time to do all the things he wanted to do. The result—unexpected to him—is chaos.

He thought he had it all figured out. He doesn't pause for a second after the official finish of his government career. The day after his retirement party, he goes to Spain on a painting tour with a group of fifty artists. That's what everybody does: the post-retirement trip to make a clean break, right?

The trip is a success. Eleven days in southern Spain. Holy week in Seville. "It was the experience of a lifetime," he says. For years, he's been doing watercolors. It started when the kids were small—twins plus one within two years. He and his wife would be traveling on vacation, and "in order to keep them busy at meals, we gave them note-books and colored pencils and asked them to draw," he says. "We started doing it ourselves." Art is an interest he wants to explore.

He comes home from Spain—not exactly a born-again Matisse, but loosened up and ready to spend more time on painting—after all, that's what he has now: time. But he finds his time eaten up. There are a couple of book ideas on the environment he's been carrying around in his head for years. He wants to get those down on paper. And confer-ences on ecology to attend, as well as committees and special assign-ments to keep him in the swim as a consultant on the environment.

He starts careening from project to project. His wife asks him how he's doing on the books. The question bugs him. Another painting trip is coming up. The pressure builds.

"The big change is that you lose a core of your life when you retire. When you have a job, you try to find time to do things around the core," he says. But without a core, "everything is chaos. *Dear Lord, what do I do today?*" When he left the government, he lost his assistant—"I refer to her as my brain. We were together twenty years. It was a workplace family," he says. He's suddenly on his own.

"I went through a period of real chaos," he says. "Knowing I had a list of ten or twelve things I wanted to do. Books to write. Major trips. Boards to be active on. I didn't have any organizing principles."

He got up in the morning. His wife went to work. He read the paper. Then he would ask himself: "Which of these things should I think about today?" he explains.

"You lose the core. You lose the importance of weekends." He con-tinues: "You get freedom after retirement. The problem with freedom is that freedom is chaotic. Freedom requires you to make choices." When you're in the zoom zone and are making decisions on the job, you have a mission and know what has to be done. As he says: "You have a high confidence that you are working your way out of chaos. You know how to do the right thing." But then you leave the workplace and it's just you: "The problem is that the right thing to do changes all the time. You are your own sextant about all this."

Bill realizes he has to get some organizing principles into his life; he has to create some structure. He starts with his body. When a gym opens across the street, he signs up for regular exercise. He now spends every Monday, Wednesday, and Friday morning at the gym.

He organizes an office on the third floor. Most important, he devises a portable filing system: a stack of different-colored 3 × 5 cards that he carries around in his pocket. Yellow cards are for Big Ideas. How to protect the waterways of the Chesapeake and develop the land at the same time. A vision for New York Harbor. The University of Rhode Island project.

Turquoise cards are for Jacob, the boy he tutors at the School for Educational Evolution and Development (SEED) in the district. Here he puts the telephone numbers of Jacob's grandmother and teachers. The blue cards are reserved for the names of potential fund-raisers to contribute to the environmental cause. If he meets someone in love with wetlands at a cocktail party or in the supermarket, he puts down the contact information on a blue card. No more slips of paper lost in pockets.

The cards become his assistant, his back-up brain. They organize his time and attention. He doesn't worry about forgetting things; he just reaches in his pocket and pulls out a card.

Meanwhile, he can see that he's making internal changes. He looks back on the painting trip to Spain. "It was very liberating," he says. "I had a constrained painting style. I was relatively unwilling to open myself up. I was careful. I wanted to get it right—I was still in that mode. I wasn't taking too many chances."

Painting is probably not going to become his next career, but it is a metaphor for a subtle yet important transformation that is taking place internally. Bill had to let go of the careful, get-it-right mode that propelled him in his old career and take some risks. "On the trip to

Spain, I was taking a chance to do something that I wasn't really good at," he says.

Painting is a complete break. He associated it with relaxing and having a vacation. That way he could shelve his zoom-zone work mentality and dream a little. Experiment on canvas. Drawing for fun enabled him to get comfortable with taking risks. After all, loosening up a painting style is a pretty safe "starter" risk. It wasn't about success—in the public arena. It was about fulfillment in his private arena. Instead of scoring in the objective eyes of an employer, he was doing something meaningful in his own eyes.

As a result, his drawing gets more creative—and his dreaming gets bolder. By shedding his rigid career mentality, he can open himself up to a broader vision of *what now?*

He starts to de-scatter. At first, he said "yes" to everything that came his way as a consultant—the meeting in Mexico, the project in New York City, the ecologically worthy conferences to attend and the white papers to write. After a whirlwind year or two, he realizes that he has to say "no." He's going to have to turn down some jobs if he's ever going to settle down.

The consultant projects serve a purpose, he says. They not only introduce new opportunities, they also massage the ego in transition. At one meeting, a colleague leaned over and said to Bill: "It's a damn good thing that you're here." Those words were important to reinforce his self-confidence. There's a lot of built-in ego-massaging in the workplace, especially in high-prestige jobs. When you leave a job, you lose that source of support. You have to find other ways to stroke the ego. Consultant jobs reinforce your professional identity. You become the pro who needs no introduction. In the process, you de-couple your reputation from a job title whether it was sixth-grade teacher or FDA commissioner. That allows you to change your approach to work. You're not climbing up some in-house success ladder. You have your own mission and a new attitude: "Instead of doing something or taking a job because of what it can give you, it's the other way around," says Bill. "It's: *I'm here because of what I can give you.* That's a wonderful feeling," he says.

Bill slows down the chaos of his calendar. He does some reckoning. What's he really good at?

"Pitching," he says with a smile. Pitching a vision of what the environment could be and getting people to respond. His field is *pitchology*, he says. "I'm a preeminent *pitchologist*." His specialty is "pitching an idea and getting it accepted."

Gradually a plan takes shape for My Time. "My passionate focus is helping people to visualize what their environment could be like," he says. His mission: "It's galvanizing other people." He likes nothing better than to take a group of people for a walk down a river and see what's there—what's possible. "I love doing that. It gets people's warm, creative juices going. I can see myself doing that for a long time."

Bill is finding his purpose: "Devoting my later years, devoting my energy, to improving the environment of the world—to improving the public's ability to improve the world," he explains.

Perhaps to his colleagues this doesn't seem very different from what he was doing at the EPA. But the change is significant. This is not about being a good government leader. This is about building an enduring legacy for future generations.

Meanwhile, he and his wife are about to go on a painting vacation together.

It doesn't matter if you are forced to dream or if you stumble into dreaming. It doesn't matter if you're still working in "the job" and start dreaming on the side. Or if you're officially "retired" and turn to dreaming full-time.

Dreaming shifts your focus to the future, to the *what next?*

PART TWO

Seeking Purpose

5

Challenging Work

Retirement is the ugliest word in the language.

ERNEST HEMINGWAY

R ICHARD SHINHOSTER of Savannah has already lived through several social revolutions. One brother worked with Martin Luther King, Jr. Another became a leader in the NAACP. The civil rights movement opened the door for his three sisters, and then the women's movement came along and opened the door a little more.

Richard, the oldest son, took the traditional path and went into education. But now he, too, is on the front lines of social revolution. The marching song is *I'm retired and I'm working.*

The revolution breaks down into two parts. The first is that most people will keep working beyond "retirement." The second is that this new generation of post-careerists will broaden the agenda of work and even change the culture of the workplace.

Richard, 60, who spent more than three decades in education, has reinvented himself as a businessman. He did it "by liking to do things that were too risky during the family years," he says. "When you deal with children, you want to guarantee a future for them. You aren't at liberty to take risks. Even though you have this in the back of your mind, you have this in your heart, you can't say: This is what I want to do," explains Richard. "I needed to have a career. I needed to acquire some wealth to provide for my family. When you get to the age of retirement, you can say: This is what I want to do."

For most people, work in the bonus decades is about doing something they really want to do. The quandary is figuring out what that is— and what is possible in the marketplace. You are not so much looking for a job as searching for a purpose. Work can range from joining a theater group to running for Congress. It can be community service work. Or creative work. Or consulting work. It can be paid or unpaid. What most people want is control over their time so they can reset the balance between work and leisure, purpose and pleasure. Many look for a flexible schedule of part-time work. But it's all work. A study by AARP (formerly the American Association of Retired Persons) found that nearly 70 percent of workers over 45 say they plan to work in their retirement years. More than half want to work on a part-time basis.

As AARP executive director, William D. Novelli, told the National Press Club in November 2002: "The American view of retirement is changing. I come from a family of steel workers in Pittsburgh, and when my parents' generation retired, they did it the old-fashioned way. They really retired. I remember my Uncle Andy. He came home from the mill one day, put down his lunch pail, sat down on the porch and said, 'That's it. I'm retired.' And he was. Except for an afternoon walk to the Italian club, his new domain was that front porch. But boomers and older Americans today tend to see retirement not as termination, but as transition—to a life that may include work, education, civic engagement, and of course, being ardent consumers."

James Firman, president of the National Council on the Aging, puts it this way: "The notion of retirement itself is fading away." In a survey by the council of more than three thousand older Americans, more than 40 percent of those 65 to 74 reported that they were working. Nearly 20 percent said they had not officially retired. Another 23 percent said they had retired but were still in the workforce.

"People will continue to work. The idea that you get a gold watch and retire to Florida is just not the reality anymore," says Firman. The bonus decades "will be defined by what one does, not by what one doesn't do."

To be sure, some people will go to Florida and play golf. But that's not all they are likely to do.

What's more, the agenda of *what one does* is different from the way it was in the early years of adulthood. People in My Time are looking for meaning in their lives. *If not now, when?* Earning money may be essential to maintain a decent standard of living. In a depressed economy, you hang on to the job you have—if you can. Or rule out nonpaying jobs if you are looking for work. Yet, for many people in the bonus years, making money is not the primary objective. It is a necessary piece of the larger goal of having a purpose. Once you are eligible for health coverage through Medicare and monthly support from Social Security, part of your financial burden is eased. Economic security allows you to take risks—and sometimes that leads to making a profit.

Richard Shinhoster took five years to make the transition from educator to entrepreneur. It involved a profound redefinition of himself and his goals, culminating in the debut of a family business. Not just any business, but an enterprise with a mission: to help other people and awaken the public to a different way of looking at the world. He's found his purpose by selling . . . bronze and copper bracelets, carved wooden antelopes, and painted ostrich eggs.

Richard, the first-born achiever, grew up on the West Side of Savannah. As he says: "We had a traditional kind of upbringing." From his mother, he got religion. She was a beautician who did the neighbors' hair from home while the kids were young. Then she worked for many years for Belt's department store. "My mother went to church all the time," he continues. His father was a foundry worker for thirty years and had taught school. "He always challenged us educationally," says Richard. Everyone in the family was headed for college.

Richard excelled in math and physics. His first dream was to become an engineer; he had a summer job at the Brooklyn Navy Yard and wanted to enter its apprenticeship program in engineering. But the Navy yard closed down the year he graduated from college. He turned to education, first as a math teacher. At age 31, he became an administrator and never looked back. Education was the path to advancement. Along the way he earned an M.A. in adult education in 1973. He's been married for thirty-four years and is the father of two grown daughters.

By the time he retired in 1998, he had secured a safe niche for himself and his family. "I'd been in education for thirty-four years. It provided me with a good life. I was recognized as a leader in my profession." He could have continued as an education consultant. He could have relaxed. The faculty gave him a complete set of golf clubs as a retirement present.

He's hardly used them. The traditional son is not so traditional anymore. Two agents of change have turned his life upside down: Africa and his brother, Earl.

Richard went to Africa for the first time when he was 54. It was a chance thing: The pastor of his church was from Ghana and wanted to go home for a visit. Richard accompanied him as a representative of the church.

As soon as he stepped off the plane, Richard found a missing piece of himself. "I walked the streets of Ghana. There were people who looked just like me. They were in control of the country. I'd never seen that. They had gray hair, a gap in the teeth. This was where I came from," he says. "The trip to Africa was a turning point. It was a tremendous experience in helping me understand who I was."

He visited the Castle, the transit station for the slave trade, and went through the Door of No Return that led to the dungeons. "It's still damp and eerie," he says. "We heard the stories." How the people were gathered from inland and jammed into the dungeons until there were enough of them to make the trip across the Atlantic profitable. "These are things we didn't learn in school," he continues. "African Americans are the descendants of survivors. It is necessary for us to build on that legacy."

His own way. And with his brother. Africa brought him closer to Earl, who was almost a decade younger—the civil rights activist who already knew Africa, who had visited with Nelson Mandela. The two brothers began to take trips together throughout Africa. Richard was still working in his education job, but the transformation had begun. "My brother; he was a great inspiration," says Richard. On one trip, they traveled from Ghana to South Africa. "To have someone to share it with—a brother who could deal with ideas and concepts. You realize you are not going to change the world. The world is tougher than I originally thought it was. You resign yourself. But you say to yourself: Maybe I can have some effect. Not to change the world, but to have some effect on it. You're more realistic. You can have an effect that will make a difference to someone other than yourself," he says.

"Earl and I talked almost every day. Earl had so many dreams. Life offered so many possibilities. We were at a point where we could make them materialize."

An idea started to take shape. After all, look at the stuff Richard was bringing back from Africa—so many presents for family and friends. The incredible crafts and art he saw everywhere he went. The carvings, the jewelry. And then Richard got angry. So much talent—and so much poverty. Richard and Earl talked about that.

The idea grew. All the talented people they met in their travels. All the real opportunities in international trade. Why not set up an import company? "One, we could provide the people with a market. And two: We could expose friends and family and others to see these products," explains Richard. A people-to-people trading company. "We do not deal with major import manufacturers. We deal with the people we met in the villages. Our business is based on our dealing with indigenous people and helping them to become economically viable in their own land," he says. Real globalization, he says.

"The business was not based on our becoming wealthy. Nonetheless, it is a business. It must make a profit."

In 2001, the family opened the Diaspora Market Place, "specializing in cultural imports from the African Diaspora." Richard realized his dream—but not without great pain. By the time you reach the bonus decades, finding purpose is often forged in loss.

A year before the opening, Richard got a phone call from his sister on a Sunday morning in June: *Earl's been in an automobile accident,* and thirty minutes later she called again: *Earl did not make it.* Car crash on Interstate 85 in Alabama. A tire had blown. Earl T. Shinhoster, a passenger in the car, was killed. He was just shy of 50.

Richard fiddles with the two copper and bronze rope-spiral bracelets on his wrist. From Africa. From Earl. His brother used to wear them all the time. Now Richard wears them. *Earl did not make it.*

"That just doubled my determination to get the business going," he says. "There was no question. Everything Earl and I talked about had to be done."

The store is where he gathers the threads of his life and the black experience throughout the world. Soap stone carvings of elephants from South Africa. Polished teakwood sculpture from Ghana: Unity sculpture of interlocking male and female figures, the woman with a water pot on her head, the hunter with an antelope on his shoulder, the shepherd with a staff.

The man who had never ventured far from Georgia now makes regular trips to Africa. He's planning to go to Brazil, Guatemala, Haiti. "It's what I enjoy. I will travel to all these places. I'll establish relationships with the people."

Meanwhile, Richard has more time to balance work and fun. "I like to get out and deal with the yard," he says. "I play with the computer. I enjoy life."

Richard's new destiny is a long way from teaching kids the Pythagorean Theorem. But it's closer to home.

And the old dream of becoming an engineer? That had to skip a generation to his older daughter—the one who got the engineering degree from Georgia Tech.

✦

Retirement is actually a relatively recent phenomenon. In 1910, two out of three American men past the age of 65 were employed. The gold-watch idea of retirement at 65 didn't take off until after World War II. It was based on the male model of job experience—working for one company or institution for many decades and earning a pension to cover a few golden years of leisure before what was considered a timely demise. By 1950, fewer than half the men over 65 were in the labor force and the leisure concept of retirement accelerated over the next decades. By 1985, only 16 percent were working.

History seemed to be at cross-purposes: People were living longer, healthier lives—and retiring at younger and younger ages. Retirement was mainly viewed as a well-deserved, extended vacation.

Now history is changing again. "The trend toward earlier male retirement has recently stopped," note researchers in *The Public Policy and Aging Report* in 2001. In a tight economy, people are postponing retirement—if they can. Meanwhile, older women have surged into the workplace over the last fifteen years, making the concept of retirement even more obsolete. As the authors conclude: "The relative attractiveness of work and retirement at older ages has been altered in favor of work."

Longer life expectancy reinforces this shift toward work. Of course, who wouldn't like to take an extended vacation for a few years after the many decades of mainstream career work? But a vacation for thirty or forty years? People in My Time want fun and leisure. But most also want—and need—more than that. As the researchers in the *Aging Report* point out: "For many workers, retirement will last longer than the period from birth until full-time entry into the job market."

"We need a transformation of work as profound as that which occurred when women flooded the labor market," writes syndicated columnist Robert J. Samuelson. Most people would like to move gradually from full-time work to full-time retirement. But that requires a restructuring of the workplace. "We need more part-time jobs, we need more jobs with flexible working hours, and we need more jobs that engage people's interests even though promotion prospects have faded," continues Samuelson, who at 56 wears the label of "mature worker."

A key aspect of the work revolution in the bonus decades is personal control. For many people, that means devoting fewer than forty hours a week to one job. But as soon as you leave full-time employment for part-time work, you can get trapped in a wasteland of the labor force. As a part-timer you may not get the respect (or the relative pay, benefits, and good assignments) that a full-timer gets. Women who work part-time to raise children are already paying the part-time price in the job market. So do men who fall off the full-time ladder. And now a new group is tripping into the part-time ghetto: those in their 50s, 60s, and 70s who have left their primary career jobs—voluntarily or not—and still need and want to work.

What is so sacred about the forty-hour, full-time work week? asks social scientist Phyllis Moen of the University of Minnesota. Moen, who conducted the Cornell Lifetime Well-Being Study, would like to get rid of the forty-hour week as the gold standard of work and break down the full-time/part-time dichotomy. Maybe the forty-hour week reflected working lives—mainly of men—in the mid-twentieth century, but not in the twenty-first. She prefers the concept of ten-hour work units. Some people might work four units in a week, some only one. It's all work, she says.

A ten-hour work unit would enable people to take on multiple roles. She talks about a "package of pathways"—the different types of important work that add up to a "career" for people in My Time. There's paid work in the marketplace. There's community work that can be paid or unpaid. There's family work that may involve caring for an older relative or a young grandchild. And there's the personal work that goes into leisure activities and pursuit of a spiritual life. "People want some of each," she says. "It's very volatile."

At this stage of your life, you want a career that allows you to grow and fulfill the psychological tasks of My Time: *generativity* (reaching out to others), *wisdom* (providing knowledge and memory), and *integrity* (becoming whole). Putting the package of pathways together to achieve these tasks is the challenge.

You may have to step back from the busy years to reset priorities. Part-time work is often the answer. Sometimes, the part-time job becomes a central passion. Sometimes, it's the means to that end—the financial boost that enables you to pursue *what I want to do* outside a job. Sometimes part-time work in the same field provides a needed decompression period. "Particularly those who were involved in high-powered, high-product oriented activities," says psychiatrist Gene Cohen of George Washington University. "They are enormously helped by a transition—a modification of what they're doing."

A common pathway is to work part-time for your former employer. These are "bridge" jobs, and they serve an important function. They give you mastery over your own time—and some structure and stability as you shift focus. But a pitfall of working part-time for a former employer is that you often wind up working full-time for part-time pay—and being extruded from the hot center, not to mention the top. You get bitter.

Another danger is that the part-time job is all you do. You don't get involved in other aspects of your life—your family, your community, your own pleasure. You cut back and close down. You feel pushed aside, marginalized. That's another way of hanging on to the past.

The point of part-time work is that people "have the rest of the week to explore other aspects to see what gives them satisfaction—what taps their potential," says Cohen.

✦

Often it takes a new career to get started on finding the next career. You may have several careers in the bonus decades and find purpose in several different areas. It's a searching process.

Nancy Sullivan is searching. She remembers the first step into her Second Adolescence. She was exhausted. She had taken a three-week break one summer—part vacation, part sick duty for her sister—the longest she had ever been away from work in twenty years. "When I got back, instead of being refreshed and ready to go, I could barely get in the car on the way to work," says Nancy, 60, a nurse-midwife who lives in Portland, Oregon. "I was just exhausted."

She decided she should retire. Not that she had figured out her *what next?* Who had time for that?

For more than fifteen years, Nancy has been a professor at the School of Nursing at Oregon Science and Health University. She ran a maternal care program for indigent women. She developed distance-learning programs to train midwives throughout the state. She was teaching and seeing patients. She loved her work and her patients—the midwife who says: *"I will do everything to be there for your birth.* Most others don't say that. You're on call but you cannot guarantee to be there for the birth. I promise to be there," she says.

Along the way she was married and raised three children. And then, the jolts started. About five years ago, she and her husband broke up after thirty-two years of marriage.

Her unlined face is framed by silver hair that falls loosely to her shoulders. Nancy retains the gentle manner of obedience from her

Catholic upbringing. Growing up in Charleston, West Virginia. Going to Catholic schools and listening to the nuns. Becoming a nurse.

But she learned how to be disobedient and make her own decisions. The turning point came in midlife when she was living in New York with young children, an ambitious husband, and the ambitious goal of becoming a midwife. She was working as a labor and delivery nurse and getting her degree in nurse-midwifery from Columbia University in New York. As part of her clinical training, she was told to see a patient and make an assessment. Nancy went in, evaluated the patient, and gave her instructor a perfect assessment. Then the instructor said: *What's your plan for managing the patient?*

"I fell apart. I couldn't do that—I couldn't come up with a plan," says Nancy.

Her instructor raised a red flag: *I think you need to get some therapy to find out why you can't decide how to manage. Why do you need someone else to tell you how to manage things?*

Nancy got some counseling. "It produced a real change. It enabled me to make my own decisions," she says. From then on, she was able to address the issues in her marriage and, after she and her husband moved to the West Coast, she was able to plan her advancement at the university in Portland. And then, to decide on an exit strategy from her full-time position so she could work part-time.

Meanwhile, she found a new purpose—related to her field, but different from her job: creating a special website of information for midwives and parents.

The project grew out of exhaustion—"when I was desperate to retire. I was so tired all the time," she says—and a visit from her son, a web designer. *Hey, mom. You could make a lot of money.* Nurse-midwives can prescribe drugs. Advertise stuff on the web. It wasn't the money, she says, though in this economy, even with her half-salary, she needs to make money. It's the idea of using all her experience to create a medically sound resource center for the general public. "My goal was getting information out to midwives and about midwives to consumers. At the time there was no good information on the web. I thought it would be a good thing."

With the help of her son, she launched *www.midwifeinfo.com*. In addition to a midwife directory and general data about pregnancy and birth, she sells items such as "birthing balls"—polyvinyl exercise balls to sit on during labor and "soothies"—gel-filled pads to put on nipples when you're breast-feeding.

"I'm enjoying myself," she says. She's breaking even. She thought the website might grow into her next career. But she finds it's not enough. Something is missing. Now that she's had time to step back and examine her life, she is dreaming anew. For several years, part-time work and the website have been a good *what next?* But what about some bigger possibilities? Something not connected with medicine? Something not based in Portland? She's free. "I'm searching. I'm definitely starting to search. I'm not there yet. The good thing is that there are a lot of enticing options. It's an exciting search," she says.

Some new careers last decades, some a few years. Meanwhile, you loosen up psychologically and are more open to change. Reinvention becomes routine. With thirty or forty years ahead of you, there's opportunity for a series of *what next?*

It gets down to what Nancy learned in nursing school: how to make a proper assessment—and how to formulate a plan of action. In My Time, you are your own case. You do this for yourself.

✦

Some people know exactly what they want to do in My Time. They've harbored the dream for years. You meet them going to parties or riding on a train or waiting in the doctors' office. "When I retire, I'm going to work with animals," says a voluptuous woman, 40, who works in public relations. Or: "I'm going to live on a farm"—from a man who dresses in a suit everyday at the office. Or: "I'm going to act in *A Streetcar Named Desire*."

Do you have a Big Dream to pursue? All through mainstream adulthood, the Big Dream churns in the psyche. Over a lifetime—paying the mortgage, going to parent-teacher conferences, making presentations to the boss, getting loans to pay for college—all during those mainstream years, the dream morphs from *what I really want to do* into *what I Will Do*. When, when. And finally—*if not now, when?*

It takes a lot of courage and a lot of planning to pursue the Big Dream. Especially if your dream is a radical departure from the status quo. And a lot of your friends say you're crazy.

But you get to the point where you can't *not* do it. When you've got a Big Dream, there's no time to waste.

Jim Taylor has that kind of Big Dream. When he was growing up in Charleston, South Carolina, he lived right on the harbor. He could see the big Navy ships and hear the pipes of boatswains as they ferried sailors into port. He liked to fish. He liked to row. He liked to sail. Right from the beginning, he was more at home in a boat than in the sandbox. Just looking at water stirred him up—the ripple of the waves, the beckoning of the horizon. He was a city boy, but the sea made him look outward, not inward. After graduating from a small college in Tennessee, he joined the Navy. The rhythm of the waves began to reflect the rhythm of his life. The Navy took him from Southeast Asia to the Mediterranean. So many harbors, so many straits.

So two things make perfect sense to him now at age 61: He has cut loose from a mainland career in the law to live on a boat in the Caribbean. He's still with his wife, Jayne, who is not afraid of the sea— or of sea-changes.

But first came that other life—the long period of adulthood that George Vaillant of Harvard calls the "career consolidation phase." In those decades, Jim became an international trade lawyer in Washington. Jayne became a chef with her own catering business. They raised two children and two dogs. They entertained a wide circle of friends and business acquaintances. Their life was as successful as it seemed serene.

But after decades of single focus, a restlessness started in Jim like the lap of the tide. As he describes it: "The case comes in. You're not as challenged by it because you know exactly what to do. You know all the stages in the relationship you will have with the client. First, there's a period of denial. *I didn't do it. Why me?* Then you finally come to the point where you can say: *Let's get down to work and defend the case.* I've done this for thirty years. Why am I doing it? How many more years— ten years? What do I do afterwards? If I want to do something else, I better think seriously about it."

Sailing is in the blood. You imagine life before the wind—roaming oceans, taming gusts, putting into port. Sailors harbor a near-mystical vision of the Perfect Boat, the one true hull. To sail is to be humbled, thrilled, and free! So free! Haze on the horizon. Winds shifting, currents turning, whitecaps of joy—and danger.

Jim always had a boat. Success at law allowed him to make sailing a hobby. Slowly his passion for sailing began to overtake his love of the law. "A lot of people have this dream—a lot of people in the sailing community. They talk about sailing around the world," says Jim. "This type of thing is a dream of most people who sail. Sailors have to do this."

After a sailing vacation with friends in Panama, Jim talked to Jayne about the dream: Cast off from the mainland and live on a boat.

Jayne's first response: *Oh Jim. This is crazy.*

"I couldn't imagine this happening," says Jayne, 52. "It's all a dream, I said to myself. I'll go along with it. Nothing's going to happen soon."

Jim said: "We've got to do this before we're too old." *Jolt!*

About a year later, a big four-inch, three-ring binder of boat specifications appeared on the bedside table. As soon as Jayne saw Jim's choice of night-time reading, she thought: "This is serious. He really wants to do this." But still, a far-off dream. And impractical. "I didn't see us sailing around the world," she says. They were too engaged with friends and colleagues. And children in college. They enjoyed people too much to set out on an indefinite cruise. "If we did that, I thought, we'll go crazy."

Jim kept talking about it. Maybe they should think about chartering—having a boat and taking people out on cruises? That way they could keep their involvement in people and earn the money they needed to support this new life. Okay, thought Jayne. We'll look at boats. Maybe they should hire themselves out as captain and crew? Okay, we'll explore that. No. Better to have our own boat. Set up our own business.

Slowly the dream morphed into a plan: They would start a gourmet charter boat business in the Caribbean and give tourists the best in food and sail. Soon Jim had narrowed down the size and type of boat: a Cantana catamaran built before 1996. There were only nineteen in the world. "Then I realized—this is going to happen," says Jayne.

It took Jim five or six years to make the transition from lawyer to cruise captain—three years alone to find the Perfect Boat. Meanwhile, he had to go back to school and get a captain's license from the Coast Guard. For eight months, he got up at 5 A.M. to study for two hours before getting dressed in a lawyer suit and going down to the office. He and Jayne had to take courses to become boat brokers. They had to learn the business details—insurance, wear-and-tear boat maintenance, consumer issues like: How easy is it to climb into bed? Jim took a fire-fighting course on St. Thomas. Jayne investigated how she could provide gourmet meals.

"Once I realized this was going to happen, I went into Type A personality overdrive," says Jayne. Jim was in charge of all things nautical. She was in charge of all things domestic. She designed the boat's interior, which included a gourmet kitchen above the water line. Now they were partners in a B&B&B: bed and breakfast . . . and boat.

Since they had fallen in love more than thirty years ago in Naples, they decided to name their renovated forty-four-foot catamaran *Andiamo*—which in Italian means Let's Go! In the fall of 2001, Captain Jim and Chef Jayne were open for business: *www.sailandiamo.com.*

All was well planned—except the timing. Fortunately, their son had finished college and was working at a bank in Washington. Their daughter was still in college. Would she feel abandoned? And what about the family dog—their beloved Irish setter? (The dog went to live with the daughter at college and became the class mascot.) And the huge task of packing very quickly—getting rid of furniture and storing boxes from the house where they'd lived for more than twenty years? And Jayne's clients? She'd had to shut down a thriving catering business. One client burst into tears. Some of their friends whispered to Jayne: *Are you really going to do this? Are you crazy?*

Dramatic change involves risks. That can be very unsettling for you and those around you. But taking some risks is usually necessary to make the transition to My Time—and taking risks gets easier and less frightening with practice.

Jim and Jayne had an advantage: They actually went through a dress rehearsal for this sea-change about twenty years earlier. At that time, Jim was on the power track at a large law firm. Jayne was raising two small children and starting her catering business. Jim had a dream of opening an office for the firm in Paris. He kept lobbying the firm. Let's go to Paris. We could be big players in international trade. Finally, he got the green light to go ahead.

"I came home and told Jayne," he recalls. They were having friends over for dinner that night. "I announced it at dinner. Everyone said— it's a wonderful idea." Jim was ecstatic. Going to Paris! It befitted his romantic impulse for adventure—and achievement. Everybody raised a glass—Paris! Fantastic! "I looked down at Jayne at the end of the table. She was crying." At first he thought it was tears of joy.

But it wasn't joy. Jayne was undone. Pick up and go? "She was thinking about all the practical issues—the kids in school, the house, her catering business," says Jim. She was also remembering her childhood as an Army brat. Her father was in the public relations department of the British Army. She moved all over the world. Her ease with adventure was tempered by the desire to give her children one firm home address. "I was a homebody," she says. "I couldn't be happier than when I'm being at home."

Jim hadn't prepared her. This was the moment of crisis that made them talk through their mutual dreams and fears. In the end, Jayne took the risk and turned all her alpha energies to making the Paris years a success. Indeed, they had three glorious years. What's more, the Paris adventure turned out to be a big boost to her career. She worked with a leading French chef, collaborated on a recipe book, and opened a cooking course during the season on St. Barts. By the time they returned to home base in Washington, Jayne was an established chef and not so afraid of taking risks. And Jim was careful to share his dreams—from the start.

As the *Andiamo* dream unfolded, Jayne could see the potential for her as well as for him.

Not that she didn't have moments of bad-mother blues. What if her daughter needed help on an art project—or had a fight with her boyfriend and needed to talk? The children reassured her. More than that: "They both said: *This is awesome*. They said: *If we are able to do what you are doing when we are your age, we would be so happy*," explains Jayne. Even the children's friends were enthusiastic. "They said: *You guys are utterly cool*."

The start-up was disastrous. There was the house they rented in Trinidad with the bats. "Jim comes out of the bathroom screaming. I'm screaming. The bat startled us. Then at night we'd hear boom, boom. A mango tree, dropping mangoes on the roof."

There was the killer storm that destroyed several other charter boats. And there was September 11.

In the wake of the terror attacks, the cruise industry collapsed. The stock market tanked—along with their savings. But that strengthened their resolve. "By then I was just determined. So many things went wrong. That made us even more determined. We had huge support from family and friends," says Jayne.

Jim had also put a safety plan into place. When he told his colleagues at the firm about his plans to bolt, he was given a lifeline. "They said: *If anything goes wrong, come back*," explains Jayne. Again, this caution mixed with risk had precedent. When Jim was considering law school, his father had given him similar assurances. A businessman in Charleston, who ran a cold-storage locker and seafood-processing plant, his father told him: *Why don't you go to law school? If you still want to come back to the company, it's there.* Jim went into law and never came back. But having a safety-net is good insurance for risk takers. It allows you to be more adventurous in pursuit of your dreams—and more thoughtful in the planning.

Today Jim and Jayne have a new life together. "I tell you, it's great. He's got his responsibilities. I've got mine. It's strengthened our relationship. We're together all the time every day. We love it. We've developed a different form of respect. We're dealing with the same things, the same issues, the same demands," says Jayne. "Jim exudes an immense amount of confidence. I feel very safe."

And it's up to her to whip up around-the-world cuisine: bouillabaisse Marseillaise, Mango mousse, Greek mezze, Floating Island with coconut crème Anglaise, Andalusian gazpacho, and Flamenco flan caramel.

They feel healthier than ever. They've lost some weight. "Fresh air. Activity," says Jim. "You swim. You're in good shape." He doesn't have a nervous stomach anymore. He doesn't have lactose intolerance. He doesn't have sleep problems. He always had to worry. That's the law. Worrying about the big case. Nothing else matters. If you don't worry, you get flushed out. The only way to succeed is to work in your head all the time. To worry. As he says: "Sleepless nights are not uncommon in the legal profession."

"We get on the boat," says Jane. "He sleeps like a baby. We go to bed at 8:30 and sleep until it's light in the morning."

But this is work. Running a small business is 24/7 work. "We're trying to break even. The goal is to do something you think you love to do," says Jayne.

✦

Jim's transition from lawyer to sailor illustrates the potential for reinvention in My Time. And so does Jayne's transformation from reluctant disbeliever to equal partner in their new life. It takes both of them to make the dream work.

Why do some people take risks—and others don't? Part of the answer lies in your past. Did you take risks long ago—in high school? When you first got out on your own? How do you respond to changes at work? In relationships? Jim and Jayne benefited from having made changes earlier in their marriage. They were more comfortable with risk—and more prepared to turn risk into opportunity.

Another part of the answer is fate. Events happen that allow you to open up and try something new—or a catastrophe occurs that forces you to change. Jim and Jayne point out that most of the other boat owners were in some way forced into it. Some were shoved out of a job—and given a golden parachute that enabled them to take the financial plunge. Or they were diagnosed with a disease and given two years to live. Or they suffered a life-changing trauma—the death of a loved one.

"We're not in that position," says Jim. But he felt an urgency not to wait too long to make the break. "I felt the timing was right," he says. He remembers another sailor who harbored the same dream to live on a boat. "He said to me: *When I finally got around to it—when my wife was willing, when the kids were settled, when the dog died—I was too old to do it.*

"Physically and mentally, this is a big challenge," he says. "You can't come into this business at 65. You're too old. You might work in it longer than 65, but you don't begin in it." And you need a certain mindset for the Big Dream. "I think you have to be a romantic. You have to be something of a romantic to ignore the hardships when you do something like this," he says.

The whole enterprise could fail. You have to confront the possibility of failure.

Take ten guys with the dream to live on a boat and sail the world, he says. "Maybe 60 percent drop out because their wives say no." At a farewell party for them, Jim and Jayne noticed a gender split. "The women would say: *Do not tell my husband what you are doing.* They were afraid. The women didn't want to do it," says Jayne. "The guys would say: *This is awesome.* They'd say to Jim: *How did you get your wife to do this?*"

Sometimes the Big Dream is not feasible. Your spouse balks. Wives—or husbands when the wife is the big dreamer—may be rooted in their own career and social network. They may not share the dream. They have a different dream. . . .

Another factor is the status of children. How self-sufficient are they? And what are your other responsibilities? Do you have a parent in an assisted living facility? A dependent sibling who needs regular attention? A friend in need?

Then there are the numbers. Can you afford to make the leap? Jim and Jayne ran the numbers before the economy turned sour. If they were looking into starting a boat business today, "it would have been irresponsible to get into this," says Jim. But he's weighed anchor. "Once you're in, you can't get out. You don't call it irresponsible. You call it—caught."

Still, he's an optimist. That's a key element of resilience in My Time. You're able to see hope in setbacks, possibility in disappointment. You draw out the positive. Jim puts it this way: With nobody getting into the charter cruise business, there is no new competition. They have market share. "We're ready to go," he says. It's even better than getting in on the ground floor, he says. "We're in on the new basement level!" And then he laughs.

Jim, with his easy manner and the hint of South Carolina in his voice, is content with his choices. Damn the torpedoes of fate: full sail ahead.

This is what he wants to do—with Jayne. "It's like the Last Hurrah. You say to yourself: I'm not going to fade into oblivion. You want to do something that is challenging. People like challenges." He looks over at Jayne—her bright green eyes, short pixie brown hair, athletic build. "Jayne will do anything," he says.

The Sailor's Dream is not for everyone. But the story of Jim and Jayne lays bare the universal anatomy of taking risks and changing your life— when you aren't forced by events, but driven by a passion.

So many factors have to line up—as though you were hitting the jackpot on a slot machine. But foremost is personal style and discipline. A dreamer has to make a plan—and implement it. How often do you say: *if only?* Fill in the blanks: *if only* I didn't have children still in college, *if only* I didn't have such high house payments, *if only* I had a spouse to do this with me, or *if only* I weren't married, I could do this. The softer refrain is *when I have time:* I'll go back to school, *when I have time.* I'll go to the Grand Canyon, *when I have time.* I'll draw up a business plan for my own company, *when I have time. . . .*

When you hit the bonus decades, you have time. You can't afford to wait any longer. *If not now, when?*

6

Giving Back

We make a living by what we get. We make a life by what we give.

WINSTON CHURCHILL

EVERYONE HAS THE FANTASY of being free—being free of work, free from household chores, free of the past. You hit the road to relax and do nothing. . . . And then something happens on the way to the fantasy.

Bob and Marge Kitterman had been on the road in their motor home for four months when they pulled into Hannibal, Missouri, and Marge started fixing dinner. Bob had retired from the banking business in Greensboro, North Carolina, and the next day they had driven off in a brand new RV. "We thought—we'll see the country, lie back, read, do nothing. That was the way we were going to spend the rest of our lives," says Bob. First stop: Tallahassee for the birth of their second grand-child, and then up to Atlanta to see their older daughter, and then they headed West. "We ended up in Missouri. I can't tell you why," says

Marge. "This was the longest time we'd been on the road without anything else to do but do for ourselves."

And frankly it was starting to wear thin. Even though they were on-the-road-again kind of people—considering all the camping trips they had taken with the kids, all the times they'd said if only there was more time just to roam and relax and do nothing. But as Bob says: "You get tired of that."

They were in that kind of mood when they got to Hannibal and turned on the TV and found out the news: Their daughter's in-laws were involved in a train wreck in Florida. "We were horrified," says Marge, 65. "A barge hit the bridge and the train went into the swamps," explains Bob, 67. The couple escaped from a burning car. Bob and Marge saw footage of the car half in water. All the while they agonized. "We can't be there. We can't help our daughter," says Marge. "We've got to do something."

They kept watching TV. Another news flash: Floods . . . Mississippi River breaking through the river bank . . . Illinois town threatened . . . volunteers needed . . . start at midnight.

Bob and Marge looked at each other. Train wreck. Flooding. Volunteers needed. "We said: We need to do this. We want to do this. We had to be there at midnight," recalls Marge. They couldn't help their daughter's family, but they could help somebody.

They finished dinner, got into their grubbiest clothes and drove the RV to Quincy, Illinois, about an hour away. "We worked all night," says Marge, packing sand into bags to shore up the river—filling sacks a little bit bigger than grocery bags to stop the waters from breaking through. "We were tired and hurt all over. But we were so happy doing something useful again," says Marge. "We needed something meaningful in our lives."

The next day Bob called Habitat for Humanity, a nonprofit organization that uses volunteers to build affordable houses for needy families. He offered to go anywhere in the RV to help out. They haven't stopped.

Today Bob and Marge are leaders of the Care-A-Vanners, a group of about a thousand people, mostly between the ages of 50 and 75, who live in motor homes and go around the country building houses with Habitat for Humanity. Marge and Bob still get to roam around in their RV, but now they have a purpose—thanks to the Mississippi floods of 1993. Instead of packing wet sand, they are insulating closets and putting on roofs.

That night a decade ago changed their life. "Thank heavens it did," says Marge. "We had to do something to give back again." It's a new life for the Kittermans, a new career of giving back. "It's hard for me to put in words. The feeling. . . . " Bob pauses and then he says: "In reading the bible, this is what you ought to be doing. Give back, don't just take."

◆

Giving back, reaching out, caring for others, helping the community, volunteering your time and wisdom—this is the developmental task that Erik Erikson called *Generativity*. Marge and Bob exemplify this stage. They had always done volunteer work with their church, the local hospital, and the PTA. But now giving back is the centerpiece of their lives, from building houses for strangers to nurturing their grandchildren. According to George Vaillant in *Aging Well,* "generativity means community building" and "empathetic leadership" and "a broader social circle through which one manifests care for the next generation."

You want to give back. You are mentor, guide, coach—grandparent, matriarch, and patriarch. Your psychological style is different from that of your younger peers. As a leader, you are warm (rather than combative), empathetic (rather than competitive), open (rather than secretive and manipulative). You use power to steer toward the greater good (rather than toward personal advancement). It takes the seasoning of age to get to this stage.

In earlier decades you were quite rightly more focused on building up your own self. You were passing tests in school and searching for a mate and raising children and finding a job and making money and aiming for promotions and seeking status and getting ahead. You were meeting the tasks of *identity, intimacy,* and *career consolidation.* Once you've done all that, you are ready to move on. You've gained enough along the way to have something to give back. You volunteer.

The giving-back impulse is the psychological mainstay of community service and volunteerism. The current buzzword is "civic engagement." For many people, the bonus decades are an opportunity to get involved in projects to help others. You now have the time and the psychosocial resources. You want to find something meaningful to do in these "extra" years. "This is an invention of a new stage of life," says Marc Freedman, author of *Prime Time: How Baby Boomers Will Revolutionize Retirement and Transform America.* "We've got to sell a new dream for this stage of life."

His dream, as president of Civic Ventures, a nonprofit organization in San Francisco, is to marshal the talents and expand the public contribution of older men and women—as a way "to help transform the aging of American society into a source of individual and social renewal."

Public contribution and volunteer work have always been a staple of retirement. There you are with a social security check in your pocket, crow's feet around your eyes, your name on a tag, a smile on your face. You volunteer at the hospital. You volunteer at the museum. You volunteer in the schools. You volunteer at the polls. You volunteer for a nonprofit organization. More than 55 percent of Americans aged 50 to 75 say that volunteering is—or would be—an important part of retirement, according to a 2002 poll by Peter D. Hart Research Associates.

The benefits of volunteering are well known. Research shows that people who volunteer live longer than those who don't. In the Hart survey of six hundred men and women, volunteers tended to be more optimistic, productive, and empowered than those who did no volunteer work. They were also less disabled by poor health.

But the world of volunteerism is in flux. The conventional labels of "volunteer" and "retirement" are becoming obsolete in a society reshaped by longevity. It's all about work. You're certainly not *retiring*. You're in the workplace. You're serving the community. As James Firman, of the National Council on Aging, says: "Retirement is irrelevant."

So, too, is the narrow concept of volunteerism—of simply offering your services for free. Not only does this definition exclude people who need to receive some kind of compensation for public service. It also has a negative candy-striper image—suggesting that unpaid work is not as serious as a "real" job.

Community service is serious work. Giving your expertise and donating your precious hours to the community is a real job. Giving back is a continuum of contribution from donating a few hours to the church to making a regular commitment to tutor in the schools—in return for some payment. Better to think of a volunteer as a "not-for-personal-profit" worker. You are still a worker, no matter what the pay, no matter what the hours, no matter what the age.

There are landmines in this redefinition of volunteer service, which is outside the conventional job market and calls for flexible work for flexible compensation. One is competence: Are you qualified to do the job? Can you get the proper training to work in a hospital or a museum? To counsel families moving from welfare to work? Another issue is exploitation: How do you make sure you won't be taken advantage of as a source of cheap labor? That you aren't taking jobs away from people in the traditional workforce? Little public attention is being given to these issues—leaving you to fend for yourself.

The critical component is motivation. When you are engaged in community service, you are putting public good ahead of personal gain—monetary gain, that is. You work out of a desire to help others and make a difference.

Still, you may need compensation. You are more likely to get involved in community projects if you do. In the Hart poll, half of the nonvolunteers said they would work at least fifteen hours a week in exchange for such benefits as education scholarships, prescription drug coverage, or a small stipend.

Receiving some kind of compensation is becoming a trend in public service as more and more people turn to giving-back work. Bob Kitterman, for example, is on the staff at Habitat for Humanity International where he gets benefits and a small salary. Marge receives a stipend for running the mission control center of the Care-A-Vanners—matching motor-home volunteers with requests for new houses. They both still think of themselves as volunteers. They depend on retirement income to put together a package of financial support. Recent losses have changed their lifestyle somewhat—but not their fundamental commitment to public service. They plan to be Care-A-Vanners as long as their health holds out.

It doesn't just happen. Building a next career in civic engagement takes the same kind of imagination and courage you need to start a business or enroll in law school or become a portrait painter. You still have to break away from mainstream adulthood. You still go through a transition phase of Second Adolescence and have to try out different scenarios of what you want to do. You still have to pay attention to the jolts—big and small. You still draw on "life power" and the core strengths that have shaped your past.

Marge and Bob Kitterman come across as down-home straight-arrows. But they have never been afraid to take risks, even when all those around them said: *you're nuts*. That's one of their core strengths.

They grew up in Indiana and couldn't miss each other at Butler University in Indianapolis: Bob is 6 foot 6; Marge is 6 feet. They married right after college and went to visit friends who lived in North Carolina.

Everybody was so nice. "We fell in love with the lady at the A&P who said good morning to us," says Marge.

They decided to leave the North and move south. Back in Indianapolis, they packed up all their stuff in a U-haul—plus the new baby—and drove to Charlotte without having a house lined up, without having a job. "Our daddies were making bets on how long it'd take for us to get back to Indiana," laughs Marge. "What a life we've had."

Fast-forward thirty years and people were making bets on them again. Here they were, living in a big house. Bob, a successful banker. Marge, a member of the Junior League. When Bob announced that he was taking early retirement and the two were going off in a new RV, all their friends said they were crazy. "They were taking bets on how soon we'd come back," says Marge.

But Bob and Marge were ready to move on. They could sense that the long chapter of middle adulthood was coming to an end. Not that Bob didn't love his work. He had ridden the banking boom to a good life. Starting in the 1960s, the banks in North Carolina were growing aggressively. As he says: "Opportunities kept opening up. It was a great time to be in there." After more than twenty years with one bank, he moved to a savings and loan institution and had another ten good years. But then, the S&L industry began to implode in the wake of scandals and government crackdowns. "I saw the handwriting on the wall," says Bob.

It was Labor Day Weekend 1992, and Bob and Marge were working in the yard. The timing was right. "We had already purchased the RV," recalls Marge. "It was a year since the last child graduated from college and the dog died." The two of them were raking leaves. "We looked at each other and said: This is ridiculous. We want to be traveling," continues Marge. *If not now, when?* As Bob says: "Our kids were getting older. They'd moved away. They were starting their own families."

Bob and Marge were free. The primary tasks of adulthood had been achieved—children raised, career completed, their Southern identity established. External circumstances reflected inner changes. Bob puts it this way: "I'd lost both my parents. It's just the realization that you're not going to be here forever."

At that point, he was 57. Marge was 55.

Everything happened very fast. Bob gave notice. They put their house on the market—it sold in four days. "We played with the finances. Our health was good," continues Bob. "We thought—let's hit the road. So we did."

In breaking away, there were no crises, no unexpected losses. Just the usual passages of adulthood—and inside, a seesaw of insight and restlessness that shaped their transition to My Time. It all added up to an urgency to get going while the going was good. "We realized that life is very fragile. We have a limited amount of time. While our health is good, we'll make a run for it," says Bob.

In making a run for it, they start dreaming again. The way they were right after college: on the road again, destination somewhere. First they try out the dream of being RV vagabonds—a dream they'd nurtured for years in their old life with a yard and a mortgage. They have to test their freedom—no job to return to on Monday morning, no children to get home in time for school. Nothing to do but relax and have fun.

Their experiment in full-time leisure lasts only about four months. "It doesn't work," says Bob. It took the jolt in Hannibal for them to make a mid-course correction. But it's just a correction. They keep the road-roaming part of the dream. They just combine it with a purpose. The dream evolves.

In the midst of their vagabond life, they get a recall: The S&L asked Bob to come back to Greensboro and help out for a while. One month turned into nine. The whole time, they lived in the RV park next to I-75—along with the followers of the Grateful Dead and the Circus. Their old friends would come over for dinner in the motor home.

"Their eyes were so big. They were thinking—*these two crazy fools,*" says Marge.

Since becoming Care-A-Vanners, they've gone through four RVs and built houses across the country from California and Oregon to Idaho, Colorado, Florida, Vermont, and Michigan. They've taken a group of RV builders to New Zealand, traveling five days, building five days—combining work with pleasure.

They reserve vacation time for the grandchildren—taking them off to Colorado and Maine. They had the lows—the time they broke down in Alaska some fifty miles from the nearest town. Bob stood out on the road to flag down some help. Every truck passed him by. "You're too big and too ugly for someone to stop," Marge told him. She went out on the road and the first truck that came along stopped. They laugh about that now. Living and working together has been good for their marriage.

They also rejoice in the highs—the thrill of making a difference. They remember their first build in Newport, North Carolina. "It was 107 degrees," recalls Marge. "We were so excited. We were just dripping." They made friends with the family whose house they were building—a couple with six children. The way it works, volunteers build the house along with family members, who invest "sweat equity." Habitat makes houses affordable by selling them at no profit and not charging interest on the mortgage.

Seven years after the house was built, the Kittermans received "payment." The oldest son in the family sent them an invitation to his Eagle Scout ceremony in the Boy Scouts. "Having his own house—having security really paid off for that family," says Marge. "Everybody wants a home. Everybody needs a home. We'll never forget that first build. We became hooked. There's a term for it—*habititis.* We got a good case of it."

You give—and in return, you get fulfillment. Marge and Bob know they have been richly blessed—strong health, a close family, material goods. They have "life wealth" to share, and in that sharing, they connect with the larger community; they connect to the future. Out of these connections comes the joy of making a difference. Their life has meaning—beyond themselves.

It's not that you don't have fun when you are making the world a better place. . . . Marge and Bob have a lot of fun rolling around the next bend in the road in their RV. They are still caught up in motor home mystique: "Every curve in the road, you see something spectacular," says Marge. "It's just magical." But they have a purpose that anchors their roving life. Having a purpose allows them to have fun *and* fulfillment.

For some people, retirement is seen mainly as an opportunity to enjoy themselves after the high-stress years of having a job and raising children. Even among volunteers in the Hart poll, about 16 percent viewed retirement *primarily* as a time to "take it easy" and "enjoy leisure" and "take a much-deserved rest from work/daily responsibility."

But leisure is the old definition of retirement. Today, most people—volunteers and nonvolunteers—say retirement is the beginning of a new chapter in life, rather than an extended vacation. Seven in ten volunteers in the Hart survey talked about having a purpose—"setting new goals" and "starting new activities" and "being active and involved"—beyond spending time with family and friends.

Forty years ago, the purpose-to-leisure ratio would have been reversed, points out pollster Peter D. Hart. This is a dramatic change, fueled by the bonus decades. You can't *just* coast. At least, not for thirty years. You want to enjoy yourself. You want to have pleasure. You also want meaning. *What are you going to do?* "It's not the idea of shuffleboard," says Hart. "These people want to be engaged. They believe they can make a difference."

✦

There are pitfalls in the giving-giving-giving work of volunteerism. If you haven't completed the earlier psychological tasks of development,

you risk getting trapped in the giving mode with inadequate resources. This is the stereotype of the continual caretaker, usually a
woman, who spends all her time giving to others—children, spouses,
relatives, friends, and dependent parents—and then takes on all the
giving work in the community—delivering meals to the frail, volunteering at the day-care center—without ever taking care of her own
self. Giving gets to be a habit. It provides you with a surface identity:
care-giver. You are rewarded with praise. Look at all the good you are
doing! And you are.

But in the process you may be carving out a hollow place inside
where you leave unanswered the basic question—*Who am I?* You're
running—volunteering—on empty. As Harvard's Vaillant warns: "When
Generativity is attempted before its appointed hour, it may fail. We can
give ourselves away only after our selves are formed."

Where are you in this process? All through life, you give and take.
It's never a perfect balance. You need to learn how to do both to grow
up and form a strong self and make intimate relationships. You may do
volunteer work as a young adult—but volunteering at this stage is usually in addition to everything else you're doing.

Volunteer work in My Time often becomes a central focus. It also
occurs at a different psychological level. It is rooted in the task of
Generativity, and that comes with maturity. Generativity is philanthropy of the soul. The great philanthropists from John D. Rockefeller to Bill Gates had to make their money first before they could
give it away. The same is true of the psychological assets that you acquire through adulthood. You have to have a portfolio of experience in
order to give back.

Research on normal development shows how your center of gravity
shifts over the life span. At 25 years of age, most of your desires and responsibilities are centered on advancing your personal agenda. At 60,
what you wish for—and where your obligations lie—are turned outward to extended family, friends, community, to the world in general.

Philanthropy—whether it's money or wisdom or service—tends to be a late-life phenomenon. By now you have something to give away.

You take stock. What psychosocial assets have you accumulated? These are stored in your safe-deposit box of "life empowerment." You have some core strengths that have kept you going all these years. Do you know what they are? Is your accounting up to date? You may not be aware of the riches you've put away over the years.

Some people get to My Time with a hole inside. Maybe you've been too beaten up by the past, suffered too many of fate's whippings. You didn't get much while growing up. You didn't get much in relationships. You didn't get much appreciation on the job. You just didn't get much, though you put out. You gave of yourself—but what did you get back?

Maybe you've lost the deposit slips. You're not using the hidden strengths that make up your life empowerment. After all, you've made it this far. One of the tasks of Second Adolescence is to catalog your strengths. You have the chance to turn past suffering into energy for the future. You need to understand the themes that have shaped your development. You've got the time. You've got some perspective. You've got a life to examine.

The bonus decades are an opportunity to give of yourself *to yourself* as a way to shore up your resources. Then you can give of yourself to others and make a difference. In the process of filling the hole inside, you blossom.

Annette Mitchell, 69, walks around the bright yellow classroom at Montgomery Elementary School in Washington, D.C. Dressed in a stylish maroon outfit with a matching cape, Annette has flare. She also has the touch with kids. It's the glint of fun in her eye. And she knows how they hurt, too. What they need is parenting, she says. She knows about Mother Hunger because she was raised by her grandmother. She loved her gramma, but she missed her mother. She's firm with the kids. She told one boy that she would not tutor him any more if he kept behaving that way. He stopped. He became a good student. She can do that to kids—she can give that to kids: a chance at life.

Annette is many things: fourth-generation Washingtonian, wife, mother, grandmother, seamstress, poet, former government worker, coat-check girl—and now "classroom academic aide," according to her job title.

She leans over one of the students and admires the drawing: a rectangular mass of pink with multicolored boxes and streamers. Underneath, the youngster has copied down: "This chair is nice and soft for my mother." Annette smiles. She has just read a story to the kindergarten glass—*A Chair for My Mother* by Vera B. Williams. And she has given an assignment: Draw a chair. As she moves from table to table, she tells the children: "You want it to be a very nice chair." They pick up more crayons. "This is an important chair." *For my Mother*.

Annette is a member of Experience Corps, the volunteer organization that sends older men and women to work in elementary schools. She works sixteen hours a week—helping out in the classroom and tutoring students one-on-one—for a small stipend.

She's been working at Montgomery for three years. At first there were some questions. All these senior volunteers coming into the school? Were they competent to work with children? "I eat my words every day," says assistant principal Mary C. Robinson. "They are wonderful. They are so dependable. There's something about older people—character and responsibility are ingrained in them."

Annette is one of the stars. This is something of a surprise to her. She'd never been a teacher before. She didn't know she had this gift with school kids. But here she is—teaching in the classroom and tutoring the ones who need help.

She's never been so happy. "I intend to stay here for a long time, " she says. "I love it. The thing is, you're helping others. I couldn't get over the fact that the kids come out of high school and they are not able to read. If I can get a kid to read in kindergarten and get that start—it's fulfilling."

Fulfilling for the kids. Fulfilling for the country. And fulfilling for Annette.

But first she had to fill the hole inside. Growing up, she was sickly. Her asthma was so bad, she missed a year of school. She didn't think she was pretty. "I had nappy hair and skinny legs," she says. She had dreams—she wanted to go to college, she wanted to learn fashion design. She wanted to study music.

She didn't do any of that. She got married and had three children. Soon it will be fifty years. A long marriage. Three wonderful children. A solid career. But somewhere along the way, she lost her self.

Once the children were in school, Annette got a job in the school system—but it was in food service and then in accounting and program development. She worked for the school system for twenty-eight years and never set foot in a classroom. How could she be a teacher? She didn't have the credentials.

All the while, she lived on two levels. As she wrote in her journal: "Acquaintances think that I'm a carefree, happy person who deals with life with an optimistic view. I try to have a very good sense of humor and perform well." That was the outside level. And then the inside level—an empty place of sorrow and disappointment. She gave herself a nickname—"Dummy."

She didn't get her selves together until she was in her 50s. The jolts started coming and shook up her life. She retired unexpectedly. Her office was abolished and so was her job. "I didn't intend to retire," she says. But it wasn't so bad. She had earned a pension. She was 56. She just didn't know what to do. She'd read in *Modern Matu-*

rity that you're supposed to plan for retirement. But as she says: "I came home with no plans. After two or three months, I was climbing the walls."

At the same time she was confronting her past. The children were grown and she had time to think. She wanted to keep the marriage—and find a place for herself at the same time.

She found that place in the garage. Years earlier she had turned the garage attached to the back of the house into a room of her own. The contractor bricked in the back and created a couple of windows. Annette put up some quiet off-white Japanese shades to let the light in. She covered the walls in honey-colored carpeting—to set off her pictures. A photograph of Malcolm X. A drawing of an American Indian—her great-grandmother was a Native American who married a black man in the Coast Guard and settled in Washington.

At one end of the room is an armoire with a TV, but she doesn't watch much TV. What she loves is music. On top of the armoire is a large box with the index file to her music collection: Brahms, Beethoven, Chopin, Tchaichovsky. And Natalie Cole, Barbra Streisand, Gladys Knight. First she had LP records. She converted them to tapes. Now she has CDs. Her mother used to play the piano; Annette played, too. At night after the children had gone to bed, she'd go down in the living room and play the piano, but she made too much noise so she had to stop that. Now she can listen to her music as much as she likes.

In the center of the room is her sewing machine and a comfy office chair. She made her children's clothes. She made some clothes for her husband. She makes her own clothes. Spools of different thread are stacked on one side of the room. Hanging on the door is a rust-salmon coat with pale blue trim. She followed the pattern for a jacket and extended it into a coat. She can do that. She has an eye, the eye of a fashion designer. She lined the coat with fancy gray silk. She likes fancy linings.

She pours her heart out on a typewriter. She has some arthritis in her hands, but her fingers tap out her soul, whether it's writing or sewing.

This is her sanctorum. It is neat and orderly. Everything is in its place. Everything is about who she is, who she has become. Here she is in control of herself. No one to tell her she's no good, no one to tell her she can't do something—though she'd like to have a dog. Once they had a dog, a German shepherd, named Blu. So she has a photograph of Blu on the wall. And photographs of all her children. And grandchildren.

It is in this room that she strengthens her self—a safe place where she comes to terms with the dark side: the trough of depression, getting into treatment, falling back into the trough again. Long ago, a psychologist suggested she keep a journal and she hasn't stopped. "I felt lonesome, nervous and became more insecure," she wrote during a particularly bleak time. Back to treatment. Back to her room. Back to her music. Her sewing. Her writing. Back to this zone of safety where she can confront danger with the help of Tchaichovsky's Piano Concerto No. 1, the silk-lined coat hanging on the door, the children smiling on the wall.

It takes Annette many years to build up her store of inner resources. In the emotional arena, she has to make up for lost time. She has to secure her persona the way teenagers are supposed to establish their identity the first time around in adolescence. But like many people, Annette arrives on the cusp of My Time with unfinished business in her psyche. She deals with her "wounded dummy" side, first by acknowledging it in her journal, then by putting it to rest in her poetry. A few years ago, she wrote in a poem: *Fortunately, God carries fools and dummies that cannot walk alone/In hope that one day they'll awaken and at least know that the sun has shone.*

Annette awakened. Meanwhile, she goes through a number of external changes—experimenting with different scenarios like a kid out of school. After she retired, she took a bar-tending course. She worked as a coat-check hostess in a hotel. "Terrible hours," she says. She didn't want to do office work anymore, but ended up as a part-time receptionist in a program for seniors in the federal government. She stayed in that job for six years.

And then . . . serendipity. She hears about Experience Corps from a friend and goes for an interview. But she has no teaching experience and is told: *This isn't for you.* Still, she's invited to come to a training session. A fluke, she says. And then she excels in the program. Her core strengths come to the surface. She blossoms in the classroom.

What Annette lacks in credentials, she makes up in life empowerment. She realizes her assets. After all, she volunteered in school when her kids were young. She was the Homeroom Mother because so many of the other mothers were working and couldn't be there with the children. She was a mother figure in the neighborhood. "There was a little boy up the street. Every day I had to stop and wipe his tears. That kind of thing stays with you," says Annette. She's always had the mothering knack with kids. "I listen. That's the main thing. It's almost like a puzzle with children. You have to listen—then you can figure it out."

She realizes that the special theme of her life is about mothering: missing her mother when she grew up, fantasizing about the mother she didn't have, turning to substitute mothers, finding her mother by becoming a mother to her own children, creating a "mother" persona to all children—in the home, down the street, and now in the classroom. She sees the links between past and present. "My children were a joy. As adults, they are a joy to us," she says. "Tutoring is an extension of parenting."

Draw a Chair for Your Mother. . . . The classroom is where Annette belongs. She gathers up the drawings. It's lunchtime. The children march out to the cafeteria, single-file, no talking, hands at their sides. First the girls in gray-green plaid jumpers, then the boys in green pants and neckties. "They are wonderful kids. I enjoyed my kids when they were little. I enjoy these kids," says Annette. "You do what you want to do. It's good. I'm doing something that's a way of giving back."

And now she's got a lot to give back. "I've done a whole lot of changing over the years," she says. "When I was young, people were trying to tell me things and I couldn't hear. Now I'm trying to tell the things I know to the kids. It might help somebody."

Annette has found contentment in her bonus years. She's doing what she wants to do. "I'm comfortable. I like where I live. I like the neighborhood. I like what I'm doing. I'm glad I worked long enough to have an annuity. I have Medicare. I have what I need."

Giving back is part of the broad psychological agenda of My Time. You can be generative in relationships—taking care of a grandchild, nurturing a sick friend. You can be generative in organizations—being a mentor, a consultant. You can be generative in creating an entity to help others: a medical project to stamp out AIDS and TB in Russia, a program to help addicted mothers. You can be generative in volunteer work—delivering meals on wheels, protecting a row of ancient elm trees in a public park from Dutch Elm disease.

The main thing is the passion you feel about what you do. You are reaching out and helping others not out of duty, but out of desire. You want to do this.

7

Expanding the Mind

Only put off until tomorrow what you are
willing to die having left undone.

PABLO PICASSO

IF YOU PUT RATS in a nice cage with Ducky doll, a windmill toy, and some mazes—they get smarter. If you feed them blueberries, they remember better where they're supposed to go in swimming tests. When you examine the brains of mice, those who lived in an intellectually stimulating environment have more brain cells than those left to their own lazy devices.

If that doesn't convince you that what you do, what you think, even what you eat, can help keep your brain vital, remember the study of London taxi-cab drivers who are famous for knowing all the streets and alleys in that city. Researchers found that they have a bigger part of the brain responsible for finding things than non-taxi-cab drivers.

In other words, use it or lose it. The brain is a malleable and dynamic organ that needs activity. "We can do much more to help the brain and help ourselves than we ever thought possible," says Marcelle Morrison-Bogorad, an expert in neuropsychology at the National Institute of Aging. "The rate of aging is mutable. That goes for the brain as well as the rest of the body."

You want a lively mind. You need to go where you can find the equivalent of Ducky doll and mazes.

For many in My Time, that means going to school.

There is an education surge among people over 50. The new face on campus is a wise face. Nearly 85,000 men and women over 50 are full-time students in undergraduate and graduate programs, according to the latest figures from the Department of Education. Nearly 435,000 are part-time students. About 120,000 are earning graduate degrees— almost two-thirds of them are women.

Millions more are taking courses not for credit. They are attending classes at universities, going to life-learning centers, seeking education vacations with Elderhostel—"The Trace of Japanese History" in Kyoto, the "Genesis of African Civilization" in Addis Ababa. They are flooding into creative arts. They are singing in choruses, going to arts festivals, joining book clubs, signing up for community theater, learning to paint portraits, taking music tours to Santa Fe and Vienna. One 82-year-old man learned German just so he could understand Wagner in the original.

The boom in education and creativity in My Time is a grassroots movement. You can't wait for the academic establishment to put together a core curriculum for those with graying hair. This is do-it-yourself learning—and more and more people are doing it. In a study of more than a hundred people over 60, education turned out to be a top priority. "I was struck by the fact that almost everybody expressed on their own their desire for ongoing education. The sheer magnitude of interest was a surprise," says the study's director Gene Cohen of George Washington University.

You go to school for some of the same reasons younger students go to school: to learn, to gain skills, to figure out your future. But your goals are different. After all, you've graduated from the real world of experience. Going to school isn't just about getting ahead. It's learning for learning's sake and putting meaning into your life. It's finding your voice—What is it that you really want to do?

Sometimes schooling is a means to an end; sometimes it becomes the end. When you're in the midst of Second Adolescence, you don't know how it will turn out.

Libby Borden, 63, has always been a woman of accomplishment. When Libby and I were in elementary school together, she had blond pigtails and the highest math marks in the class. In the first part of adulthood, she lived in New York City, raised children and used her math skills to help run a publishing company that she and her husband had started.

About ten years ago, she developed an interesting hobby. She began noticing obituaries of women who made major changes late in life. One woman began mountain climbing in her 60s; another took to writing mysteries. By the time Libby was 55, she had put together a whole scrapbook of these late bloomers. "At that point, I knew I would be facing this. I was gathering courage by reading positive life stories," she says.

In the space of a few years, a cascade of jolts forced her to contemplate a totally different life—she just didn't know what.

First, a divorce after more than two decades of marriage and three children. Still, Libby and her husband remained close. After all, when they started the company, it was just the two of them and a secretary. In the end they had seventy-five employees and ten million dollars in annual sales. "We were joined at the hip," she says. And then, soon after the divorce, her husband was diagnosed with cancer and he came back home. Libby took care of him. When he died, she was by his side. She was 51.

Life went on with her children, with friends, old and new. She ran the company successfully for six years. Then she decided to sell it. One afternoon shortly before the sale, she went to the farmhouse in Norfolk, Connecticut, that she had bought twenty years earlier for weekends. A quiet, rural place. She felt herself suspended between past and future. "I came up for an afternoon just to think," she says. "What will happen to me if . . . ?" If she didn't work at the publishing company anymore? If she sold the New York apartment and lived somewhere else? If she broke up with a man she was seeing at the time?

"All the main things in my life—I was going to sever. Sometimes you get so afraid. You think the structure of your life is what is buoying you up." But her structure was about to crumble.

In July 1998, Libby ended her connection to the company. She was 58. "The morning I got up and I wasn't going to go to work, I got really, really depressed and down in the dumps. What am I going to do? I got back into bed and let it pass over me," she says. She just lay there and let it all sink in. "Then when I got up, I was fine," she says. This was the way she would confront the future. She would let it all sink in and then get going.

"I had absolutely no plans," she says. "I decided I wasn't going to fill my life with a bunch of stuff. I was going to wait and see where I was going to go," she says. "Some days—I would have nothing to do all day."

For many, this is a frightening prospect. A wave of anxiety can build up in Second Adolescence when you have nothing to do all day. When you take too long to read the paper and wonder what to eat for lunch. When unwanted thoughts keep intruding like—what are you doing, who are you, does anybody care . . . and what's your life about anyway. You're not used to not having a plan.

But by resisting the temptation to get too busy, Libby opens the way for the unexpected to come her way. Like the Beatles refrain: *She came in through the bathroom window!* Sometimes, the breakthrough route to the future is the least obvious. This is the bathroom window solution.

But to let the unexpected unfold, you've got to keep the bathroom window of your psyche open, or at least ajar.

Libby's *what, next?* "evolved with no big plan," she says. "But every time I took a step, I just knew it was right. Then I took another step." Like the day a friend canceled lunch, and she signed up for an Outward Bound excursion. That took her outdoors—and inside her head to review priorities. She liked that. And every time some environmental group would send her mail, she'd join up. A friend put her in touch with the Wilderness Society and Conservation International. She liked that a lot, too.

One day when she was riding the train from New York to Boston, she looked out the window at the marshes near New Haven—the sweeping grasses in the silver light of the sun, so much beauty, so much harmony—so different from downtown Manhattan. She thought about living in the country.

And through the bathroom window came another idea: Why not contact Yale University about taking some courses on environment? By this time she was getting hooked on the outdoors. Why not apply for a master's degree, suggested the director of admissions. *Why not?* So Libby applied. When she was accepted into the program at the Yale School of Forestry and Environmental Studies, she said to herself: "Oh well, I might as well go."

Just as teenagers revise their dreams of the future as they go through adolescence, so did Libby. She grew to love the solitude of the house in Norfolk and decided to make it her home. "It's very isolated. I love it. I'm happy to be here," she says. The environment with its natural beauty and unspoiled land was slowly becoming her destiny.

The transition was huge. She sold her apartment. Goodbye City Girl. She moved to Norfolk. Hello Country Girl. She went to Yale. Hello Student!

Once Libby started in the master's program in the fall of 2002, her life reshuffled. Her children were on their own—a married daughter with a two-year old in New Haven, a son working in New York City, another finishing up college in California. At 62, she was on a new path as an academic pioneer. In the program of 120 students, the average age is 28. "I am definitely the oldest," says Libby.

The beginning wasn't easy. Going back to school can unleash all the insecurities of being a kid again. You are no longer in control, no longer the boss. You remember what it was like to enter a new school. Suddenly you don't belong. You don't know the rules.

"What I felt . . . I am an outcast. I am an impostor. I am taking the place of somebody who should be here instead. I felt that I didn't fit in," says Libby. "Sometimes I forget what I look like to other people. I'm acutely aware of my age."

After a lifetime of being in the center of things, Libby found herself on the margins—at first. "I was out of it," she says. "I thought no, I'm supposed to be in the middle of it. . . . I've always been in it."

Libby grew up in the "don't trust anyone over thirty" generation that wore miniskirts and rebelled against the rules of "Father Knows Best." As a "war-baby" she's always been on the forefront of social change—a pre-boomer who paved the way for the seventy-eight million Americans born between 1946 and 1964, who are just now hitting the retirement zone.

She is used to paving the way. Libby soon made friends with her classmates. She remembers one young woman who came up to her and said: *I called up my parents immediately and told them all about you. . . . We really admire you. You're older than my parents!* Imagine! Libby laughs. The woman was only 27.

Libby settles into a rhythm. Every Sunday, she drives to New Haven and stays in a student apartment. On Thursday, she comes back to her rural solitude. She is single and likes it. Not being married or in a relationship is an advantage, she says. She is free to focus. She needs this period of singlehood to reset her compass. "The world is yours. The difficulty is deciding what you want to do. That's the scary thing," she says. "You have to listen to your inner voice and see where it is leading you."

The challenge in Second Adolescence is to open yourself up to uncertainty and let different scenarios pop up on your radar screen. What is your gut telling you? Do you want to continue in your same field, but in a different role? *The surgeon who stops operating and sets up a public health campaign to stamp out tuberculosis in Russia.* Do you want to switch fields? *The engineer who makes jewelry.* Or you just don't know?

The danger is that you don't listen because it would mean making major changes in your life and making changes is scary. "The lessons that I think I've learned are how important it is to take risks and how debilitating it is to be immobilized by fear of the unknown," says Libby.

When you've been racing ahead on a predictable schedule, you forget to step off the track and start thinking and dreaming and letting vagabond ideas take shape. It's as though Libby had to get away from the noise of the city and her past to hear the siren call of what she really wanted to do with the rest of her life. For so many decades, she had focused on others. "You go through life being reactive. Your children—you're reacting to their needs. Your husband—you're reacting to his needs. You don't have the luxury to take a look and take a step for yourself," says Libby.

"When you're not married you can be proactive. Being proactive is hard."

It's also exhilarating. In this process of transformation, "I'm so enjoying learning about all the natural phenomena that you just take for granted," says Libby. "It's so much fun."

She's found a purpose. She'd be a good Number Two in an organization, she says. She's using her old talents. "I'm lucky I'm good at math. I have a little specialty," she says. "To have a little extra teeth is an important asset." Extra teeth can be many things, she says—"being an artist, being a writer, having big boobs. You have to have a little hook."

With her old math hook and her new academic degree, she'll be ready for her next career. The workplace might not be ready for her—ageism is a potent enemy for My Timers. But Libby is used to breaking down barriers. She also has a different attitude: Instead of focusing on the job she might get, she's excited about the job she could do. "Think of the enormous problems society faces," she says.

Libby is also grateful that she has financial resources so she doesn't *have* to work. But no way could she stop working and just play golf all day. She knows people who do that. "Think of those hours going to waste on the putting green."

By going to school, Libby is also increasing her odds for a long healthy life. Education and intellectual activity are correlated with longer life spans and a reduced risk of Alzheimer's disease. People who aggressively use their minds from early childhood through their 40s and 50s maintain their memories better as they age.

PET scanning studies find that college graduates have higher activity in the posterior cingulate, a key part of the brain involved in memory performance. Gary Small, director of the UCLA Center on Aging, sums it up in his book, *The Memory Bible:* "Mental stimulation, or exerting our brains in various ways intellectually, may tone up our memory performance, protect us from future decline in brain function, and may even lead to new brain cell growth in the future!"

Just as rodents do better in stimulating environments, so do you. "Continual, lifelong mental stimulation is healthy for human brains as well," continues Small. "Mentally and physically active people over age 65 have been found to have higher IQ test scores and higher blood flow into the brain compared with those who remain inactive over a four-year period."

Mental activity may be just as effective as physical exercise in extending your life. In one study, couch potatoes over the age of 65 were compared with those who did vigorous exercise. These sofa slugs were engaged in "social and productive activities" such as book clubs, church groups, bridge games, travel groups, cooking schools. After eleven years, the socially and intellectually active couch potatoes had the same positive outcome as those who did physical exercise. "Social and productive activities," concludes the 1999 study, "lower the risk of all [causes of mortality] as much as fitness activities do."

Translation: Mental activity lowers your risk of death.

There are normal changes in the brain with age. "Decreased speed of learning and processing information," says Morrison-Bogorad of the National Institute on Aging. You're not as quick at picking up new things as a youngster. You have more difficulty "performing divided-attention tasks," continues Morrison-Bogorad. It's harder to do many things at once. You have more trouble recalling a name. But overall, you know more than younger people. You have a larger vocabulary and more experience to draw on. You are also more stable emotionally and can handle stress better.

But you may be a little rusty if you've been out of a formal classroom for several decades. As Libby describes the first semester: "I had no science background—it's all science. I'd forgotten all my algebra. It was a combination of senior moments and panic attacks. I couldn't remember the most obvious things. My mind is so much slower."

She even gave herself mental tests to make sure she wasn't suffering from Alzheimer's disease. "You do worry about your mind slowing down and your ability to remember things. I was going in there with the handicap of an overstuffed and less retentive mind. That meant I worked all the time: work—work—work."

But she also has advantages. In a course on climate, there was a lot of discussion of atmosphere, prevailing winds, and geographic locations. Libby realized that she was way ahead. "I know more place names," she says. Hey, she's traveled to many more places. "I have a maturity and experience in work that younger people don't have," she continues. "I have run a company. Running it and succeeding at it is pretty challenging."

This is what you have over younger students. You have experience and knowledge—life empowerment. You're walking around with a rich internal library. What you lack in speed, you make up for in clarity of purpose.

✦

Today, people over 65 are better educated than ever before. In 1950, the median level of schooling was about eight years. By 1990, it was more than twelve. As gerontologist Gene Cohen observes: "There's been a tremendous increase in well-educated older people and in well-off older people."

This sets the stage for the emergence of a Creative Society—a culture that values learning and artistic expression across the life span. Expanding the mind is also a way to gain social wisdom, so you can make sense of your moment in history. So you can safeguard what's been available to you and pass it on. Where do you fit in? How do you define your generation and its role in the body politic? What do you want your grandchildren to know about the times you lived in? What do you want to preserve as knowledge?

Some people go to school simply to learn. Like a medieval monk freed from pedestrian chores, you study to become a guardian of the culture. Or in George Vaillant's phrase—*Keeper of the Meaning*—as he puts it in his landmark Harvard Study of Adult Development. You want to tie the past to the future. You want to be wise.

Bob Dodds looks back on his more than three decades as a lawyer for Mobil as a clearly defined era. High-wire stuff negotiating deals with foreign governments—Indonesia, Nigeria, Qatar. The discovery of new oil fields, mergers and acquisitions. Putting in eighteen-hour days, beating out the competition, surviving trench warfare in business suits. Zooming along and into the finale with the merger of two giants, Mobil and Exxon—and the clash of corporate cultures.

Now at 63, he's a student of classics at Georgetown University. He wants to understand things better. Big stuff, like the use of power, the rise of resistance, the expression of dissent, the role of poets and humor. How do you explain the behavior of nations? Of organizations? Of individuals? He's lived *inside* the big stuff for years—made a good life for himself and his family—but what does the big stuff look like from the outside? What does it look like in history?

Bob exits the corporate circus ring at age 60, a few years earlier than he thought he would. He'd completed a special assignment for the merged company. "I loved my work but it got wearing. At the end, I was burned out," he says. He knew he was going to cut the cord. His wife grew a little nervous—would he be at home all day?

Bob smiles. Trim, smart, energetic. There's something of the boy in him still—as though he'd like to talk over some things with his father, the Quaker from Philadelphia with Quaker values on the big stuff. But both his parents died when he was in his 20s, leaving him a kind of adult orphan. He's had to make his own way. A good way, it's turned out—strong marriage for almost forty years, three grown sons, successful career. But he has questions. He remembers the classics course he took in college, "Classy Civ-10"—a little Thucydides, a little Herodotus. But it wasn't enough. "I knew there was a rich lode there of knowledge and thought," he says. He remembers saying to himself: "Someday, I've got to get back to that."

Going for the gold in the international oil business put his mind on a different track. And then? The bathroom window solution. . . . "Serendipity," he says. His wife suggested he take a break from "corporate mergeritis" and go with her on an art tour to Sicily. Their guide was a professor from Georgetown University who lectured about the Greek myths.

He holds on to this thread. After he retired, he signed up for the graduate program in the classics at Georgetown as a part-time student. He wants to take his time. He's working toward a master's degree and

he might go on and get a Ph.D. But that's not the point. "I'm here because I love the stuff. I want to enjoy it to the full. I don't care about
grades or getting the degree. I don't want to rush it," says Bob, who's
just finished his fifth semester. Last year it was Thucydides and the
poets of Alexandria. This year, Virgil and Plautus. "It's the trip that's
fun, not the ending."

He plunges into the big stuff. Propaganda. Who tells the story? Take
Cleopatra. "The Romans did a job on her," he says. "She was used as
this symbol of decadence and female guile. The Roman propagandists
portrayed Marc Anthony as a wimp—falling for the wiles of a woman,"
he says. The truth? "Cleopatra knew five or six languages," he continues.
"She was the first of the Ptolomys to spend the time to learn Egyptian."
Not exactly a shy blue-stocking. She was impressive—too impressive.
Powerful, smart, sensitive to her people—she was too much competition, Bob explains. That was her problem—and he knows all about
competition. And the old dirty trick: badmouth the competition. It's
how myths get started—in business, in politics, in history.

Bob is excited. He's embarking on his own R&D – Research and
Discovery. Many people in My Time go back to the great works of the
past to find echoes of insight into the present.

Maybe you were forced to read some of these tomes in school and
you've stored away the plot in your brain. Then you re-read *The Iliad* or
Anna Karenina or *Moby Dick* — and you discover a different book. A
new gold mine of intellectual excitement. The words haven't changed,
but you have. Now you know something about the grand themes of
love and hate, ambition and failure, birth and death. You start to wonder why these classic works are wasted on 18-year-olds.

There's another bonus to this kind of learning in My Time: You're
working your mind for pleasure; not a paycheck.

Bob loves wallowing in the big stuff of the ancients. "I'm just happy
doing it. I love libraries. I love research. I love getting into the nooks
and crannies that not everybody knows about. It's fun," he says.

"Every once in a while, you get a zinger of insight. Pieces of the puzzle fall into place. Take Athens in the Peloponnesian War. You quickly see analogies," he continues. "Where Athens got into trouble . . . people objected to its *hegemony.* They objected to the thrusting forward of an energetic, self-confident nation that had come to depend on colonies." Bob points to an incident when a U.S. spy plane was forced down by the Chinese. In the official press release, the Chinese objected to U.S. *hegemony.* "They used Thucydides' word: *hegemony.* I loved that connection," says Bob.

By pursuing the classics, Bob is fleshing out a purpose. The next challenge is making use of what he learns. "The great thing now is that I am doing exactly what I want to do and at my own pace," he says. "I like that spark of creativity. I'd like to be more creative. There are large parts of my brain that didn't get used for the past thirty years," he says.

The ancients are waking up his mind and helping him chart his own Odyssey to My Time.

◆

What parts of your brain have you left unused over the past decades? When was the last time you tried something that you weren't particularly good at? Solving a crossword puzzle ... taking photographs? You probably have some mental muscles that need exercise. What about expressing yourself – on stage or in a poem?

Intellectual activity often leads to a burst of creativity. "I feel that creativity is in the species," says Cohen, author of *The Creative Age: Awaking Human Potential in the Second Half of Life.* His formula for creativity in My Time: $C = ME\text{-}squared$. Creativity equals the Mass of Material inside you, what you've gained through Experience, multiplied by lots of Energy and Effort.

Loss is often the muse of art, he points out, and by the time you get to the bonus decades, you know something about loss. Grandma

Moses did needlepoint until she was 78 and then her arthritis got so bad, she turned to painting. That's when she came into her own, he says. She painted her last painting at the age of 101.

Age does not necessarily diminish talent. In fact, creativity is a growth stock of the intellect. The poet Ruth Stone recently won the National Book Award at age 87. She got tenure at the State University of New York at Binghamton when she was 72—and retired only three years ago. As she writes in her new award-winning collection of poems, *In the Next Galaxy:* "Things will be different./No one will lose their sight,/their hearing, their gallbladder."

Folk art is dominated by older people, notes Cohen. Of twenty artists featured in a retrospective show at the Corcoran Gallery of Art in Washington, sixteen had begun their work after age 65. Some started after age 80. "If Mozart had lived to an older age, think what he might have done," exclaims Cohen.

You don't have to be an award-winning poet or a musical genius to tap into your creative potential. You can just turn your mind to what gives you the most pleasure.

When Janet Williams was a little girl in school, no teacher ever put her drawing up on the board. That always bothered her. Her mother became an artist after age 50 and gained recognition as the first married woman allowed to graduate from the High Museum of Art in Atlanta.

At the time, Janet was married with two babies. Her husband was a man twelve years older, who proposed a month after they met. He said: *You'll keep me young and I'll raise you.* He told her he wanted lots of children—and for the oldest to be a girl because girls are a civilizing influence.

And that's exactly what happened. Janet, 80, and her husband, Emory Williams, 92, have five children—the oldest a girl. They are both in good health and celebrated their sixtieth wedding anniversary in 2003.

Janet looks back. After World War II, everybody was trying to pick up the pieces. Emory was home from overseas and found a job. The first baby was a toddler. And her mother decided to paint the little girl's portrait. She prepared the canvas. Her plan was to paint portraits of all the family.

But it was not to be. Emory had to break the news to his young bride. Janet's mother was killed in a car accident. She was 52. Life interrupted; art interrupted. Janet was 25.

Janet and Emory went on to a long, satisfying stretch of adulthood. They moved to Chicago where Emory became a successful businessman and civic leader. Janet's purpose, she says, was being the best wife and mother.

Then, when she turned 52—the same age when her mother died—the secure world she'd built around family started to shake. The landmark birthday brought back the tragedy and reconnected her to her mother's story. Meanwhile, Emory "retired"—a jolt—and immediately began a new business career. The youngest daughter graduated from college.

Janet held on to her family focus—though the children were scattered in their own lives. She designed a dream house on the coast of Florida to gather in the expanding family. An octagon-shaped Great Room with cathedral ceilings, clusters of comfy sofas, a grand piano, bookcases, and a fireplace looking out on a pond.

One day she bought two large vanilla lamps—and thought they looked a little bland. *Why don't you decorate them,* a friend suggested. Why not paint some ferns and flowers on the lamps? *But how?* asked Janet. *Why don't you go to art school,* said the friend.

At age 62, Janet went to suburban art school in Chicago, once a week for two hours. She started out in charcoal. Class assignment: Draw a Raggedy Ann doll in a basket. The teacher looked at her work and said: *I think you have a good eye. What do you want to do?* Janet told her she wanted to paint in oils. One painting, two, three. The teacher said: *You really have a talent*. Janet was thinking: *This is so much fun*.

For five years, Janet studied with her teacher, learning different techniques, churning out paintings of landscapes, flowers, portraits—one a garden of hot red tulips, another a glistening salmon shell, another a fisherman with pelicans entitled "Sharing the catch." Finally the teacher said: *Go for it. Go for it, Janet*.

She got her first commission at age 67, her first big art show at the University Club of Chicago at age 77. Her paintings now sell for thousands of dollars. "I hoped to reach professional status," she says. "I am a professional artist."

Janet's journey through art instruction and emergence as an artist taps into a long-ago dream. It also fulfills her need to be family guardian. One of the first portraits she painted was of her mother, taken from a photograph: a lovely young woman with bold blue eyes and dark hair, wearing an off-the-shoulder black sequined evening dress against a background of curtains in contrasting light and dark blue—hues highlighting her mother's enduring blue eyes.

And then portraits of all the thirteen grandchildren. And a portrait of Emory for his 90th birthday. And portraits of the adult children. Janet keeps her family close by putting them on canvas. The house in Florida is called "Lembrancas"—lembrancas in Portuguese, she explains, are remembrances, keepsakes, memories, reminders. Just like her paintings.

Janet has found her talent—and her purpose in My Time.

◆

Once you reach a certain age, you worry about your brain. You misplace your car keys. You can't remember a name. "It's Alzheimer's," a friend says to me. She's joking, of course. A little humor to neutralize the fear. The AD fear. Over the last decade, as medical scientists have stepped up research on this devastating brain disorder, the fear of Alzheimer's disease has spread. The idea got started that if you lived long enough, you would end up with this terrifying dementia. In one estimate, researchers projected that 50 percent of people over 85 would succumb to the disease. Who would want to live so long?

But these figures are now in dispute. The revised estimates are much lower. According to Trey Sunderland, an expert in Alzheimer's disease at the National Institute of Mental Health, at age 65, one in twenty people will have AD; at 75, one in ten; at 85, one in five. "It's not normal aging," says Sunderland, chief of the psychiatry branch at NIMH. "It's an illness. There is brain pathology."

Most people—80 percent of those over 85—will not have the disease.

Meanwhile, researchers are racing to design ways to prevent and treat Alzheimer's. Current drugs can stall symptoms, but they do not affect the underlying pathology of the disease. IQ is no defense: The disease strikes ex-presidents and Nobel laureates. But mental activity may serve to stave off symptoms. The famous Nun Study, which analyzed the lives and brains of 678 Catholic nuns, showed that fostering linguistic ability in childhood and stimulating the expression of complex ideas may protect against Alzheimer's disease.

What emerges from research on brain diseases and stroke damage is how flexible the organ is. "The brain has alternate routes. We have five different ways of saying something. If you lose two or three, you've still got two," says Sunderland.

This flexibility explains why the mind is so resilient and creative across the life span. It allows you to have a second, third, and fourth chance to try a creative pursuit or get an advanced degree. In the absence of disease, you can always increase your brain power. True, you're fighting aging stereotypes. *You can't teach an old dog new tricks.* But this is geezer myth. "Research shows that older people can, and do, learn new things—and they learn them well," conclude researchers John Rowe and Robert L. Kahn in *Successful Aging*. You just have to change that old-dog internal message that undermines your confidence.

You are never too old to go to school. Some people don't *begin* their education until they're midway through adulthood.

Aida Nydia Munoz Rivera dropped out of school when she was 17 and went to work as a sales clerk at W. T. Grants in the ladies underwear department. "I was folding nightgowns. Making $28 a week," says Aida, 70. She worked there for a year—a teenage Puerto Rican girl in New York City right out of "West Side Story": flashing eyes, street smart, pretty, and poor. "I had a little bit of a mouth," she says.

Today, she divides her time between Long Island and Puerto Rico. She's changed her hair to red. "I'm old and I'm red," laughs Aida—mother, grandmother, and holder of two graduate degrees. She's still very pretty, with flashing eyes. She likes to dance—Salsa, Tango, West Coast Swing. She stays out of the sun and eats flax seed with every meal. And she's not so poor anymore.

She is doing what she loves to do: counseling women who are victims of domestic violence.

All because she went to school after age 60 to get the necessary degree to become a therapist. She didn't get her college degree until she was nearly 50. For the first half of her life, she was a high school dropout. Education, she says, was her route to salvation in the second half.

Her story begins in a one-room basement apartment in the city where she lived with her younger brother, her mother, and her mother's boyfriend. Her mother was out cleaning people's houses, trying to learn English. "The most I remember," she says, "my brother and I slept in little cots next to my mother and her boyfriend. When my mother was away, the boyfriend would get in bed with me. What I remember," she pauses, "something hard and warm in between my legs. I don't know if he penetrated. I'd just cry a lot. I cried and cried. My brother would wake up and hear me crying." Then the man would stop.

Aida was 7 or 8. She buried it. The boyfriend was beating up her mother, too. "He would hit her. He would throw her up against the wood cabinets in the kitchen. I took my brother and we would hide under the bed and wait until it was over. My mother had a black eye and broken lip. She would tell everybody she went into a door. I knew if you said something you would get into trouble. You learn to shut your mouth and not say anything."

So she shut her mouth and shut down her psyche. That's the one-two punch of trauma: first the assault, then the cover-up. The abuse lay dormant, a smoldering fuse of sorrow until it exploded in her life two decades later.

Aida remembers the moment. She was pursuing the upwardly mobile dream with a husband, four children, and a house on Long Island. Aida always dressed her daughters in fluffy dresses. One day, after they came home from visiting her in-laws, her 3-year-old daughter said to her: *Why does grandpa wipe me so hard?*

"I thought I was going to die," says Aida. Time stopped with a sudden crushing, whirring inside her chest. She could not breathe. She tried to remain calm. She asked questions: *Oh . . . when you go to the potty? He rubs you hard . . . down there?* Scenes flashed through her head: grandpa taking her daughters upstairs to go potty, grandpa playing with her daughters in the backyard, playing piggy-back. Scenes flashed in her memory. She reassured her daughter. *That won't happen again.* She turned to her older daughter: *Does he do that to you, too?* All the while, the crushing, whirring in the chest. She saw her daughter stare at her. "She saw the horror in my eyes," continues Aida, that telltale look of horror. Her daughter paused. *No,* she said. "She had learned to keep her mouth shut," says Aida. "She had that look—I better not tell. That was enough to start fireworks."

The "fireworks" blew up the marriage as she confronted what had happened with her daughters and severed relations with the grandfather. She and her husband lived in a marital war zone. She sank into depression. She went into therapy—to sort out the marriage, to unravel the abuse she had suffered. After a few years, she got divorced—and quickly remarried.

And then she got lucky. Not with men. That would take many more years. But she got lucky in academia. Though her second marriage ended in divorce, it opened the door to education. That changed her life.

Her second husband was a teacher. He couldn't believe she was a high school dropout. She covered it up so well. She didn't even tell her children. After all, she had gotten a job in the school district as a bilingual tutor. Her second husband encouraged her to go back to school. "He helped me with a few papers. He got me rolling," she says.

At age 45 she got her high school equivalency degree and won a scholarship to St. Joseph's College. She began to separate from her chaotic midlife and set her sights on the future. She got a taste of what her life could be. "I was a college kid. I was doing what I always wanted to do. I was learning every day," she says. Here she was—with four children, one divorce, and a second marriage on the rocks. What she studied in books reinforced what she knew from experience. She made the Dean's List. She wrote her first paper on *A Midsummer Night's Dream*. "Shakespeare is my teacher about life," she says. Life in all its darkness, all its playfulness. All its potential.

Once she went back to school, she didn't stop. After her B.A., she earned a master's degree in bilingual education. All the while, she was working full-time as a teacher. With her new degrees and 3.80 average, she got a $30,000 raise in one year.

As a young woman, she used to have a recurring dream: It's the first day of school. She arrives with her books but she doesn't know where she's supposed to go. She doesn't have the schedule, she doesn't know the curriculum. So she can't go to school. Can't have a life. Shut out. Shut down.

After she went back to school, she never had the dream again. She had gotten a life. "Nothing stopped me," she says. "I'm very determined. I'm very focused."

And then, when she was nearly 60, she earned her master's degree in social work—opening the door to her current career as a family therapist. "That's the one that put me over the top," she says.

Now her life theme has come full circle. Except that she is the one who helps those who suffer as she once suffered. As she explains: "I was abused—I didn't know it." Empathy and experience are combined with the skills she acquired in the classroom. She knows what it's like to be poor, abused, and trapped. Through education, she knows the therapeutic techniques to treat the wounded. She has found her calling. "This is the core of my soul," she says. "I see Hispanic women who are sexually abused and battered. They have no awareness that they are being abused. They say to me, 'I feel so bad.' In five minutes I figure out that they are being battered emotionally. And some are being battered physically," she says. As a therapist, she can help them get on the right track.

"People say to me: Don't you get depressed doing this work? I say: No, I'm opening doors for women. I show them what they need to do. I show them that they are not stuck," she says. "This is my life. I love it. In helping others, I'm helping me."

For the last two years, she's had her own independent practice. "I am my own boss," she says. "I have more clients than I can see." She has a government grant to work with Hispanic families.

And she has a life. She has grandchildren. She has a boyfriend. "We talk every day. It's a new relationship," she says. "See how long it takes before you heal your childhood wounds?"

My Time is turning out to be Aida's best time.

8

Leaving a Legacy

I am a messenger who has been sent on a long journey
to declare that there's hope for the world.

ISAAC DINESEN

YOU WANT TO LEAVE something behind. Something that tells your story and puts your life on the record. The bonus decades are an opportunity to review your life and create something positive that will endure for future generations.

A legacy can be grand and public—like the Guggenheim museum or Thomas Jefferson's design of the University of Virginia. It can be small and personal—a necklace given to a niece, a bible handed down from father to son. It doesn't have to be a thing at all. It can be a philosophy, an act of love, a display of courage. Usually, it's a combination of abstract and concrete, of thing and meaning. It's your message to the future. As gerontologist Robert Butler says: "You have a sense of legacy. It's important to leave something."

But what traces of yourself, your times, your values, do you want to preserve? Most often a legacy is a testament to struggle. You take your own struggle and transform it into something that will help other people as they struggle in the future. With a legacy, you recognize the generational imperative to change in the face of change. You think of the ancient Greek philosopher Heracleitus who saw that all things flow—in the river of a life, in the river of history.

In its primary form, a legacy is a reminder of the flow. "I want you to have this bone china," said an aunt to her niece. It was family china that had come from her mother. At that point, the aunt was in her 80s. "She saw the end. She wanted to unload her stuff," says the niece. But now the niece has four grandchildren and sees the china from her aunt in a different light. "She left a legacy to me. She wanted to connect to me in the hereafter." The woman recently replaced some of the plates so she could pass on a complete set to the next generation—so that the bone china could keep flowing down the river of a family.

It might not occur to you that you are creating a legacy in this way. But the inclination is so strong that you can't help but leave traces. The challenge is to see what in the cupboard of your experience is worth passing on. Then you have to make an effort to leave your mark.

✦

Sometimes, creating a legacy just evolves. It starts out as a little something and grows like a wild vine, seeping into corner after corner of your existence until it becomes a defining purpose—a unifying principle of your daily life. You are a messenger of a larger legacy. You bring to it your struggles and resources, and you give it a shape. But you are not doing it *for* yourself. You create a legacy for others.

John and Juanita Jackson are a love story. They met in Cincinnati more than forty years ago. Juanita—who has a pieta Madonna look, with her deep dark eyes, dark hair, and dark skin—was separated, raising her two small children and living in an apartment. The apartment below became vacant and she worried about who would move in. The last tenant had been a single woman, a trouble-maker. Juanita voiced her concerns to the landlord who decided to rule out tenants who were single. When John, divorced and single, applied for the apartment he was turned down. "I was really mad," he says. "I faced racial discrimination for years—but discrimination because I'm single?" He went back and convinced the landlord that he was a desirable tenant and neighbor. Reluctantly the landlord let him move in. "There was some apprehension of this 'old biddy' upstairs," says John, 68, with a smile. They look at each other and giggle.

Their cars were parked on the same side of the garage. One day, John was working on his car and "she came through! I put the spark plugs in upside down. I got the wires crossed. It was such a mess. She really shook me up," says John. They both laugh. "He never got that car to run right," jokes Juanita, 71. "I could really wear a shift then." They became friends—slowly—and married several years later. "We had both been married before," says John. "Juanita said this is 'til death do us part. If you don't behave, death will do us part." They both laugh again.

They found that they had much in common: a commitment to education. They both came from families of college graduates, teachers, and school principals. A commitment to religion. They shared similar faiths and went to church. A commitment to their heritage. They were both African-Americans of similar background. They even learned that their families must have crossed paths. One day, Juanita used the expression *Hard times will make a monkey eat red peppers!* John was stunned. His Aunt Ruth said she had never heard but one person use that expression, a man she had known at Knoxville College in Tennessee—a man they realized was Juanita's father!

John and Juanita led an adventurous life and moved around from Ohio to Massachusetts, New York, and Washington, D. C. John went up the career ladder at General Electric Co. Juanita, an educator and musician with a rich contralto voice, sang in the choir, raised the children, and did volunteer work. "We've moved so much. Every time we'd go to a different community, I'd have to reinvent myself," says Juanita. Or as John says: "We are both people who like to live and do new things."

By the time John and Juanita reached 50, they were living in Albany and heading into a typical Second Adolescence. Their children had finished college. John looked at his life. The industry was stagnating. He wanted a change, but what?

"Why don't you go to law school," suggested Juanita.

"Because I have to earn a living," said John. Of course: the familiar trap of midlife, when economic demands conflict with internal needs.

"Not for three years," said Juanita.

Not for three years, when he could go to law school while she went back to work. They were like that as a couple. "He's encouraged me to do so much," she says. And she's done so much for him. Why dither about going to law school? She'd go to work to support the family while he was a student. "That way there was nothing to prevent him from doing it," she laughs.

So they turned their lives upside down. John left GE, went to Albany Law School, and made Law Review. "I was the most senior among the students and faculty," he jokes. Meanwhile, Juanita ran a Head Start program in upstate New York. Later she became the director of a business development center for women and minorities, established by the Chamber of Commerce, the State University of New York at Albany, and the Urban League.

In the midst of all this, Juanita was asked to put together a church program for children for Black History Month to explore the role of African-Americans in U.S. history. With her education background and deep, haunting voice, she sang spirituals and recited African-American poetry. She explained that slaves weren't allowed to be taught to read and write, so they sang. Their history is written in music—*My Lord, What a Mournin'* and *Steal Away.* The children loved the music, loved the message. Juanita loved performing—and passing the message on. Soon she was asked to perform the program in schools, in community groups. Slowly the program, called "Honoring the Legacy," began to take on a more permanent shape—the legacy of the spiritual and, later, of African-American poetry.

By the time John and Juanita had moved to Virginia in 1990, they were on to a different life: John concentrating on a career in the law, Juanita giving priority to her music. And they had the outline of what would become a major commitment in their life—to honor the legacy.

Today their modern stone and frame house in Northern Virginia overlooks the woods. In the center of the living room is the grand piano: Mehlin & Son, 1917. On the coffee table sits a thick book, *A Year in Chautauqua*—the arts, education, religion, and recreation community in New York where they go every summer. A print by African-American artist Paul Goodnight of dancing black female figures in bright-colored dresses hangs over the sofa. The title: "Figures of Speech."

Message. Music. Faith. These motifs run through the house, through their past, through their relationship—and they run through their efforts to create a legacy that will carry on the larger legacy of history.

John, a lawyer at Howard University, is a lay speaker in the Methodist Church. Juanita, former president of the Women's Committee for the National Symphony Orchestra and current president of the Association of Major Symphony Volunteers, is also a lay speaker.

The program for school children in Albany has blossomed into a major project on the spiritual as historical text. Juanita performs variations of this program in churches, community centers, nursing homes, and arts festivals—educating mostly white audiences on the black experience. John helps her develop variations of the program and sometimes joins her as a narrator.

As the program has grown, so has its vision. At first the goal was to present the music and the words to make a story. Then it was to use the story and the power of song to open people's hearts and minds. Now the program has become a moving collage of song, poetry, and history—with a purpose.

As Juanita performs the program in different settings, she fulfills a mission of teaching audiences—black, white, and mixed—the "figures of speech" of blacks. With each spiritual, verse, and prayer, she lays down a common foundation of historical experience—providing a unique perspective on the past to facilitate understanding in the present.

John and Juanita don't talk about their program in these terms. Juanita talks about her passion for music and her faith. John compliments her. "She has moved this small lesson that she put on for youngsters in a church in Albany to a multidimensional program," he says.

The program speaks for itself.

A legacy is a kind of memoir. It's a record of who you really are, what you believe in. It captures your life themes. So it is not surprising that John and Juanita would aim high—and it's not surprising that they would share their healing legacy with all who would listen, regardless of race. After all, that is how they have lived and worked throughout their lives.

Sometimes Juanita performs on Mother Nature's stage. On Easter at dawn, she always sings *Were You There When They Crucified My Lord?* from a lookout in Great Falls National Park. "You did it again. You made me cry," says a woman in the crowd.

Sometimes Juanita and John perform together and fashion a worship service with spirituals, scripture, and prayer that presents Christianity from the perspective of African slaves and their descendants.

Sometimes, the performance is educational. One week in August, in the Hall of Philosophy at Chautauqua, Juanita teams up with music professor Horace-Clarence Boyer to show the audience how to interpret the spiritual as historical text. *Follow the Drinking Gourd.* "Follow the drinking gourd—follow the Big Dipper," exclaims a man from Iowa when he learns how slaves used the ancient guidance and navigation system in the sky to take them north to freedom. "It expands your knowledge of history—it expands your spirituality," he says.

On the last day of the Chautauqua program, Juanita and John weave together poetry and song. John talks about "the struggle to overcome the legacy of racism and slavery." Juanita sings: *Nobody Knows the Trouble I See.*

Slowly, slowly, with each performance, with every variation of music and verse—on stage, in schools, by a rocky cliff at dawn—wherever they speak and sing, they make their gift. They are living "figures of speech." And like the print on their wall, the spirituals and poetry that they recite will go on and on and on.

◆

The timing has to be right. You have to reach a certain maturity to build a legacy. John and Juanita are not distracted by the primary tasks of adulthood. They have both made their mark in the workplace. The children are married with their own children—four grandchildren in all.

You need freedom and opportunity to focus anew. You've got to get past middle adulthood and the demands of getting ahead. By now, you have internal and external resources to leave something behind. This is why making a legacy typically occurs in the bonus decades. Now you have something to leave behind.

Creating a legacy is rooted in the same developmental phase that fuels public service—Generativity. You want to reach out and give of yourself. With volunteer work, you are giving to others in the present. With a legacy, you are giving to others in the future.

It's a gift with a message. You want to speak to the next generation. You are transmitting the past to the future. In the process, you become a guardian of the culture—whether it's the culture of a country or the culture of a family. You define that culture, transform it into a unique package, and pass it on.

You become a "Keeper of the Meaning," as George Vaillant describes it in *Aging Well*, based on the Harvard Study of Adult Development. "The focus of a Keeper of the Meaning is on conservation and preservation of the collective products of mankind," he writes. The virtues of this role are "wisdom and justice," he continues. Its danger is "rigidity" and partisan conviction. You are so convinced of the rightness of your "meaning" that you hammer away in a vacuum of self-deceit. The safeguard is openness and reaching out beyond the self to the larger community—present and future.

Gene Cohen of George Washington University talks about "the desire to find larger meaning in the story of our lives, and to give in a larger way of the wisdom we have accrued." In the last half of life, people want to "make strong lasting contributions on a personal or community level, to affirm life, take care of unfinished business, and celebrate one's own contribution," he writes in *The Creative Age*.

There are many ways to craft a legacy. You have to think: What has your life been all about? A legacy may come out of your own experience. It may come out of a distant moment in history.

Some legacies are quirky. Charles C. Dent of Fogelsville, Pennsylvania—pilot, business magnate, world peace activist, founder of UN WE BELIEVE (now known as the Business Council for the United Nations), art collector—founded a project in his bonus decades to create the giant bronze horse designed by Leonardo da Vinci that was never completed. He wanted to present the grand horse as a gift to the Italian people to thank them for the Renaissance. The project took almost twenty years. Dent died five years before the fifteen-ton statue was finally installed. But the horse monument lives on, a testament to Dent's long commitment to international peace and goodwill.

Whether your legacy is rooted in world history or a private moment, what you want to leave behind—and how you go about leaving it—is still a story about you.

David Graham, 61, is a proud son of Ohio. He's retired and lives in Columbus. A "whiz tech," he loves machines—the more complicated, the better. He's always been a computer jock—a numbers analyst—beginning with a stint in the Air Force and all through his career with NCR Corporation. He loves his wife of more than thirty years, a piano teacher who plays all three services at Hilliard United Methodist Church. And he loves his country. He feels something is lost today—something precious in the nation's soul. Where is the heroic goodness he remembers as a kid playing with toy soldiers just after World War II?

David is setting out to find it. He is doing oral histories of World War II combat veterans who fought in Europe. He travels to battlefields to mark foxholes. He goes to reunions to talk to the men. He has made videotapes of several dozen veterans. He doesn't know what he will do with his interviews. He doesn't have a coherent product—yet. He's deep in the process of collecting the voices and searching for patterns.

He wants to send a message. "There is something unique about the generation that had to deal with that war," says David. "The characteristics of those people are those that are necessary—would be necessary if we are faced with a war again. If we are faced with it now."

This project is also about him, a member of the Vietnam generation, a boy from the heartland who served in the military but hated *that* war. The Gulf of Tonkin resolution? "A lie!" he exclaims. A phony excuse to give President Lyndon Johnson the power to escalate U.S. intervention in Vietnam—and it got David drafted. But he served. He could have gone to Canada; the border was only 100 miles away. But he didn't. He believes in military service. He believes in standing up for your country.

For many decades, he put all that behind him and rode the corporate escalator to an interesting life with NCR, traveling across the country and to Europe to inspect manufacturing facilities that produced the company's business machines. But the military stuff gnawed at him. Toward the end of his formal career, the merger craze on Wall Street accelerated and his company changed hands. He could see what lay ahead. He took a sweetheart early-retirement package. He had already started visiting battlefields in Europe. He was already making the transition from one life to another. He was 56.

And then, the bathroom window solution. . . . He went online to look for volunteer opportunities. Up popped a project for the local Jewish historical society to interview Jewish combat veterans. David, though not Jewish, had the skills and the interest. "I came along and they gave me that project," he says. "It's led to fantastic discoveries." It has also given him a framework to shape his larger agenda of documenting the "good soldier."

It's as though David and a whole generation were robbed of a "good war" and the country lost its integrity. Going back to the combat veterans of World War II is a way to restore that integrity—for himself and future generations.

Not just the glory. But the horror and the failures. How do you survive the dark side of history? David interviewed Felix L. Sparks, retired Brigadier General in the 45th Infantry Division of the U.S. 7th Army. The Division is revered for helping to win the battle at Anzio. Sparks himself is hailed as the liberator of the Dachau concentration camp. But David talks to him about the debacle at Reipertswiller, France, during the Battle of Alsace when Sparks lost hundreds of men who were pinned down on a hill and surrounded by German troops. He commandeered two tanks for a rescue mission and, under fire, brought some to safety. But most were lost. The Reipertswiller battle stands as one of the great losses in the war in France.

"I want to walk in the shoes of General Sparks when he tried to rescue these men. So I've walked up that hill. I've dug in those foxholes. I've handled the old weapons," says David. "I talked to a man the other day who was captured and lost an eye."

How do you take the stuff of nightmares and turn it into a badge of courage? Combat covers a multitude of sins—killing and so much else.

It creates more dead and broken men than surviving heroes. But in the rawness of hell, character is defined. What is the "good soldier"? David wants to document that character and keep those coals of integrity burning. "I've got the men. To me, that is the ultimate. I see and I hear their voices," says David. "I do have a treasure."

The project plays to his strengths. He was a history major at Ohio State University. He was in the service—though not in combat. As he says: "I wanted no part of the Vietnam War. I found another way to serve." He signed up for four years so he could select the service. For most of the time, he was stationed in Europe as a Russian linguist. "I have the benefit of military experience. I could talk to these men."

The project gives him an opportunity to use his technical skills and take advantage of the latest super-gadgets such as new software connected to a Global Positioning Satellite to pinpoint foxholes.

The project also flashes back to David's early childhood. He was almost 3 when Sparks lost his men in the Battle of Alsace. David remembers how returning veterans were treated like gods after the war. World War II was the transforming event of the twentieth century; he grew up in its shadow.

He couldn't have done these interviews before now. The disadvantage is that so many voices are gone. He doesn't have the perspective of the 35-year-old lieutenant with four children who landed on the beach on D-Day. He's interviewing men who were 18 and 19 in the war. Still, it's something. He was too young to do this earlier. The veterans were too distant, too mythical. How could he go up to a general and ask him if he has nightmares? But now he has the confidence to question and the maturity to understand.

And there's another thing—deeply personal. His grandmother was the daughter of German immigrants. "I loved my grandmother dearly," he says. For a long time, he couldn't focus on Germans killing Americans and Americans killing Germans. During his military service, he turned his attention to Eastern Europe and the Soviet Union. But now he is able to focus on the Western Front and gather the details of being a soldier. He's learned from history. Look at the Civil War! "It always surprises me that after a terrible war of conflict and hatred, then you go fight together in the next war. Kids from New York and Alabama are foxhole buddies."

Something about being a combat soldier, something about character, something about history's imperative to use force—this is what David wants to pass on to future generations.

He is going around the country gathering the stories. He's in a hurry. The exact shape of his legacy is evolving; that's part of the exhilaration he feels in pursuing the interviews.

David has found a purpose in his bonus decades. He is using his talents and life experience. He knows he has a treasure to give to the future—and crafting a legacy is giving him a great sense of fulfillment.

✦

Leaving a legacy is a "desire, so profound in older people, to leave something behind when they die," writes Robert Butler in *Why Survive? Being Old in America*. It is also a sign of developmental growth and well-being. As Butler continues: "The older person who does show social knowledge of and personal concern about 'leaving traces' and preserving a heritage for the future tends to reveal greater psychological health."

A common way to leave traces is to put together an autobiography. This literary form speaks to that yearning to explain your life to future generations. There are expiation memoirs such as *In Retrospect* by Robert S. McNamara, his mea culpa tale of the Vietnam War. There are attack memoirs—the Mommy Dearest slam that leaves the next generation to pick up the pieces. And there are instructional memoirs such as Katharine Graham's *Personal History*. "We see a flowering of the memoir," says Butler who heads the International Longevity Center in New York. "It's the signature of the times. It's the effort to write the truth, to write the story of lives."

Sometimes a legacy is a private explainer to anticipate the questions that might be asked in the future. Emory Williams, 92, whose wife Janet became an artist late in life, has written a memoir for his grandchildren. A successful businessman and civic leader in Chicago, he grew up during the Great Depression. His father was an engineer in a small town in Mississippi and he went broke while Emory was in college. "He had no time to recover," says Emory. When Emory got out of college, there were no jobs for a year. And then came World War II. A commission in the Army and assignment to India. A younger brother in the infantry in Europe.

Emory never stopped working. Even after he retired from Sears Roebuck at age 63, he found another career and went into banking. After that, he chaired a railroad holding company. When he was in his 80s, he started a concrete block company in China that he now runs with his son.

What was it all about? Along the way, he wrote an account for his grandchildren—250 pages, single-spaced. "It will be something for them to refer to," he says. "I think they will want to understand the times that their grandparents grew up in. I wanted to answer the question: What was it like?"

The flowering of the memoir is tied to gains in longevity. Only when people reach a certain point do they look back and make a record. Only when readers are a certain age do they have the interest and time to plow through a memoir. While younger people tend to write novels, older people write autobiographies. Both are relatively recent literary forms. "We didn't have the novel or autobiography until the 17th century," explains Butler, pointing out the connection between longer life spans and the emergence of this kind of story-telling genre. There were sagas and legends, history, poetry, and plays. But when life expectancy at birth was only thirty years or so, there wasn't much interest in the story of ordinary lives.

Today, with the bonus decades creating a new stage in the life cycle after 50, the memoir, or "docu-fiction," is becoming a staple in bookstores. You don't have to be a public figure to tell the story of your life. Doing the personal essay is a frequent assignment in writing workshops. Searching for roots and crafting a story for your grandchildren is a popular pastime.

While a legacy reflects your life, it is focused on *them*—the ones you hope will live out your legacy. And in most instances, the desire is to have a positive impact. You want to pass along something that will guide the children of tomorrow. A legacy may embrace the dark side of life, but it is meant to be helpful, inspiring, enriching . . . for others.

✦

Sometimes your legacy is very private. Public legacies are the ones that get notoriety in the press or on a plaque. Personal ones are the legacies that your children will live by. You may make a public gift to the future. But most common are the personal legacies. These are intimate gifts that you want to pass down to your children and your children's children.

The elements in an intimate legacy are the same as in a public one. Your gift transmits the past to the future. It reflects the essence of your life. It has its own identity. It can be a thing—big like a family homestead, small like a collection of Charles Dickens. It can be an experience—vacations spent with grandparents. It has special meaning, which you have spelled out. It is intended to guide future generations. It involves action on your part to make sure your legacy gets handed down. Sometimes an intimate legacy takes decades to form. Sometimes it occurs in a moment that endures for generations.

I remember the day my father gave me the legacy of my mother's sculpture. It was the bleakest of times. The family house was to be sold. My mother was in a mental institution. After decades of illness and draconian treatments, she was foundering. She would die about five years later. My younger brother, who was born brain damaged, was in a facility for children. My sister had fled to Colorado to escape the darkness. My father, the stoic, would go on to another life and a second marriage. But this moment was the end of everything—the demise of a family, the fall of the house that bore their sorrow, the collapse of the code that had held them together.

I was the oldest child. It was my job to pack up the house with its lovely old broken-down furniture and long-neglected drawers of unpaid bills, unanswered letters. I was 25, just married, righteously practical, and buoyed by my own escape into adulthood. I attacked this stable of chaos, packing up boxes and labeling them. My father came by to lend moral support. After a while, I noticed that he had disappeared.

I found him in the driveway. He had gone to the rafters of the garage and taken down six huge wooden crates and opened them. At first I was angry. We were supposed to be packing boxes—not unpacking them. Then I saw that he was weeping. Just standing there, shaking his head and weeping. I looked down at the ground. He had broken apart the crates and set up a row of heads and busts and bodies in stone.

I had never seen my father weep. I had never seen these pieces of sculpture, which were done by my mother when she was a young woman. "You must take the sculpture with you," he said. A female figure. A head. Two busts of men with African-American features. A second bust of a woman—I recognized my mother—sculpted by another artist and friend. Before. "This was your mother," said my father, tears rolling down his cheeks. Before the darkness. Before the war. Before the dead baby and the depression and the pills and the white-knuckle nights and shock treatments and years of more pills and booze and institutions with locked floors called Codman II. Before my father, an infantry lieutenant in E Company, fought through St. Lo, Failaise Gap, the Meuse River, Monshau, Hurtigen Forrest, Mariaweiller, Remagen on the way to Bittefeld and VE-Day.

The sculpture had been packed away all these years. This was the mother I never knew—the woman of joy and talent, who once was and might have been. "You must take the sculpture," my father whispered. Yes. Yes. Of course. *This is my mother. I am happy to have her, this piece of her that she left long ago.* My father kept shaking his head. There was no way to penetrate this mystery, to comprehend the way mental illness hijacks people and brings on the darkness. All that was left was the loss, the memory of love, and the sculpture.

But in the sculpture was hope—a solid sign of potential and vitality.

Today the sculpture sits on bookcases and in corners in my house. It's a legacy from both parents. A legacy from my mother, who made the sculpture. A legacy of my father who made the gift when my mother couldn't. They were a good team. The legacy tells their story of early triumph and long struggle.

Looking back, I can see that my father was on the cusp of My Time. He was 55 when the house was closed. The first chapter of adulthood was coming to an end. He had accomplished the main tasks—raising the children, settling into a law practice. He was moving on to a second chapter. He would have new love. He would leave other legacies, more public ones with the music he composed throughout his life. This was a legacy from the first chapter. In the upheaval of transition, he was reckoning with the past, bidding it farewell and salvaging the best of it to pass on.

It took a conscious effort to make the gift. So much easier to have left the sculpture in the crates and kept the pieces in storage. But he didn't. He also had to break the stoic code of E Company and a Yankee family's tight control of emotion by weeping openly to let the wholeness of the story out. And he had to make sure I got it.

This was his message to future generations: No matter how dark, no matter how great the loss, there is always a nugget of promise and life in full-force. I see it in my grandchildren—toddlers still—who go and pat the larger bust sitting on the floor in the dining room as though it were a pet. I feel it in my own life with its ebb and flow of light and dark. I use it in my job. When I interview people in crisis—and that's usually what makes news—I can empathize with the dark, but I always know to look for the sculpture.

You don't know how your legacy will fare in the future. That's part of the risk you take in making a legacy. You have to trust that the recipients of your legacy will go forward with it, amending the legacy to suit the times. Chances are they will. What were the legacies given to you that helped shape your life? At this age, you see how the generation wheel turns and old legacies are reinvigorated.

A legacy embodies your strengths, your purpose, and it marks your spiritual shift to coming generations.

Then you have to let go. A legacy is a gift. It has its own destiny. In the face of mortality, you have to give up control and put your faith in the future.

PART THREE

Nurturing Love

9

Refreshing Friendships

We only die when we fail to take root in others.

LEON TROTSKY

THE E-MAIL POPS UP on the screen. A holiday greeting: "What's most important in life is friendship. I don't know what I'd do without my friends. . . . " The sender is a classmate from elementary school. We've started to have reunions now, though we've scattered across the country. It's a surprise to see how much we care about other, how much this connection means after forty or fifty years.

Friends are always important throughout life. In the bonus decades, they become precious. My Time is the Era of Friendship.

During the middle years, you were too preoccupied with raising children, settling in—or out of—marriage, finding your niche in the workplace, securing your status in the community. Relationships tended to flow from family and work. Time was scarce for one-on-one friendship—though you made friends wherever you were living. But friends from far away or from earlier parts of your life drifted to the

Christmas card list, the fleeting phone call, a chance meeting at a wedding or funeral.

Suddenly you have more time for friendship. Your children are grown. You've established yourself on the job. You've widened your social circle. You are more available to play and have fun with friends. You also have more experience to meet the needs of your friends and care for them.

And you might be heading into a vulnerable zone yourself. Fate throws up its special list of misfortune for those over 50. You may develop a health problem or lose a loved one. You are more likely to find that you are living alone. Who is there for you at the Ground Zero of your life?

Your future depends on a friendship network. Researchers call it "social capital." They talk about the importance of "social engagement" and "connectedness." You need a social network to sustain you through the bonus decades. This is true of men and women, though women seem to be better at forging a community of friends—a talent that partly explains why they outlive men.

At its most basic level, friendship is a human connection that involves affection and commitment. With those in your inner circle, there is a continual sharing of the most important details of your life. Close friends are "those to whom you feel so close that it is hard to imagine life without them," explain John Rowe and Robert Kahn in *Successful Aging*, a popular account of the MacArthur Foundation Study of Aging in America. Whom do you confide in on a regular basis? Whom can you call upon if you need help? Whom do you call when you want to celebrate?

The main thing is having a close connection with someone—better yet, several people—to share your life. "There are lots of ways to get love and intimacy," says Harvard's Lisa Berkman, chair of the Department of Society, Human, Development, and Health. "You don't have to be married," she continues. "It doesn't matter whether it's friends or relatives. You have to rely on somebody for emotional support."

I walk into the old farmhouse and the floorboards creak just as they did when I was 6 years old and this was where I would spend hours playing with my friend. Her family had a farm across the road. Her mother was my godmother, and she mothered me. My friend, a year older, watched out for me on the school bus. We formed a club called "owl pals" and we had our own song: *Together, sun or rain. . . . Strolling arm 'n arm down the lane*. We learned about sex when we sneaked into the barn and watched as a bull was brought in to breed a cow—and we agreed not to do that for a while.

Now her father lies in a hospital bed on the first floor; he is dying. Her mother has been dead for almost a decade. My friend and I sit close to the bed. Her father is comfortable, alert. He starts telling stories. We laugh. We sing. We say good-bye. We hold one another.

Here is the circle of kinship—our families have been entwined for generations. Here is the circle of friendship where beginnings and endings merge.

Friends are precious. When you get to My Time, they can help you close the circle of your life and integrate the past with the present.

✦

One of the hallmarks of My Time is the recovery of old friends. You go back to the past. This is a way to get started on refreshing your web of kinship. You go to class reunions. You go online to find lost sweethearts. *What ever happened to . . . ?* You revisit old neighborhoods. You contact far-away friends. You start over.

The five women grew up together in the small town of Mayville, New York. Anne Smith, 65, and Nancy Goodrich, 66, met in kindergarten. Nancy Reitkopp, Sandra Fry, and Verna Torres—all 66—joined them in the third grade. Anne's father was a family doctor, Nancy Reitkopp's father was the pharmacist. Nancy Goodrich's father ran the grocery store. Sandra's father was the high school principal, and Verna's parents taught in the school. Every day after school, they'd head for someone's house to play dolls or make fudge. "Our mothers were home, too. This was when women stayed at home," says Anne.

After high school graduation, they scattered across the country and into different lives with husbands and children and jobs. The decades went by. Then, six years ago, a crisis brought them together. Nancy Goodrich's husband died of cancer and, one by one, the group gathered to give Nancy support. "We didn't keep in touch until then," says Anne. "We were all focused on our families." Oh sure, they exchanged holiday greetings and saw each other at weddings. But they weren't involved with each other—not in the intimate way they had been as children.

When they regrouped, they were in a different stage of life. They were all in their late 50s. They had finished the primary tasks of adulthood. They were open to each other in ways they hadn't been before. Over the next six years, they would spend a week together every summer and get to know each other all over again. They call themselves the "Homies."

The beginning phase of recovering old friends is fueled by nostalgia. For hours and hours, the Homies reminisce: About sticking messages in a long stone wall just like Nancy Drew. About the elephant named Lena and the five-legged cow named Shirley Temple that Anne's father had bought from a bankrupt circus. Remember how Anne's father used to ride the elephant in the Fourth of July Parade?

Day after day, the memories keep flowing. About climbing to the top of the pine trees in the big lot where Catholic missionaries lived in a large Victorian house. "The priests were sure we were going to fall out and kill ourselves. They couldn't keep us out of the trees," recalls Nancy Goodrich. "So they cut all the branches off the trees. We were crushed. Those were our trees." Today the church home is a funeral parlor behind a row of very tall trunks. Makes them laugh every time they go back to Mayville.

Reminiscing is an important part of recovering friendship. With each memory, you construct a joint narrative of the past and lay the foundation for new connections. Slowly the Homies work their way up to being in Girl Scouts, becoming cheerleaders, falling in love, getting married.

The second phase is one of revelation and discovery. You find out what happened to everyone during the adult years. Who did your friend become? What kind of person emerged from the tomboy who liked to climb trees? Can you see the link between then and now? What were the shadows in childhood that you now see through an adult lens?

Meanwhile, you tell your story—and each time you go deeper into who you are, what your life is all about. This period of mutual revelation can last for years as you share the "lost" decades and get to know each other anew.

After her husband died, Nancy Goodrich put together poster boards with photos of their life together and showed them to the group. There was her husband, the Scout leader. There he was with the cancer. When he started chemotherapy, he went bald and couldn't have cared less. "We talked about the pictures. We laughed about things," recalls Anne. The Homies saw that Nancy and her husband had eight great years after he was diagnosed with lymphoma. "He did what he had to do to live," says Nancy, who is a nurse. They went to Italy to seek out Nancy's Italian roots. They went rock climbing and para-sailing. They went down in the whirlpools in the gorge of Niagara Falls. "The most frightening thing I'd ever done," says Nancy. Meanwhile, she and her husband had raised two sons and became foster parents for hard-to-place children. "Nancy was extremely busy," says Anne in admiration.

With each revelation, the fullness of life takes shape. Verna Torres went the farthest away. After graduate school at the University of Kansas, she headed for California. She met a Methodist minister in Santa Monica, married him, and then he became a college professor.

They had two sons and started a computer company on the side. When Verna was 52, her husband suddenly died of an aneurysm. For the next decade, she ran the company. The annual August reunion with the Homies "is very special," she says. "We all shared the same tent at Girl Scout camp. . . . We really like one another."

Sandra Fry, who lives with her husband in Erie, Pennsylvania, had suffered a brain tumor. "I was getting deaf. I had trouble with balance," recalls Sandra, a music teacher and mother of two. She needed brain surgery, but doctors couldn't predict the results. Some patients end up with permanent damage to the vocal chords. "Music means everything to me—after family and friends. Music is a way of expressing yourself," she says. "I went in not knowing what was going to happen."

When she woke up from the operation, she was alone. Her head was wrapped in bandages. She couldn't move. "I started to sing," she says, and slowly the thought formed in her head: "I'm still here. I can still sing. I can vocalize. . . . " She would be all right. "I was on Cloud Nine, " she continues.

Her recuperation took two years. She lost hearing in one ear. "It was difficult," she says. "It took me a long time to be one-eared." But she learned things, too. How peaceful she was the night before the surgery when her sister washed her hair. How grateful she was for anything wonderful and good—"because most things are," she says.

Especially the Homies! "It's a wonderful thing to have," says Sandra. "I came home."

But it's not just going back. By sharing their adult lives, the Homies connect on a new and more profound level. In the process, they create a mutual support system. "The most amazing thing is that we're so kind to each other," continues Sandra. "There's a kinship there. You'd never do anything to hurt anybody."

Too much has been shared. Death, illness, sorrow. "I lost my parents. I lost my younger brother. These are people who knew my parents," says Nancy Reitkopp, who lives in Rochester.

Too much is at stake. The Homies are now involved with each other in an activist, intimate way. Every summer reunion is an old-fashioned pajama party where they laugh and cry and transform the links of childhood into ongoing adult relationships.

"It's like family," says Nancy Goodrich. "I can be myself. I don't have to watch what I'm saying. It's very comfortable. We discuss everything. We discuss our children honestly. No one is putting on airs or trying to outdo one another."

As Anne says: "You're there for each other. That's the way I feel about it."

✦

Not having a close friend can be hazardous to your health. Study after study shows that people who are socially isolated are more likely to die "prematurely," as the researchers put it. The relationship between isolation and risk of death is so strong that it stands out whether or not you smoke, drink too much alcohol, eat a lousy diet, or lead a sedentary life. Not having someone you can relate to and count on makes you more susceptible to a range of disorders from heart disease and stroke to depression.

According to Berkman, social isolation is "a chronically stressful condition." The human organism responds "by aging faster." You just don't do as well as those who have a social network. You are likely to have more health problems and more "functional decline," says Berkman.

Even the common cold is worse for the friendless. In one study, those with more types of social ties were less susceptible to common colds. If they developed a cold, they were able to fight off infection more effectively.

All this suggests that social bonds have physical effects and can influence the immune system. What's more, biology and bonding may be a two-way street. There may be biological roots for bonding, and social scientists believe they have identified possible biochemical pathways involved in friendship. The ability to relate to others seems to be encoded in the brain as an evolutionary advantage.

There are gender differences. Lisa Berkman points out that in studies on friendship, if you ask a married man who is his closest friend, he'll likely name his wife. If you ask a married woman, she is more likely to say her confidant is another woman.

Women are also more likely to be single in the bonus decades. They turn to each other to create a network of support and companionship.

"Friendship matters to women; it matters a lot; women today—with lives often in transition—depend on friends more than ever," say Ellen Goodman and Patricia O'Brien in their book on friendship: *I Know Just What You Mean*. "Many who once believed family was the center of life, with every myth and movie and fairy tale having the same married-happily-ever-after ending, now know that friends may be the difference between a lonely life and a lively one. As they turn over the Big Birthdays, women are taking deep breaths and looking around at the other women who are their fellow travelers and saying—sometimes for the first time—this person is important to my life; indeed this may be my most sustaining relationship of all."

Making friends turns out to be a pretty basic instinct. In research on stress, Shelley E. Taylor and her colleagues at the University of California, Los Angeles, have shown that women may have a different response to danger and challenge. Instead of flight-or-fight, they "tend-and-befriend."

"We are fundamentally a nurturant species," writes Taylor in *The Tending Instinct: Women, Men, and the Biology of Our Relationships*. "The brain and body are crafted to tend, not indiscriminately so, but in order to attract, maintain, and nurture relationships with others across the life span," she continues. "Threatening situations especially evoke tending of all kinds. Signs of real or potential dangers alert us to join forces and watch out for one another."

Tend-and-befriend behavior is not only rooted in the culture of care-giving and raising children. It may also reflect the release of certain chemicals in the neuroendocrine system, such as the pain reliever oxy-tocin, that are enhanced by female reproductive hormones. Much more research needs to be done on this biochemical model of bonding in the face of stress. But the tend-and-befriend theory provides more clues as to why women seem better at attachment and turn to each other in stressful circumstances.

"I see it in my cancer patients every day," points out psychiatrist Judith Eve Lipton in her review of the tend-and-befriend theory. "Admittedly, many caring husbands and male health care providers step up to the plate too, providing help and comfort for these women," continues Lipton, a consultant to the Comprehensive Breast Center at Providence Hospital in Seattle. "But the heart to heart stuff is female. . . . We women talk to each other, confide, whine, wail, plan, and just plain kibitz, and stress subsides once we feel heard and understood."

◆

Traditionally, women have been the arbiters of social connections. They tend to set the relationship agenda within the family—with children and in-laws as well as more distant relatives. They are usually in charge of the social calendar—they organize who is coming to dinner. With car pools and play groups, they are often more rooted in the neighborhood. Women are also more likely to be part of the volunteer network in church or at the library. In the stereotype of the gender gap, women can spend hours talking on the phone with a friend while men can spend hours in the bar making jokes with buddies. Women share the most intimate details of their lives; men discuss football strategy as they root for the Dallas Cowboys.

But this stereotype gives short shrift to men's capacity for friendship and their need to be heard and understood. Men may have different manners in friendship and use a different language to connect, but the basic ties are similar.

Men, like women, rely on friends all through life—in school, on the job, in formal retirement. One of the lessons of an unstable workplace is that loyalty—and identity—are forged not so much by a company or institution as by the people you have worked with throughout a career. After a certain age, the workplace becomes less secure and hospitable. Friendship among colleagues helps you navigate the shoals of ageism on the job.

Friendship also bridges generations. In relationships with mentors and those you mentor on the job—as well as peers—there is always the thread of caring. This kind of bonding in public life—among firefighters and nurses and airline pilots—is essential for both men and women.

Meanwhile, the gender revolution that has changed the lives of men and women from the bedroom to the boardroom has also blurred the traditional divisions of responsibility in the social arena. Today, men as well women arrange the social calendar—calling up people to ask them for dinner and cooking it, too.

In times of stress, both men and women reach out to friends. In flight from danger (getting out of an abusive relationship) or in a fight for survival (who keeps the job when the company downsizes), you need people to lean on. By the time you get to be 50 or 60, life has usually offered up plenty of opportunity for foxhole bonding.

You find out that one way to transform loss into gain is through friendship. For many people, friendship has been the mainstay all their lives, making up for what they didn't get—or aren't getting—in family relationships. In My Time, this kind of kinship can have a renaissance.

Al Gottesman, 70, has always been a little restless. As he says: "I'm a serious New Yorker." He's never spent more than two months away from the city—and that was basic training in the Army. He is also the friend's friend. Right from the start, growing up in the Bronx, playing in the street, he was part of a group. They called themselves the Royals—occasionally the concourse Roayls, named for the main avenue that ran through the Bronx.

Al went on to a successful career as an entertainment lawyer—for many years he worked with Jim Hensen, creator of the Muppets. Al has the people touch; he's smart, funny, good-looking—and he's playing the best game of tennis since he was 25.

Still, there are shadows. He's been divorced and has recoupled, happily so. But there are lingering questions in his life—why he did certain things, felt certain ways. He has always relied on friendship. Literally, as in the Beatles refrain, he's been getting by with the help of his friends.

It started in childhood when he made a kind of family for himself out of his friends in the street. "When I was 6, my father had a nervous breakdown," says Al. "Paranoid schizophrenia; he had delusions." His father went away to a state hospital. His mother took over the family printing business. Al didn't see his father again until he was 23 and he went to the funeral home where his father lay in a coffin.

"What happened was my mother kind of closed off my father from me. I was too young to visit him in the hospital. I compartmentalized. I closed it off, which allowed me to pick up the rest of my life—to play, to be funny, to go to the movies. I remember my childhood very fondly, despite not having a father, despite that loss," he explains. "That's where friendship comes into play. I think back a lot to how important it was to me—not having a typical family structure. My friends became an important part of my life."

Al had all the seeds of resilience. He was good in school, good at sports. Back then, the Bronx was a stable neighborhood. Most of the families were Jewish or Catholic. Al and his friends went around together from first grade through high school. "There were twenty of us.

We played stickball, we played softball, we played football, we played basketball—we played everything together. That was our structure. We knew one another. We'd go to the movies on Saturday afternoon. I was successful in that structure. I had a sense of humor. I was an athlete. I was a nice guy. That was my world."

The street became his home. "The other mothers looked after me," he says. "It was a warm, comforting childhood in spite of the loss."

After high school, the Royals dispersed—until they were all in their mid–50s. It was during a crisis in Al's life that he rediscovered his childhood friends. He was 54 and his marriage was breaking up. "I was very much in love" when he got married, he says, and the breakup hurt. He moved into a bachelor apartment. And then, he got a call from an old friend from the Bronx days in a similar situation. "He was having a difficult time separating from his girlfriend. He knew I was separating. When he left her, he needed a place to go. He moved in for a week. That rekindled the friendship," he says.

After high school, they had circled each other for years. They both went to law school and became lawyers. They were friendly during their first marriages, but not close, and they had drifted apart.

The condition of being single—and vulnerable—gave them the opportunity to connect and comfort each other. "It's that common background. We know from whence we both came. He knows that I know who his parents were. He knows my family," he says. "We have a lot in common—our perspectives on life, sense of humor."

Not that friendship is supposed to be a rescue operation. For that kind of support, Al had turned—as before in his life—to a good therapist. With his childhood friend he had more of a comradeship in the void. "It's good to be involved with a familiar person—someone you can do things with. I don't know how supportive we were to each other. I didn't look to him for serious support. Nor did he," he says. Yet the two men shared the details of their private lives and talked about how hard it was to break up a marriage. "We exchanged the basics—it was very meaningful," says Al. "I was a sounding board. I remember telling him why my marriage broke up, how responsible I was," he continues. "We were comforted in talking about it."

It was also during this period that Al started to review his life and reach back to his childhood. He ended up co-organizing a reunion of the Royals.

Of the original twenty, sixteen were located and twelve returned; nearly half had become lawyers, a similar percentage had gone through a divorce. The reunion events started in his bachelor apartment—just the men—and moved on to dinner where the group was joined by wives and girlfriends. One by one, the Royals stood up and described their lives. "Throughout, it was as though the gap of forty years had not happened. We picked up as friends. We talked the same way to each other," says Al. "That was very meaningful to me."

Someone had brought an old photograph—there they were at age 13 at a Bar Mitzvah. "We stood in the same places and had our picture taken again," says Al. The circle from childhood to adulthood was complete.

But friendship needs more than a shared past to blossom. "That's not enough. You have to have the high-energy stuff going for you in the present to make it meaningful," he says. Like: Who are you now? What are you doing? "It's not just the past. The present is very important."

Al remains very close to two men from the old gang. He talks to them regularly on the phone. Al and his friends have passed through the unsettled phase of transition and gone on to new lives. Still they hold on to each other. They spend time together on vacation. They celebrate birthdays together. They are on each other's team as they cruise along in My Time.

✦

On a basic level, friendship is how you parent yourself as an adult, points out psychiatrist Harvey Rich. It can make up for the parenting you didn't get as a child. Al found this out early when he turned the street into home and the Royals into family. He reaffirmed the parenting role of friendship in Second Adolescence when he reached back to the street for reinforcement.

Friendship can also extend the positive nurturing you got in childhood. You remember the selfless love of a parent and parent figures that got you started. With friends, you can continue to draw on a protective source of emotional nourishment and acceptance.

"Friendships can carry us through life," writes Rich in his book on psychological touchstones, *In the Moment*. "Just as when we were young children, and one parent provided a safe 'other' for us to discuss our struggles with the other parent, friends provide a safe 'other' to whom we can bring the struggles of our lives."

In adulthood, friendship can fill the gaps in marriage, soothe disappointments—in children, in yourself, in work—and ease the struggles of making a place for yourself and your family in the world.

Rich describes the lifelong friendship between his mother and her female cousin. "These two friends sustained each other through poverty, joy, death, illness, great sorrow, marital disappointments, and all the exigencies life placed before them," he explains.

"Ideally, friendship offers a source of essential support, refuge, and modeling of healthy relationships and self-expression. Friendship can affirm and reinforce the echoes of a nurturing beginning. We also find in friendship the sacred space to explore new faces of our character."

You need friends to provide a safe testing ground for personal development. That's why many people make their lifelong "best friend" in late adolescence when they are laying down the foundation for their adult personae. "The big change in personality occurs in adolescence," explains Paul Costa, chief of the Laboratory of Personality and Cognition at the National Institute on Aging. "The most dramatic changes take place between 17 and 20." As teenagers mature, "they become lower in neuroticism and higher in agreeableness. They are less emotional and better socialized," continues Costa, who is also a professor of psychiatry and behavioral sciences at Johns Hopkins University School of Medicine.

This is the period when you leave home and are on your own. You are becoming the person you want to be. You try out different personae. You choose your friends. If childhood friends are friends of circumstance, college friends are friends of choice. They reinforce who you will be as an adult. They are agents of awakening.

As Anais Nin wrote in her diary: "Each friend represents a world in us, a world possibly not born until they arrive, and it is only by this meeting that a new world is born."

The lifelong friend from this period, who bears witness to all the different phases of your adult development, provides the thread of continuity and affection that can hold you together in the bonus years.

Al's closest friend is the one he met in law school during those formative years of first adolescence and early adulthood. After they graduated they shared an apartment in New York City for three years until his friend went off to Europe to live. Eventually, each got married. "He was best man at my wedding. I was best man at his wedding," says Al. Even though his friend has lived in Europe for the last forty years, they have remained close. They talk on the phone to each other every two weeks. They know each other's kids. They have side-by-side vacation places in rural Connecticut. They discuss politics and world affairs (they disagree at times). They discuss relationships. "We share the intimacies of our life."

This is the friend who knew Al as he was going to be. When they met, the friend was the outgoing one and Al, the retiring one, particularly with women and other friends. The friend drove an MG and smoked a pipe—people responded to him easily. Al appeared to be the more realistic and level-headed one. They gave each other a piece of themselves. Al's friend became more grounded. Al became more adventurous—and he's not so retiring anymore.

The two men can be completely open with each other. When Al's marriage unraveled, he turned to his friend for intimate support. There are things you can say to a friend that you can't say to anybody else.

"Friendship is where disappointments can be used safely. In marriage the stakes are too high. In child/parent relationships, they could be crushing. In business, disappointment can be costly or disastrous. In friendship we exist on a playing field of life where disappointment can play out and even enrich us," writes Rich.

Friends also keep you from getting stuck in a dark corner. They help you grow and move forward. Friendships, continues Rich, "create new opportunities for us to evolve as adults, in ways different and apart from the context of family. At every age, friendships give us room to grow, and some degree of emotional safety in which to do it."

✦

You start to wonder: Do you have to be single to make friendship a priority? The answer is no, but you do have to have a sense of your own "singleness" to form relationships on a one-to-one basis.

There are advantages to being single. Kay Logan, who was widowed at 54, explains it this way: "I have my first really close women friends. Being a couple can be constricting. It's nice, but you don't get a chance to develop your potential," she says. "I don't think you realize this until you're not married."

Certainly there is more opportunity to explore friendship when you are single. There is no "other" to disapprove and rein you in. "There's nothing to stop me from what I want to do," she continues. She is free to have fun—and she does. "I enjoy food and wine. I haven't had a glass of milk since I was 17," she says. "I'm at the point—if it's not fun, don't call me!" Her Virginia license plate is YOPTWO: You Only Pass This Way Once.

The main issue is availability—and opportunity. In My Time, you have a new sense of freedom (or you should have). You may be more involved with friends if you are single—but many married men and women are able to make room for each other to explore friendships outside the marriage.

Perhaps you look back on a recent period of singlehood when you re-discovered the importance of friendship. Even when you recouple, you make sure that the friends from your single network remain active in your life.

A close friend who was divorced with three young children at age 44, didn't remarry for almost 15 years. At the wedding reception, she made a toast to those who stood by her during that time. "I'll never forget my women friends," she said. And she hasn't. They remain a constant presence in her new life with her husband and stepson.

In My Time, the solidarity of friendship often becomes a framework for other relationships. You weave the friendship thread into your experience with lovers, companions, spouses.

You find that it also fits into your bonds with adult children. As the parent-child relationship changes, the obvious hierarchy of dependency gives way to a more equitable relationship. There's a mutual sharing of life's details.

You use it to strengthen your relationship with new acquaintances. You know enough about people not to waste time. You can connect faster, deeper. You widen your net of intimates as well as the larger universe of social connections. There's a ripple effect as one friendship leads to another.

All in all, you give more priority to relationships. Your philosophical center of gravity shifts. As Al Gottesman puts it: "That whole mix of people is to me more important than career used to be—more important than my identity as a successful person."

In My Time, your goals become very different. "I used to have three standards: having an interesting job, having financial success, doing a job that is meaningful," says Al. Now his priorities have changed. "Friendship and people," he says, are his new standards.

My closest friend is poet Heddy Reid. We were roommates in college; we are neighbors in adulthood. We've shared the major passages of life: death, birth, marriage. Held each other in grief and in joy. Spent years talking deep, talking dirty, giggling and dieting, singing and kayaking, wiping tears, giving hope, making jokes, and playing patty-cake. We've guarded each other's dreams: falling in love, learning French, writing poetry, searching for God. And we've embraced each other's loved ones: husbands, children, relatives, and friends—ever increasing the circle of kinship.

This kind of friendship has a simplicity to it. You are there for each other no matter what. The bond endures forever—in the face of mortality and inevitable separation. It's a metaphor for intimacy with all those you love . . . more than yourself.

Heddy describes this bond of selfless love in a poem written about a woman whose younger sister had suffered a stroke. It captures the essence of true friendship:

> *I'll go first*
> *and throw the rope*
> *back for you. I'll*
> *go first, and tell you*
> *if it's safe. I'll go first*
> *and make a place*
> *where you can rest.*
> *I'll go first, carrying*
> *you in my heart*
> *the whole way,*
> *but you won't know.*
> *When you come over,*
> *I'll be waiting for you.*
> *We'll be laughing,*
> *and I'll braid your hair.*

10

Exploring Romance

A single event can awaken in us a stranger totally
unknown to us. To live is to be slowly born.

ANTOINE DE SAINT-EXUPÉRY

"I T'S BETTER THAN BEST," says a close friend, 63, who recently found her love on the Internet. In the bonus decades, you
often discover a romantic freedom that you never had in earlier years.
What is there to hold you back? Marriages may see a renaissance. New
relationships start off with some logistical advantages.

"We have no issues. We don't have to do children. We don't have to do
money together," says my friend. She feels she has finally met her soul-
mate. "I always wanted someone who understood China. His great-grandfather was a Methodist minister in China. He was born in China," she
continues. "We each had two messy divorces and three spectacular children. He calls us the 'old wrinklies.' I feel 45. It's like being young again
without having to be young—without the disabilities of being young."

Longevity has turned the manners of romance upside down. The old
wrinklies are on the loose. It's two in the morning—Do you know

where your grandparents are? Heading to a hotel room in Rome, camping out in a national park, dancing in the street for Mardi Gras.

Sometimes parents and children switch roles in recognition that romance can occur in My Time with the same chemistry of desire and sexual intensity as it did in youth. Middle-aged children now try to fix up their single parent at a neighborhood barbecue the way society matrons once paraded their daughters before eligible men at a waltz evening.

For all ages, the Internet has become a 24/7 dance hall. My friend went online after her daughter had met her husband-to-be on the web. She tried it as a lark: "TROUBLE-MAKER SEEKS ACCOMPLICE: Currently passionate about language, Bach, deep country, large dogs, textiles, historic preservation, sustainable forestry. . . . Checkered career includes Proper Boston, excessive education, varied travel, anthropology, procreation. . . . Looking for company to explore any of the above."

He noted in his initial bulletin: "I like the whole Bach family, Handel, Mozart, and jazz—Brubeck, Coltrane, Benny Goodman. . . . I paddle a sea kayak. . . . I am a fair cook. . . . I like to go for walks, cook, sail, camp, watch movies (occasionally), listen to music, talk, hug."

They hook up in cyberspace, e-mails zinging back and forth. As he says, the Internet is the "great cocktail party in the sky." Eventually they meet in the flesh—and go on to take walks and listen to music and talk and talk and after a while, they hug. "It was real," she says. "This is a man who can understand me. I kept after him. I was really in love with him. I could hallucinate him next to me." One year together, two years. When she has a stroke, he comes to her bedside, supporting her for weeks during rehab, and he keeps hugging her as she recovers. She helps him, too. "He has really been there for me. I want to be there for him."

✦

In My Time, there is less pressure to get married and more opportunities for different kinds of relationships. Friendships and love affairs flourish. Living-together partnerships and traveling-together relationships become more common. For many, it is a time of romance that is much more imaginative and fulfilling than during the middle years of adulthood or the distant passage of youth.

Just when you might be thinking—*Oh, I'm too old, too worn out. I've seen it all*—a new door opens and you may find yourself running through, giddy with romantic imaginings.

It is the night before New Year's Eve in California, a formal party of sixty people, candles flickering, music playing, champagne flowing. He rushes down the stairs and accidentally bumps into her. "Oh," she says, "are you asking me to dance?" They look at each other. "Yes," he says and he takes her hand. *Wham!*

"He's a wonderful dancer," says Dorcas Preston, 64, of Corona del Mar. She remembers every second of their meeting. "The attraction was immediate. As soon as we started dancing—the physical attraction was there."

This is the eternal *wham* of falling in love. It can happen at any age—when you're 14 or 64 or 104. It can happen at first sight, as it did with Dorcas. It can grow out of a long friendship. It can be rekindled in marriages. It can explode outside of marriage.

But when it happens in My Time, it's different. You are more stable than younger Romeos and Juliets. You have more confidence to build on the spark. You are not as likely to end up so broken-hearted if it doesn't work out. You may feel just as silly as a teenager. And you are not immune to making foolish choices and causing havoc to yourself and those around you. But you are not a novice. You bring a long history of past loves to a romantic relationship—for better or worse.

My Time is socially more fluid than earlier adulthood. More people are single, and being single becomes a norm again. People, especially women, find a new comfort zone in being unattached and open to new possibilities. There's more going out in groups, taking trips in groups, hanging out in groups—the way you did when you were a teenager.

You have a lot more flexibility. For starters, you don't have to worry about getting a baby sitter. You don't even have to worry about getting a baby. For most, the biological clock has stopped ticking. (Unless you're a man who marries a much younger woman and has more children, a whole other story, which puts the My Time chapter on hold.)

You are not restrained by what your mother thinks—or you shouldn't be. You're no longer preoccupied with what your children think. In general you don't care so much what anybody thinks. You are finally able to do what you want to do.

This has a double effect on romance. You are less cautious. You don't waste time—*if not now, when?* And you are more cautious. You know better what you want and you don't want to repeat the mistakes of the past.

"Falling in love—it happens. A lot," says family psychologist Constance Ahrons in San Diego. People are thrown together—taking trips, playing golf, volunteering in a soup kitchen, going back to class reunions. "It's proximity. Or it's finding old lovers—that's become quite a big thing," continues Ahrons, former professor at the University of California, Los Angeles. And now that you have more time to spend with friends—going to the theater, going on an Elderhostel tour—"people in bad marriages find each other," says Ahrons.

◆

By now you know that the Hallmark Greeting Card of living happily forever after doesn't automatically happen. As a romance plays out, you resurrect the ghosts of past affairs and marriages along with your relations with parents and siblings. Romance becomes the arena in which you expose the dark corners of your self, opening up a space where you can get to the bottom of your psyche.

Falling in love during the bonus decades is often part of the reevaluation phase. It forces you to examine why you're attracted to certain types of people, how you behave in close emotional quarters, what you do to promote intimacy, and perhaps how you deceive yourself, sabo-taging your pursuit of love.

Since the mark of success is not necessarily a wedding ring, you can concentrate on the quality of the relationship . . . and see how the mys-tery of love can transform the sense of self—regardless of the outcome.

Dorcas Preston has fallen madly in love before. Pretty, petite—with a timeless teen-queen glamour—she moves easily among the rich and fancy in California. But she's also a preacher's daughter, and that's complicated. The day after Cupid's arrow struck at the dance was the Millennium—New Year's Eve 2000. Dorcas, who was raised to get ready for Armageddon, spent the evening by herself. "I refused to go out," she says. As a child she had spent every New Year's Eve on her knees, in case "Jesus comes," she explains. "I was in a meditative mood all night and watching TV. I was alone."

She grew up right after the Depression. The family moved around—West Virginia, Indiana, Texas, Michigan, Alabama, Missouri, Ohio, Washington. In her early childhood, people were too poor to put money in the offering plate, so her mother made a grocery list and put slips of paper into the plate for a can of beans, a loaf of bread. "Instead of putting in money, parishioners would draw a slip and then bring us the item on the slip," she says. "I would go to school in old clothes. When it was cold, mom let me wear her sweater with holes in it."

All the while, she lived under glass. "People were looking at me all the time—being the preacher's daughter," she continues. "I had to be perfect. I never felt comfortable if I hurt people's feelings."

Her God was fierce and so was her dad. How her father adored her. How she pleased him. She had a voice. When she was 3, she sang "God Bless America" at the Church of God convention in Tennessee.

And then, when she didn't please him, he'd beat her. He belonged to a generation that believed in "spare the rod, spoil the child." "He had a temper. He grew up with someone beating him all the time. He did the same thing to us," she says. "We had cuts and bruises all the time." Once, when they were living in Michigan, she was sent to the grocery store to buy food. "There was a penny change. I bought a piece of bubble gum," she begins. "I was so scared. When my father asked for the change, I lied." Her father found out from the grocer that she'd spent the penny change on bubble gum. "Dad got out his belt. He was beating me so hard."

After the beatings, "he'd kiss me and hold me and say: Your daddy had to do this." And after the bubble gum beating, "I never lied."

Today, her father would be in jail, she says. She knows that from her work with the Orange County Child Abuse Prevention Center. She keeps salving her wounds by helping others and raising money for the abuse prevention center. "I have such compassion for children," she says.

Still, she knows that the imprinting of abuse and poverty in her brain has influenced her behavior in love. "My experience is—I don't pick the right men," she says.

She reviews the falling-in-love pattern in her marriages. They all started with the *wham!* and, for different reasons, she ended up crushed. The first time, she married at 19. When they broke up, she quickly remarried. "I met him right away. I fell madly in love. He had charisma," she says. After nearly ten years, they broke up and she married her third husband. She didn't dare refuse. "I was too afraid. I really fell for him. He was handsome, powerful in that way of being very interesting and intelligent. I was fascinated with someone so bright. He had Paul Newman's gray hair, beautiful blue eyes—he was a cross between Newman and George Segal. He played football at Michigan State," she says. They were together nearly twenty years. On her 50th birthday, he threw a party for her—lots of friends and singing. "He gave this little talk. He had people rolling on the floor. I was madly in love with him." But there was a dark streak there too. The relationship began to crumble. She felt increasingly crushed.

Seven years later they got divorced. Dorcas was 57.

As she plunged into Second Adolescence and got through the turmoil of the breakup, she realized she wanted to change the script. First, she didn't get married again. She resisted "falling madly in love" again to relieve the pain. Since 1995, she's been living on her own—a good place, she says. There have been men in her life, but she's held on to her independence. "I stayed single. I was happy that way," she says.

She also realized that while her marriages failed, she had gained much from them. She has three sons who are now grown and one grandson; they are a close family, she says.

She became stronger. "The thing my last husband did was to build up my confidence. Being a minister's daughter, you had to be humble all the time. He helped me become stronger. When he was in a good mood, he put me on a pedestal. He just adored me. It helped my self-esteem," she says.

She got over being poor. She became a successful real estate broker. Her third husband had financial resources. "I could buy anything I wanted," she says.

She rediscovered her singing voice. Like many others in My Time, she resurrected an early talent and rebuilt her life around it. The preacher's daughter who used to sing from the pulpit went to music school. She now sings opera—roles in *Orpheus and Euridice, Dido and Aeneas*. She sings with the Pacific Symphony Orchestra and the Pacific Chorale. She sings in church. She sings at weddings and funerals. The singing frees her. "I'm doing it because it's what I love," she says. "It keeps you young. It gives you a purpose. It gives you a reason to live."

Dorcas had also dealt with the legacy of her father, the mixture of love and abuse that echoed in her relationships. A few months before he died nearly twenty-five years ago, they had a reconciliation. "He said he was sorry for anything he had done that was bad. He held me and cried. I cried," she says.

The wintry night he died in the hospital, Dorcas went out to the parking lot. A cold wind was blowing. Her car window wouldn't close. How could she drive away with a stuck window? As a friend tried to fix the window, "I was sitting there crying," she says. "This bird flew down and sat on the hood of the car—singing away, looking at me." She stared at the bird in disbelief. Then she said to herself: "That's dad saying: *Don't cry!*" "That's dad telling me: *I'm okay.*" Then the bird flew away.

Decades later, she is driving home from an audition to sing with the Pacific Chorale. She is scared—thinking that she has failed. She wants this job, wants a new life. She stops at the light. "I put my window down because I heard a very loud sound," she begins. Then she sees where the sound is coming from: "A hundred birds are on an electrical wire, singing away." She smiles and says to herself: "That's my dad saying: *Don't worry. It's okay; you made it.*" That evening she finds out that she's got the job.

As Dorcas becomes more independent, she puts the past in its place. Recently she went back to the church of her childhood in Alabama. That day she sang from the same pulpit that she had sung from when she was 11 years old. "The church was smaller than I remember," she says.

The man who asked her to dance at the party called her two days later. "Right away, we started an affair," she says. "The sex is great. He has a strong sex drive and I do, too."

He is half Swedish, half Italian. "He's so classy," she says. "He speaks so many languages. He's so sweet. He's always so sweet." They both hate to hurt people's feelings. They want to please. "I never knew there was a man like me," laughs Dorcas. "He loves to dance. He loves people. We are a lot alike."

But she is not racing to the altar. They are spending time getting to know each other. When they are apart, they e-mail every day. He has moved into an apartment near her home. They are meeting each other's friends, seeing each other's children. They travel together. She is waiting to see how their romance deepens. She's developed a different attitude about love. Passion is no longer the agent of rescue; it's the prelude to a relationship.

"I have the butterfly theory of love. I believe true love—it's like a butterfly. You hold your hand out. If it starts to fly away and you hold on to it. . . . " She makes a fist, crushing the butterfly. "If you keep your hand open, it will fly away and come back. That's the way I want a relationship," she says. "I don't feel like I ever want to be in a marriage again."

Maybe. She's trying a different scenario. That way, she hopes to change the second act in this relationship, as the sexual attraction pulls them closer together.

✦

You may not have such a painful legacy in your past as Dorcas. But everyone has dark corners in the vault of previous relationships. You also have some treasures. This is part of the empowerment of My Time. You bring your past loves to the present.

One of the themes of My Time is the recovery of lost loves—whether you are in a relationship or not. As Harvard's George Vaillant writes in *Aging Well:* "When we are old, our lives become the sum of all whom we have loved. It is important not to waste anyone. One task of living out the last half of life is excavating and recovering all of those whom we loved in the first half."

By the time you get to this stage in life, you have lost love. A parent who succumbs to disease and dies, a spouse taken away by early death or divorce, a child killed in an automobile accident. You weep and learn to grieve. You find that the capacity to mourn is the twin of the capacity to love.

Whether you hook up with a loved one in fact or in your thoughts, you are awakened. You resurrect a whole store of past loves—spouses, relatives, friends, and lovers. "No one whom we have ever loved is totally lost," continues Vaillant. "Just as rivers expose buried geologic strata, so may the erosion of living uncover life-saving memories of love, formerly obscured by pain, resentment, or immaturity."

The trauma of losing a loved one can shut you down. But as you gather up your old loves, you may be released from loss and more open to new love.

On a gray afternoon I had tea with George McGovern, former senator and presidential candidate. He had written a book about his beloved daughter who struggled long against alcoholism. She died when still a young woman. George was a neighbor. I was interviewing him about his book. I was also seeing in his loss my own loss—the loss of a man I loved so much and the collapse of a marriage.

As our conversation wound down, George turned to me and said: "You only really learn about love when you lose love."

The energy of romance is entangled with your sexual identity. In and out of relationships, sexuality is a constant throughout the life span. As a recent Surgeon General's report on sexuality makes clear, everyone is a sexual being from birth to death. Sexual identity grows along with other aspects of development. It doesn't depend on any particular sexual activity or on having a partner. It's a body awareness, a source of vitality, a spirit of joy and connection. It is nurtured in different ways all through life.

Part of it is physical. You have to pay attention to your body. As Dorcas Preston says: "I got busy in my 40s. I stopped eating fried foods. I worked out. I got back in good shape. You have to take care of yourself and treat your body like a temple."

Part of it is tactile: You make sure you stay sensitive to stimuli. The feel of Egyptian cotton sheets on the skin. A Swedish massage. "Little by little, you realize you deserve nice things," says Mary Kunze, 64, of Elm Grove, Wisconsin. She fills her house with flowers, buys nice lingerie, gets a pedicure. You learn to indulge yourself.

Part of it is style and attitude. Marian Taylor Giles, who lived in a nursing home, held on to her romantic self in the face of physical limitations and a paucity of men. "It's really hard because I love men," she said. But her identity as a sensuous woman got affirmed in ways large and small. "On my birthday, a gentleman who's been nice to me came up and brought me a pretty card. I told him how much I appreciated that. He said: 'Marian—every time I see you smile, I remember why I love women.' When he said that, it just made my day."

Part of it is medical, mechanical even. In recent years, medical science has enhanced the possibilities for sexual expression. Just as hip replacements and angioplasty have given a better life to thousands of men and women, new drugs and technologies have brought the sexual revolution into grandparents' bedrooms. Medicines such as Viagra have not only helped many couples have intercourse; they have also gotten men and women talking. With Viagra celebrity Bob Dole on the airwaves, it's now fashionable to discuss impotence and other important issues like lubrication, desire, and pleasure.

"There is such a hunger for this information," says psychiatrist S. Michael Plaut at the University of Maryland School of Medicine in Baltimore. "There are no standards of good or bad sex. It's what makes you happy. Anything two people want to do together should be okay— as long as they are not hurting anybody." He continues. "For some, sex gets better. You have more time," says Plaut.

Plenty of people are content *not* to have sexual intercourse. In the bonus decades there's less inner pressure from hormones and less outer pressure from society to pursue sexual activity. Obviously, says

Plaut, "I would never insist that people have to have sex or have a partner." Yet, you are still a sexual being.

Sometimes you have to fight for your sexuality in a culture ridden with negative stereotypes about sex and aging. The Reverend Joan Brown Campbell, who retired recently from the National Council of Churches, saw how difficult it is for doctors to talk about sex, particularly to older women, when she underwent a hysterectomy. Hospital policy required doctors to ask patients about their sex life after this kind of surgery.

"I remember the young doctor," she begins. "He looked down at a piece of paper with a list of questions and said: 'Well, ugh, Reverend Campbell, are you sexually active?' He didn't look at my face. He didn't look at my eyes. He was too embarrassed. It's all still mystery land. But people have a lot of interest in this. We cannot just giggle. We have to talk seriously."

There are also gender myths. "The assumption about older women is that they don't want or need a sex life," she says. If there's a sexual problem, it doesn't matter. "Women are expected not to need it or want it." But a sexual problem in a man is different. "With men, it's a crisis," she says.

Yet, a sexual life is important to both men and women in the bonus decades. "It's just like eating vegetables. It's good for you," she says. And the good thing is, you get to choose the vegetables. How you express your sexuality is up to you.

✦

In the pursuit of love in the bonus decades, there is a phenomenon of "coming home." You are more likely to be attracted by shared values, to be drawn in by the familiar. You've been through a Marco Polo phase when you sought those who were opposite, even exotic. This is why, when you hook up with a childhood classmate, reminiscing about the science teacher in third grade can be an aphrodisiac. It's also why the habit of shared experience and remembering the "time when" is a staple of long-lasting marriages.

But nostalgia is no shortcut to love. It still takes courage and effort to connect and commit, even if it's the boy next door. "Falling in love is, by its nature, predicated on risk-taking," writes psychiatrist Ethel S. Person in *Dreams of Love and Fateful Encounters*. "In order to achieve mutual love, one must gamble on opening up psychically to achieve real intimacy and mutuality."

Loving is also a double script. While the face may turn out to be familiar, the familiarity you feel in the initial moment may be an illusion. You don't really know each other that well. You can be just as disappointed at 50 as at 25.

The man doesn't understand what happened. He's 55, smart, sexy, single—and there are lots of great women out there. He wants My Time romance—free and flexible. But his ex-wife warns him: *No matter what a woman says, what she wants is a ring and a baby.* Not him. He's got two children. The youngest will be headed for college in two years. He's a conscientious dad. He doesn't want to go through the whole child-rearing experience again. He stays away from the very young things. He wants an independent woman. Someone his own age who is not going to get pregnant. Who likes to laugh and do her own thing and not hang on him.

He finds her. An old girlfriend from college, who lives a safe two thousand miles away. She's an artist who lives in a shack on a mountainside in Colorado overlooking a gorge. She's had a couple of shows. No children. Laughing green eyes, a gorgeous figure. They fall in love. They want the same things. They are the same age. They're grown-ups, right?

After a year of back and forth visits, she loses the lease on her shack and, before he knows it, she's moved in with him. She has no money. She has no job. She has no friends. All she has is him. She calls him five times a day. She keeps getting lost driving around town. He's in a meeting, the cellphone rings. *I'm stuck in traffic on Pine Street, where should I turn?*

What happened to that independent artist he flipped over when she lived two thousand miles away? Suddenly it's like he's got another child to take care of. He can't breathe. His allergies have kicked in. He thinks of the Bob Dylan refrain: *To be stuck inside Mobile/With the Memphis blues again.*

He's not 40 anymore. He doesn't want to live like this. He wants to figure it out. He certainly doesn't want to end up in his bonus decades with the Memphis blues again. It's a rocky Second Adolescence as he confronts his script—and hers.

◆

Psychiatrist Ethel Person describes the process of falling in love as "magical re-enchantment"—the recapture of the mother-infant bond. It touches that place of original mystery and union. With the mention of the beloved, your eyes light up. Your heart rate rises. You get that look—that falling-in-love look. You have the love-struck aura.

Listening to Mahler's fifth symphony one June evening, I am swept away by the agonizing swells of Mahler's passion—music so full of sorrow, as I am full of sorrow. Alone, after the end of a marriage. But this goes deeper. Gustav Mahler grew up in loss, with the deaths of his siblings in youth, the deaths of his children in adulthood. The composer died in 1911 at 51. I am heading towards my 60th birthday. The man holding my hand is about the same age, and I am falling in love. When he speaks, I hear the voice of my uncles, my cousins. As Mahler's music pours forth, louder and grander, I can hear the notes in my father's music and my own early symphony of loss and love. We are a family that always communicated in music. Growing up I could always tell what was really going on at home by listening to my father play the piano. Mahler's musical wave rushes over the audience, a hurricane of feeling; the man next to me squeezes my hand. The music turns loss into wonder, into beauty. Warmth rises in my chest. I can hear the music and feel the passion that once flooded my early life. "I am deliriously happy," I whisper. I had finally come home.

The romance was a wonderful spark, although it did not become an enduring relationship. Looking back I can see that it probably had more to do with Mahler and me than with the man who happened to take me to the concert. But it was a turning point in my passage through Second Adolescence. It awakened me from my slumber of sorrow.

"Regardless of duration, passionate love is not only exultant but also transcendent and transformative," writes Person. "It changes thinking, feeling, perception, even the very sense of self."

The experience of passion is much bigger than one relationship. It's not even dependent on the other person. Romance is a sense of excitement that comes from within. It's important to find this energy—whether or not it springs from a relationship. Romance can become a force that infuses your whole life.

The process of magical re-enchantment is the engine of renewal. You can see it in the love-struck aura of grandparents as they stare at a newborn grandchild. You can hear it in the sighs of an opera buff at a performance of *La Boheme*. You can sense it in places of worship, feel it on the beach at sunrise. It is the energizing force of enchantment.

Falling in love is also dangerous. Sexual passion can come on like a summer squall. It's the French *coup de foudre*—the bolt of lightning—and it can light up the sky and torch the earth. Sometimes it just happens, whether you're looking for it or not. It may also be the clap of thunder to wake you up. What do you do if you are stuck in a stagnant relationship? Or you're just plain lonely?

You don't have to study Freud to understand that these feelings go way back. As the suitor in Shakespeare's *Twelfth Night* wistfully explains: "I was ador'd once, too." Adored by former loves, all the way back to Mother and the promise of perfect love in the Garden of Eden. No wonder you want to get back to that ideal when you fall in love later in life. To be so completely adored. There is no return to the Garden, of course. But you are seduced by your own longing to be adored.

A common scenario for finding adoration in the bonus decades is compartmentalization. By this time, you have acquired many pieces to your life. You may be in a long-standing marriage. You have a house, you have grandchildren, you have a reputation. You don't want to lose those pieces. But: *Where is the love?* You divide up your life into separate compartments. You lead double, triple lives. The affair becomes a romantic fix to an incomplete life.

You may think you're in control. You're keeping everybody happy, as you go from compartment to compartment. And you may be very content. But compartmentalization requires a web of deception—and the one you deceive the most may be yourself.

Falling in love is "dynamite," says Maryland therapist Danille Drake. "It's jumping off a cliff."

And there may be a lot of rocks below.

✦

What follows is a modern tale of compartmentalization taking over a man's life in his search for love. All the names and identifying details have been changed. The plot and quotes are intact.

I call him Tim. He doesn't want his name to be used because he doesn't want his wife to know. He would never get a divorce, he says. Cara is his "executive wife," he says. They live in Seattle. They have two daughters, two sons, all grown. He retired from Boeing in 1990 and started his own little aerospace company—just him and a couple of assistants in the office. He's 71, lanky, no health problems. He travels. He's proud of his wife—of the way she entertains and runs their sprawling house on a ridge. They have not had any sex in years. She can't, he says; it's a physical thing with her.

But he can, and he believes you can love more than one person, especially the ones you loved long ago. Number One is Mary—Mary, Mary, Quite Contrary, who lives across the country in Gray, Maine. His first love, the one he kissed on the street in Brunswick when he was 16, the youngest student in the freshman class at Bowdoin College, and far, far away from home in the rolling hills of Eastern Kentucky.

"We went for a walk at night. It was dark and cold. We stopped under a street lamp," he says. The Kiss. As rock singer Gwen Stefani wails: *Kiss me over and over forever and ever my love.* "Mary is very romantic," he says. "She never got over it."

He was on scholarship and worked in the kitchen. Mary's dad was a coach in the athletics department. Tim started playing baseball, going over for Sunday lunch, going to church, and becoming part of the family—an oasis of warmth in a school where the winters were cold and Yankees were everywhere. His classmates talked about sailing and going to Europe like Hemingway. He could show them a thing or two about shooting rabbits, but he kept that to himself because he wanted to do better than all of them. And he did.

After college, he went to graduate school at UCLA, where he met his executive wife, and then on to a successful career in the aerospace industry. He didn't go back to Maine until his fortieth college reunion. He came alone; his wife doesn't want to have anything to do with his Maine chapter. He asked around—What ever happened to Mary, the coach's pretty daughter?

He tracked her down to a trailer by the side of a brook. "She didn't look any different in the year 1992 than she did in 1952," he says. "This part got a little bigger. That part got a little bigger. She was still the same girl."

Mary lived alone. Her husband had died of congestive heart failure a few years earlier. It was not a happy marriage, with him on disability, sitting in front of the TV and drinking. One daughter, who lived nearby, and a beloved grandson. The daughter was a waitress at the local diner where they all went for dinner the first time he came to visit. He stared at Mary—at her sweet, square Yankee face, her simple blueberry-pie warmth and lack of pretense. So different from his executive wife. A wild rawness in Mary's unplucked eyebrows, her bold freckles and deep smile lines. After reminiscing for a while, he noticed that she was repeating herself and sometimes she'd doze off. Her daughter took him aside; early stages of Alzheimer's disease, she said, and she was so glad he had come back into her mother's life.

He decided to invite Mary to the forty-fifth reunion. After all, Cara had refused to come. As he explained it to the organizers of the reunion—Mary was the daughter of the family that had taken him in and she is slipping into Alzheimer's. What a nice thing to do. "I had laid the groundwork carefully," he says. "Everybody understood. I wasn't sneaking around on my wife."

All went well at the reunion. Mary knew many of his classmates. So nice to see the coach's daughter! He watched out for her. Then, as he escorted her back to her room and kissed her on the cheek goodnight, "she did a lip slide. She slid her mouth on mine," he says.

He said: *Mary, you're quivering. You're breathing hard.*

She said: *You are, too.*

As he recalls it: "It was absolutely seamless. There was no gap of forty-five years. The same person I kissed forty-five years ago—the same feelings."

He began visiting Mary regularly on his business trips. There were problems. One time when they arranged to meet in Portland, the police brought her to the hotel. They had picked her up in the Old Port. She was lost. Her daughter had pinned his name on her coat. She began to cry and kept saying the name of the hotel. Luckily he was outside waiting for her.

He explained to the police who apologized. From then on, he always went to her place. The relationship deepened. So did their sexual life. She got a new double bed. "I was forever kicking the dog out," he says.

But he was careful to compartmentalize his life. As he explained to Mary's daughter and grandson at their initial meeting in the diner: "I'm a married man. I have four children. I grew up with your mother's family. They adopted me when I was a student. I still consider myself a member of the family." And he told them about how Mary was a soccer star and a basketball star. How she played the trombone in the marching band. How she was class valedictorian. *Grandma! You never told us about that,* said the grandson. "That's why I have to come up here and explain things to you," he replied.

When his college class organized a tour to Mexico, he asked Mary to come with him. After all, Cara wouldn't go. The trip would be his grand gift to Mary after all her family had done for him.

Oaxaca was Mary's favorite place. She loved sitting in the square in the glistening golden sun, sipping margaritas, gazing at the bright colors of the bougainvillea—startling swatches of purple, pink, red. Holding his hand and listening to the bells of the cathedral. They visited the ruins of Monte Alban and he made sure she didn't get tired. "My eyes were bugging out," she says. "We walked and walked and walked."

Their hotel room looked out over the square. He had gotten a new pair of pajamas for the trip. As he lay on top of the white lace duvet, Mary went around to the foot of the king-sized bed. "She grabbed the end of my pajamas and pulled them off," he says. "She said she'd never been with a man like me." He smiles.

At the group dinner on the last evening in Oaxaca, after tortilla soup and chicken with mole sauce, he made a toast to his classmates and their spouses. His mission, he explained, had been "to show this lady my friendship of fifty-five years. I want to tell you it's been a memorable week." Cheers from the group. "Everyone has made her feel comfortable. It's a success. She told me this morning how much she's enjoying it."

Everyone clapped. Mary smiled, looked up at him, patted his arm. A nice blueberry-pie woman in a down jacket wearing glasses.

On the way home on the plane, Mary would lean over every fifteen minutes and kiss him. He'd kiss her back, hold her hand. The flight attendant brought the lovebirds extra champagne. Turned out she was from Hazard, Kentucky, not far from where he grew up. She brought them more champagne and said: "Why don't you do the honorable thing and get married?"

"I am married," he replied.

Once they landed in Houston, he'd planned to put Mary on the plane to Boston and then take a flight home to Seattle. But when they got to her gate, she refused to board. *Kiss me forever* . . . He took her aside, as though she were a child. Now Mary. Mary, Mary, Quite Contrary. "No, I'm going to stay right here with you," she said. He took her arm and steadied her: "Now you know what would happen if you did that. I'd have a lot of explaining to do," he said, winking at her, making a joke of it. "That would be right," she said, giggling. Last call for boarding. "Remember the toasts at the dinner. You had the most beautiful look on your face," he said. Mary smiled and moved up in the line.

Back home and three thousand miles apart, they talk to each other every couple of days on the telephone. Is he the love of her life? "Absolutely! We were something," she says. She reminisces about The Kiss when he was 16, she was 17. "Oh my. You know when you're very young. Kissing is so exciting," she says. "We stood on the corner. I had my wonderful red coat on. . . . It came down to the ankles."

He worries about Mary. The Alzheimer's is getting worse. She can't travel anymore. But then, Mary has started him thinking about love, and love lost. And that started him thinking about some of his other old girlfriends. The one that summer when he was working in Dallas. The one in L.A. before he met his wife.

He goes on the Internet to look for them. "Once I found Mary—that turned out to be so rewarding, I thought I'd go and contact the rest of them," he says.

Where does it end? The man is being swept along as he is swept away.

✦

Certainly "living in the moment" becomes sweeter, and sometimes by default, it may seem to be the only choice in the bonus decades. The danger is that your moral compass begins to swing wildly as you focus on what's missing in your life and you feel the pressure of having a limited time to find it. You get creative. Solutions that might have seemed outlandish or impossible a decade or two ago suddenly present as not only possible but desirable. The sense of "getting away with it" may even be rewarding in the short term, particularly if other parts of your life seem hollow and unsatisfying.

But there is another side to all this. Countering the trend to compartmentalize is the yearning for authenticity—the desire to be whole and bring the different patches of your life into one quilt of experience. My Time is when you try to integrate past with present and tie up loose ends. What is your romantic truth? You want to know before you die.

An increasing number of couples seek therapy at this stage. "For some, the newly awakened romance feels a bit like being caught at the crest of a wave—with little control over its speed or force," says therapist Danille Drake. "Couples often benefit from therapy by taking the time to explore the ways they are well matched in attitudes and values and by negotiating the sticking points."

She finds that people in the bonus decades are better at negotiating conflict and being truthful. "With greater wisdom and maturity—

and without the surge of hormones—they often are able to be more reasoned when conflict arises," she adds. "They also are able to cut each other slack—they are not so judgmental as they once might have been." They are not as distracted as younger couples. "They no longer need to prove themselves in the marketplace or in society. They are freed somewhat from those pressures. They appreciate the beauty of just being."

Then, too, couples tend to be more understanding of what it's like to be vulnerable and sick. "That seems to help them be more gentle with each other," she says.

Whatever happens in a relationship, most people believe that they have been enriched by the rediscovery of love. "They tend to use words such as 'bliss' and 'glorious' to describe their emotional state. They say it is every bit as wondrous and transforming as it was when they were 16," continues Drake. "This conveys to me the possibilities that can happen in middle and late age."

◆

You never know when it's going to happen. But you're willing to take some chances. In My Time, what have you got to lose?

The bus pulls up to the museum in Moscow. It's the last day of the tour to Russia organized by the Dallas Symphony Guild, and Pat Mattingly has sort of had it with museums. "This gentleman was in the back of the bus. So was I," she begins.

She said: *I cannot do another museum.*

He said: *Well, I can't either.*

She said: *Well, I'd like to go shopping.*

He said: *I'm dying to go shopping.*

She said: *I've seen a little place. . . . Right around here . . . a little shop that sells religious art.*

He said: *I know just where you're talking about.*

"We go bopping off down a side street," says Pat, 66. Turns out he's a lawyer who collects antiques. He loves music. So does she. He is divorced. She's never married; she's just retired as the head of a private school. They each buy a little something. They miss the bus and walk back to the hotel. How will they get through customs? They conspire. He said: *You could wrap it up in your negligee.*

"We bonded in a significant way," says Pat.

Most significant was the discovery that they share a common trait: They are both rebels. Before arriving in Russia, the tour director had laid down two cardinal rules: (1) Never leave the group. (2) Do not bring back art objects that might cause difficulties getting through customs. "We had broken the two rules of the group. It was this secret between us," she says.

Part of the joy of falling in love is feeling that the real you is known and celebrated by the other. Pat, who excelled as a leader in education, had cloaked her ambition and success in a warm, unthreatening, soft-spoken manner. But she was a powerhouse. She had broken the rules in private education by becoming a pioneer woman to reach the top of her field. Here was a man . . . like her. A risk-taker in playful rebellion who had charm, warmth, and expertise. She validated those qualities in him as he validated those qualities in her.

"From that time on, he called me. We went out. We always had that story to laugh about," she says.

The meeting in Russia was the prelude. They are now figuring out a relationship. They travel together. They go to music performances together. It's all part of a larger life for Pat since she shifted her focus from the school to a broader circle of friends, interests, and emotions.

"People say to me: *You look so happy.* They try to attribute it to him," she says. "I like to think I could have been this way whether I met him or not."

11

Redefining Family

If we have no peace it is because we have forgotten we belong to each other.

MOTHER TERESA

As A CHILD, YOU ARE BORN into a family. In My Time, you make your own. There are no rules—and few role models. You need an intimate circle of people you can love and who love you. Without it, you are at greater risk of an "early" death. That's the conclusion of Harvard's Lisa Berkman and other social scientists—not to mention the wisdom of the ancients. . . . *Now abideth faith, hope, love, these three; the greatest of these is love.*

To create family, you draw on those you inherit—siblings, cousins, parents; those you choose—friends, lovers, companions, and spouses; and those you help raise—children and grandchildren and the children of others.

My Aunt Melinda used to say that family was like a harbor: the place from which you go forth to discover the world, and come back to for safe-keeping. But who maintains the harbor?

In My Time that may be you. The harbor has gotten bigger now that the family expands over four generations and includes friends as well as relatives. The nuclear unit of young adulthood has given way to a much wider network of kin. You face different tasks in caring for loved ones. You develop a code to guide you in intimate relationships – whether it's with a spouse or a grandchild. In this period of personal change, all your significant relationships are changing too.

✦

Marriage remains a basic unit in the family. Most people in the bonus decades are married—or they have been married. And those who are single have usually bonded with others in marriage-like arrangements and close friendships. Coupling weaves together the tapestry of a tribe across generations.

But couples are tested in My Time. The agenda of marriage is different. There's no more staying together for the sake of children. For most people, it's being together for the sake of each other. You look across the breakfast table—or across the bed—and ask yourself: Another forty years?

There is a marital paradox in the bonus decades: The relationship opens up as each person is freer to pursue a more independent course—and the relationship becomes closer now that there's only the two of you. Or then again, the relationship may open up and you slide further apart. The main thing is that the dynamics of marriage change.

Bill Matuszeski, 62, has always had a safe-harbor kind of marriage with his wife—poet and educator Mary Procter, 61. In the career consolidation phase of adulthood, they had three children within seventeen months (including one set of twins), which led to an intense period of child-rearing. All the while, Bill focused on his career at several federal environmental agencies.

When he left the government at age 59, he went through his own transition to My Time. In the process, the marriage changed.

Bill relishes his new independence—and he is glad that he has an independent-minded wife. He went to Spain by himself on an art tour. He went bicycling with his brother and sister on the back roads of Chile and Argentina.

But he always comes back to the family harbor. It's just that the moorings have been moved around.

The biggest change is the career switch. Mary is soaring in a demanding job with the Charter Schools. After a career at the State Department, she recently switched to education. For most of their married life, Bill's career was dominant. "She had to deal with that," he says. Now Mary is in the zoom zone. "Her job has priority," he says. "She's in her ideal job right now," he continues. "No job had given her the kind of excitement she was looking for until now. . . . She's done very well."

But where does he fit into this role reversal?

"You have to spend a lot more time talking about how you feel—how you feel about each other. Your own sense of yourself is changing so quickly. It's real easy to knock each other off balance," he says.

"It's more important that I hear more about her work and what's going on in the job." If he's reading the newspaper when Mary comes home, he can't just keep reading, he explains. He has to stop and pay attention. "I'm the guy who is supposed to be listening," he says. He gives back what he used to get. "You're more aware of the need for ego massaging."

Meanwhile, he's taken over the domestic side of life. He had always turned to cooking and gardening for relaxation. Now he cooks, gardens, and does the laundry, too. Someone has to keep the harbor cleaned up!

The generation that blurred gender roles in the workplace is also blurring gender roles in My Time. Bill fights the who-does-the-dishes

stereotype of marriage. He also resists the mindset that husbands always die before wives—and anyway, women are more suited to widow-
hood. "It's really important for me to get over that psychology of dying
first," he says. And he makes it a joke with Mary. "I am going to outlive
her. If I died first, the house would fall down. The laundry wouldn't get
done. I have to outlive her."

Truth is, he cares too much about her to imagine her alone. They
have become essential partners to each other. And when Mary begins
to feel the rumble of anxiety and thinks about changing her life and
taking a sabbatical, he's her advocate. He can empathize. After all, he's
gone through it himself.

As Bill and Mary become more independent, they draw closer together.

✦

It gets down to a basic question: How well do you love? You want to
combine the selfless love of friendship (empathy) with the re-enchantment of romance (discovery) and anchor the relationship in a safe family harbor (trust). To flourish, it seems, intimate relationships are built
on a triad of empathy, discovery, and trust.

You have some advantages. Empathy is often an acquired emotional
talent. Through life empowerment, you have gained enough confidence
that you don't have to concentrate solely on defending yourself in the
intimate zone, or on playing a certain role. You can put yourself in
someone else's shoes and care beyond yourself.

Discovery is another pillar of maturity. It's an ability to see new things
in a loved one and to be surprised rather than frightened—delighted
rather than disapproving. Obviously some changes are devastating—the
ones caused by debilitating illness. But many changes are growth spurts
in personal development. John and Juanita Jackson of Virginia have been
married more than thirty-five years, a second marriage for both. "I'm always discovering new things about her," says John with an adoring laugh.

The romantic excitement of discovery revises Shakespeare's adage: "Love is not love Which alters when it alteration finds" but, rather, *love is love that alters in awe when it alteration finds.*

Personal upheavals in health and work are played out in the marital arena. "It's a little bit like the transition to parenthood," says psychologist Philip Cowan, co-author with his wife Carolyn Cowan of *When Partners Become Parents: The Big Life Change for Couples.* "Couples that are doing well do better," he says. "Couples that aren't doing well, once the kids go off to college, they are separating and getting divorced."

There are no good data on how couples fare in the bonus decades, the Cowans point out. Therapists notice a clustering of breakups around the time children leave home—because one of the main reasons students come for counseling at university health centers is to seek help in dealing with the divorce of their parents.

Another break point comes when a spouse officially "retires." Two people may be in very different places in their personal trajectories when they get to this stage. "Where is your partner? His dream takes him this way. Her dream goes another way," says Carolyn Cowan. "You don't know what it will mean to take this path or that. It is risky. You get used to stability. To open it up again means exposing yourself to all this risk."

Yet, marriages are generally healthier and happier in My Time. The divorce revolution that began several decades ago has washed out the really miserable marriages. As Philip Cowan explains, most of the breakups have already taken place before the age of 60. "Couples in the most serious difficulty are not together," he says. "On average, these [older] couples are happier than younger couples."

Some long-standing marriages come into a flowering. "You reap what you sow," says a friend. You finally get the rewards for sticking it out, she adds. The edges get smoothed over, conflict and competition subside. When she underwent a hysterectomy recently, her husband slept in her hospital room. "He never could have done that when we were first married." Then, too, when he had a heart attack, she was at his bedside. All those temptations and detours of the middle years get put away in the storage file of "near misses." "Thank God, I didn't leave him," she says. "Thank God, he didn't leave me."

✦

There are gender differences in marriage. After age 65, men are more likely to be married than women. Since women live longer and tend to marry older men, the marital gap widens with age. According to a 1997 Census Bureau population survey, about three-quarters of men 65 and over were living with a spouse compared to a little over 40 percent of women. Among women 65–69, more than 55 percent were married. After age 75, fewer than 30 percent had husbands—and more than 60 percent were widowed.

But mating patterns may change as the baby-boom generation hits My Time. People in their 50s and 60s today have already experienced more serial marriage—largely because of divorce. They seem more willing to risk change to renew a marriage—or to get out of it, rather than waiting for 'til death do us part. The trend toward multiple marriages is evident even among pre-boomer men and women. In 1996, a quarter of men 60–69 had been married two or more times—and so had one in five women.

Meanwhile, the life expectancy gap between men and women is narrowing. Dramatic declines in heart disease deaths have added statistical years to men's lives. Once you reach 100, the pool of healthy men and healthy women is about the same. To be sure, women outnumber men at that age, but men have fewer disabilities. "The men who survive are very healthy physically and cognitively," says neuropsychologist Margery Silver, associate director of the New England Centenarian Studies. "The really healthy are about the same numbers."

Gains in health span offer greater opportunity for "bonus" relationships in the decades ahead—with profound implications for the extended family. Grandma has a special friend, a younger man who is a traveling companion. Uncle Fred just got married again. Cousin Sue and her partner Jane just bought a house together. Every Thanksgiving, places at the table change to accommodate a new configuration of relationships.

Some people come to Second Adolescence with two or more family units, and this complicates the trajectory to My Time. If you still have young children to raise, you don't have the freedom—psychological or financial—to change course the way your contemporaries with grown children can at the same age. Yet, you still get the jolts that signal you are entering a different stage of life.

A popular image of serial marriage is the 70-year-old grandfather who marries a much younger woman and has a baby. In reality, this is not so common. If you've had two or more families, you're more likely to be 60 with a child still in school or college. You juggle caring for dependent children, keeping up relationships with adult children, and meeting your own need to regenerate. For some October mothers and fathers, having a child in their 40s or 50s skews the transition to My Time. They get stuck for a while. But most people adapt the script to reconcile the tensions between late-life child rearing and regeneration.

Stephanie Pincus, 59, got married her first year in medical school and had two children during her residency at the University of Washington. She divorced at 40, remarried, and was almost 45 when her third child was born. "Having a child at 45 means I'll be 65 when he heads to college," she says. She's already been through this. As a parent, she is stretched between two generations of children. Last year, she had a wedding for her daughter. Her young son has yet to take his SATs.

"Hopefully, by the time he's in college, there will be grandchildren somewhere," she says.

Meanwhile, she is making the transition to My Time. At age 56, she switched careers and left the University of Buffalo, where she had headed the dermatology department for eleven years. "Enough already. I want to do something different. I want to use my energies creatively," she says.

In 2000, Stephanie became the Chief Academic Affiliations Officer for the Department of Veterans Administration—and turned her family life upside down. During the week, she lives in Washington. Her husband, also a highly successful academic physician, stays at home in Buffalo with their son.

"What is different is my attitude," she says. "I used to think it was more important to be in control of things." But as a commuting wife and mom, she has to step back. "I'm learning to let go—I'm learning that life happens and it will be all right." She starts shedding the competent-woman armor of middle adulthood that enabled to raise her first two children and work her way up the ladder of academic medicine. "I realized I didn't have to do everything for everybody anymore."

She is also living alone for the first time in her life—in a small apartment she has decorated in soft whites with photos of the family all around. "It looks restful and peaceful," she says. She has time to read. "Part of my transition—I treat myself to good books. It's okay to spend the money on the hardback." Fifteen years ago, she wouldn't allow herself to buy the hardback. All she read were paperbacks on airplanes.

Meanwhile, her husband and son have thrived. "They learn how to do things independently." Giving up daily control has improved her marriage, she says. "I'm much easier to get along with," she says with a smile.

She has found a new harbor for her family . . . and herself.

Sometimes, you're not even ready to settle down to family life until My Time. The flamboyant Charlie Wilson, 70, former Democratic congressman from Texas, didn't get "really" married until about five years ago. His first marriage ended in divorce. "It was 100 percent my fault," he says. After that, the man who grew up in a small town of 1,700 people and 33 churches became a political soldier of fortune, romping his way through wine, women, and song. (As he points out, voters in the Bible Belt love a sinner and Charlie was *their* sinner.) In Congress, he was able to orchestrate a secret war in Afghanistan against the Soviets—chronicled in *Charlie Wilson's War* by George Crile. And one day, a doctor told him he was going to die. The booze had caught up with him. (As he says, his idea of heaven used to be a tall, leggy blond with a nice cold Tanqueray martini in her outstretched arms.)

He gave up drinking, went back to it, gave it up again. "I was a functioning alcoholic," he says. On April 15, 1998, "I finally quit," he adds. "I'm not saying I'll never have another drink—but not one tonight."

That same year, he fell in love with a former sweetheart. This time it would be different. They soon married. "I never forgot this woman. I couldn't be happier. A lot of people say that and it's bullshit. But it's really true. I finally got there, " he says.

"It took me a long time to wean myself from the leggy blonds," he continues. "It's a tough thing to walk away from." There he was, a single congressman in the candy store of power politics. When the two first met, he was hardly marriage material. "I was in love with her," he explains, but "I wasn't finished yet with the other life. I still had a wild hair up my ass. I finally outgrew it."

After a hiatus of seventeen years and separate lives, they re-met. "This is a very special woman," he says. "We are very very happy."

Most people outgrow the "wild hair" during their first adolescence. Still, you may have to get "finished with the other life" – the unfinished emotional business of middle adulthood to go forward in intimate relationships in My Time. For some, who have lost a partner, a new marriage can jump-start the process. Long-term couples also need to find ways to energize the triad of love.

There are a lot of marriages—old and new—that don't bloom in the September sun. The couple drifts along in a state of functional stagnation. Along the way, each spouse shuts down. Family counselors recognize the signs of foundering. "You see no growth, no movement," says psychotherapist Douglas LaBier, who heads the Center for Adult Development in Washington. "You see a continuous repetition of the same themes. The relationship becomes dead. The couple sinks into a functional relationship devoid of connection and energy."

In the early years, there are enough distractions to mask a stagnant marriage: getting children through school, making your mark in the workplace. Now the children are gone. The career may be gone, too. Now, what? Maybe you just don't want to think about it. You slide along.

"People who have the most damaging experiences are those who stay in a 'bad' marriage. They have given up," continues LaBier. "They have a transactional partnership, a functional relationship. It's a vulnerable time. They're stuck."

Until something happens that shakes up the status quo. Even "good" marriages get shaken up by change.

◆

For many couples, sexuality becomes a major issue in the bonus decades. It's part of your identity as an individual. It is also a second language. It's how you express yourself and "talk" to a loved one. When sexual function declines, it can be a double loss: the end of a specific sexual activity and a break in a vital communication link. Without that link, a critical mode of connection gets severed . . . and the relationship may start to fray.

The medical community has been slow to recognize the importance of sexual fitness in the bonus decades. But for a number of couples, recovering a sexual relationship becomes the arena for redefining the marriage.

The Lakens—Keith, 58, and Virginia, 57—are straight out of Garrison Keillor Country. Their house in Minnesota overlooks the Mississippi River. They met in science class at a small Lutheran college. Keith kept falling asleep, sliding his body against her. On a date he tried to French-kiss her. She didn't like that. She thought he was pushy. He dropped out of school and didn't go back until after a stint in Iran where he worked for an aerospace company. By then they were married. He was ready to study—earning his B.A. and master's in business administration—and eager to take on the world. Keith was the pilot, the adventurer, the aggressor, the risk-taker. Virginia was the cautious one, the "good" girl, the pleaser.

The years rolled along: two fine children, successful career for Keith as a manager in an electronics firm in Winona, successful part-time career for Virginia as a communications specialist. Children's weddings, visits with grandchildren, a swelling 401k retirement fund.

Sure there were rough spots. Keith came from a family of "screamers." Virginia's parents never argued. "A couple of times I said to myself: I'll pack up and go to Mexico and start over," says Keith with a laugh. But mostly they were rooted in the marriage. "I could never think of going any place but home at the end of the day," says Keith.

Like many couples hitting My Time, they were ready to discover why they married each other in the first place. They had survived the stressful transition to parenthood. "When the kids came, the competition really began for our time," recalls Keith. "Expected family obligations— have to be here at Christmas, have to be at church, have to be at PTA. Have to be." Now, the have-to-be era is over. It's just the two of them. "We are back to what our marriage was first like. Mentally, we're at a place where we really like each other."

Then came the jolts.

For several years the Lakens had been living in PSA angst, the anxiety of annual prostate-specific antigen tests to screen for cancer. Keith's results suggested something, but what? Right away they started fighting. What if? "Watchful waiting" or treatment? They knew the side effects of treatment—the risks of impotence, incontinence. But if this is cancer? He was worried about losing his "manhood." She was worried about losing him.

After nearly thirty years of marriage, they were foundering. Neither could understand the other. Each thought the other was nuts, dense. The empathy gap widened.

When Keith underwent prostate surgery, doctors reassured him that because of his young age and good health, he was unlikely to become impotent. But the doctors were wrong. The Lakens now believe that the risk of impotence after prostate cancer treatment has been greatly underestimated. In part, this is medicine's bias to focus on the disease rather than on the patient. A young resident summed up this attitude when he said to the Lakens: "You're probably *cured* of cancer. How can you complain about your sex life when you're lucky to be alive?"

Keith was 50 and he rebelled. So did Virginia. They refused to go away quietly and just hug. They began to see that they were on the same side. They became collaborators in the frightening twilight zone of a life-changing illness and set out to get their sex life back. At first, it was all about fixing Keith. Viagra was not effective. The doctor prescribed injections in the penis.

Injections produced an erection, but sex was not the same. For years they tried to get it back . . . and they failed. "We were fixated on having intercourse," says Virginia. "The spontaneity went out of our relationship. It wasn't natural." Ever the pleaser, she was determined to make it right for Keith. It didn't seem possible, but "we got very bored with oral sex. We started fighting again," she says.

"I started feeling like a hunted animal—like prey," says Keith. "With the shots, it was the first time I learned to fake an orgasm. I just had no interest here. She had taken an aggressive role. I felt hunted. I understand now when a woman says she doesn't want to be hit on."

All couples go through sexual adjustments over a long life together. Hormone levels decline, gradually in middle-aged men, more abruptly in women after menopause. Physical conditions, such as impotence and pelvic pain, can interfere with sexual activity. Feelings are as important as function, and couples need an ongoing dialogue in words and behavior to maintain a relationship. But a lot of people take their sex life for granted and don't talk—until they lose it.

Keith slipped slowly into a real depression. He gave up the injections. "Things now were at the bottom. We stopped making love. We stopped hugging and kissing and touching for the first time in thirty years. More detrimental, we couldn't talk about it," says Virginia. "We were both fearful for our marriage."

One evening, as they lay there in bed, Keith said he'd had it. No more trying to have sex. That part of their life was over.

"We both cried over what we had lost. That was the first time we acknowledged that we had lost something. We weren't going to get it back," explains Virginia. "Only when we cried for what we lost, could we deal with it," she continues. "I was in denial. Keith was in anger. We had to mourn the past to move on."

As with the transition to My Time, when you have to say good-bye to middle adulthood, the Lakens had to say good-bye to their old sex life. Keith got therapy for his depression. They began to think about what kind of sex life they could have together. Injections did solve the erection problem. Then, what? What were they trying to say in a sexual language?

Their goals broadened. As Keith puts it: "There is goal-oriented sex—go for the orgasm. [And then] there is pleasure-oriented sex:

What are we going to do [sexually] with our time? What are we going to do with our relationship?"

Their shift in sexual goals echoed a general shift in values—from scoring to caring, from winning to well-being. They began to focus on pleasure. Keith could experience an orgasm without erection or ejaculation. He discovered many ways to ensure that his wife did, too. "I actually think for the first time I was able to derive pleasure from giving pleasure," he says.

They became more adventurous and open with their bodies. They saw humor in their plight—like the time they had to drive to the emergency room in another town because the injection dose was too high and Keith's erection wouldn't go down. Turned out he was the third man that night to come into the ER with a permanent erection. (Does the World Health Organization know about this silent epidemic?)

Today, Keith and Virginia have a new sex life. They make sex dates. They laugh. They talk to each other—even though talking may be the scariest sexual activity between a man and a woman. "I needed to tell Keith: This part of our relationship is important to me. I want you to be a good lover," says Virginia. "I'm asking him to satisfy me. I can suggest alternatives. Prior to this I would say to Keith: I don't want to have an orgasm. I just want to satisfy you. . . .

"We've never had better sex—never," continues Virginia. "I've taken on some of his philosophy. It feels good, why not? What is the worst thing that can happen if I have more than one orgasm?"

They wrote a book about their experience to help others and educate the medical community: *Making Love Again: Hope for Couples Facing Loss of Sexual Intimacy*. The book is dedicated to Virginia's dad. Before his death, he had confided to Keith that after his heart attack, the medications he had to take made him impotent. "He told me: *This is the worst thing. This is the worst thing I've had to deal with*," says Keith.

That's the difference between then and now. Today you can expect to have a sexual life, just the way you can expect to play golf, work in the community, go to school. Instead of shutting down your sexual identity in the later decades, you open it up. Much like the whole passage to My Time, instead of winding down after age 50, you gear up.

This bonus sexual revolution is having an enormous impact on the quality of life for couples in My Time. To be sure, many couples are happy to engage in less sexual activity than they did in earlier years. There's a new sense of freedom when you are no longer driven by hormones or measured by performance. But you still use a sexual vocabulary to talk to each other—the caress, the kiss, an awareness of each other's body and mind.

In creating a new sex life, Keith and Virginia strengthened the triad of love. They closed their initial empathy gap. They enchanted each other in discovery—she with new boldness, he with new tenderness. They learned to trust each other with their worst fears.

"It forced us to think about communication," says Virginia. "When you have to say to your partner: This is what I want you to do with my body. And: I can't do that physically. Here are my warts and failings that I can't change. What are we going to do? What are we going to do to give us pleasure? That's as basic as it gets."

The challenge is to say: "I can't do that. I'm not the person I was," continues Virginia. "What's the highest honor? Trust. When you are able to trust someone with all of your frailties." She looks at Keith. "He's the only one who knows all my frailties. Once you voice them, it sets you free of them."

The lessons Keith and Virginia learned in the sexual arena laid the foundation for My Time. When the next jolt came, they were ready.

Still, it was a shock: Keith was asked to "retire" from the company where he had worked for more than twenty years. This was "job divorce"—another assault of self-esteem. Meanwhile, the stock-market slide had emptied their 401k of much of its value. The lovely house by the river—all was at stake.

"Initially, when we were confronted with his termination, we did just what we did when we were confronted with his impotence," explains Virginia. "We tried to get back the exact same thing we had lost. We went about the job search looking for the same kind of job, position, salary that Keith had had."

Keith worked out a severance package and consulted an executive head-hunter. After all, Keith was a doer; he could turn around departments, get product lines up and running. He sent out 6,000 résumés to companies across the country. He got about 1,000 responses—all with the same message: *We're impressed with your résumé and we have nothing for you.* The most thoughtful rejection was a handwritten note from a CEO: *Normally we'd be interested in someone like you, but next week I have to lay off 800 people.*

When do you admit that you aren't going to get back what you had before?

"We were both having a really bad day," begins Virginia. First the impotence. Now, no job. What next? He said: *I have to vent.* She said: *I'm feeling the same way. I just want life—I want things to be stable.* She started crying. Keith said: *I'm so glad you said it. Now I can say it.*

They looked at each other. *Jolt!*

"Life is never stable," says Virginia. "There's no guarantee. It's only the moment that counts. If we can stay in the moment—we have each other. We have a house to live in, food on the table. Tomorrow who knows. You look around you—How bad is my life? What about so-and-so? Okay, calm down. If you can say it out loud."

They were pretty fluent now in talking to each other. "The ability to say something to your partner—as bad as it is. The worst fear loses its sting when you say it. What if I didn't have someone to say it to?" she says. "Until you get past the fear, you can't be creative."

Virginia looks back. They got through the "anger, denial, fear—emotions which kept us focusing on our losses and prevented us from looking at our situation in a creative and positive way," says Virginia. "We've also moved into the mourning state, really beginning to assimilate that our loss of lifestyle, at least for a while, is permanent. But we're ready to move on, to tackle the future, to deal with what we can change and control and let the rest unfold as it will," she continues. "We are able to get by with less money than we originally thought. We also decided that what we really want to do is to be part-time retirees. We want to work—actually we have to work—but we also want to have time for choices and pleasures."

Keith starts over. He has consulting work. And along comes a bathroom window solution with new challenges. Their son-in-law decided to move his family from the West Coast to set up a drive-in coffee business in Minnesota. Keith and Virginia now have their daughter and five grandchildren nearby. They are helping their son-in-law build the new company. They are immersed in the lives of the extended family. Daily life now embraces adult children, grandchildren, and themselves.

They see themselves going down a railroad track. "We are really going down two rails. One is—oh, what if. The next is—oh, my gosh," says Virginia. Keith puts it this way: "Both of those rails come together on the horizon. Neither rail is the right rail. It's an acceptance of a lesser-known future.

"When I was young, I used to say: Why is wisdom wasted on the old? Now I know. Often wisdom comes at the expense of life learning. Life learning takes time."

The Lakens are now in the dreaming phase, barreling along toward new possibilities in work and relationships as they maintain the harbor of family. "We're not closing any doors," says Virginia.

◆

The typical family in the twenty-first century includes dependent children, young adult parents, My Timers, and Centenarians (the 90-plus generation that is hitting the 100-year-old mark). The two ends of the family spectrum can now count on two middle generations for support.

For centuries society has looked to one middle generation to raise the younger generation and take care of the older generation. Now there are two generations to do the job. Probably the most radical demographic change is the explosion of activist grandparents.

More and more My Timers are helping their children raise their children. Once a revered rarity, grandparenting is becoming a common reality. Half of the baby girls born today will reach 100. That leaves many decades to nurture children, grandchildren, and great-grandchildren. Men, too, who are living longer, have more opportunity to discover the rewards in caring for youngsters. And so are aunts and uncles, godparents and mentors. For many in My Time, the link to those in the newest generation becomes a primary bond.

I remember my grandmothers. I was lucky among my friends—two grandmothers who saw me into adulthood! One large with watery blue eyes, the other delicate with warm brown eyes. One was divorced, one widowed. One read Edna St. Vincent Millay, the other played Mendelssohn on the piano. One drank, the other didn't. One commanded in a deep voice: "Young man, get me a drink." Just out of the Navy, he saluted. Yes, sir. The other asked in a soft voice: "Could you do something nice for me?" No one ever refused.

My grandmothers taught me the triad of family love. There was empathy, for sure. One day, when I was in the midst of an arsenic period of adolescence, I was having lunch with Gran at the Wenham Tea House in the small, semirural Massachusetts community where we lived. Gran's eyes were liquid, her voice gravely. She took my hand and said: *Darling. I understand. Being a teenager is hell.*

There was discovery, too. I was enchanted with their stories. I especially loved it when I was a little girl and Granny would talk about her beaux. I'd take my dolls to her cabin in the Maine woods for a tea party with lemon sugar cookies and we'd talk about true love. How she turned down the one whose family manufactured bathroom fixtures after she got lost in a warehouse full of chamber pots! I laughed so hard I can still taste the bits of lemon sugar cookie. *Oh Granny . . .* She went on, describing how some of her beaux could dance but had no depth. Grandfather had depth. They met at a boat race. She grew up in New York City when the streets were filled with horse carriages. Before cars! Before telephones! I imagined George Washington was one of her beaux. *Granny, Granny, tell me—what did you do in the revolution?* She put down her teacup and smiled. *My dear, I'm afraid I'm not old enough.* She died at 98—after I was married and had children.

To a small child, a grandparent is timeless. There is adoration and absolute trust—by virtue of a grandparent's status in the family hierarchy, much like the professional trust a physician commands over patients.

Years later, I wondered why my grandparents wanted to spend so much time with me. They gave so much. What was in it for them? Now I know. Empathy with a grandchild brings back the best of your own forgotten childhood and catapults you into the future. My 3-year old granddaughter Sophia likes to make brownies with her mother. She and I talk on the phone about what fun it is to get chocolate on her fingers and slowly lick it off. And sometimes smudge the chocolate in her hair, I suggest, or all over the cheeks of Lila, her baby sister. Sophia shrieks with delight. Her mother rightly restrains her and washes her hands. But Sophia and I giggle and conspire. I can't wait to tell her all about my beaux. Chances are I will see her grow up and have her own beaux.

Discovery is a two-way street. As a grandparent, you get to see a whole new life unfold. You are above the fray of the intense, hands-on parent-child relationship. Says one grandfather: "It's all the love without the baggage."

Finally, you get to make a difference in someone else's life.

The grandparent explosion is a worldwide phenomenon. Sixty percent of people over 60 years of age live in developing countries, according to the International Longevity Center. Many more older people live in China, for example, than in Japan and the United States put together. As the longevity revolution spreads around the globe, family structure is being turned upside down. As an economist from Beijing exclaims: "Four grandparents for one child!"

Instead of growing horizontally within a generation, the family is expanding vertically across several generations. In the United States, young adults are having fewer children at later ages—and each child has a longer life expectancy. The pyramid of aging has become a rectangle of generations. Meanwhile, the roles of men and women continue to merge, with mothers of young children holding jobs outside the home and fathers taking on more responsibility for household chores—though mothers still do the lion's share of child raising. The fairy godmother in this workplace-childcare juggling act is often a grandparent.

Sometimes, you provide regular childcare if the grandchildren live nearby. Sometimes, you provide financial support. Sometimes, it's an informal arrangement of visits and phone calls. Sometimes, it's the special vacation trip. Marge and Bob Kitterman, who run the Care-A-Vanners for Habitat for Humanity, take their grandchildren on a trip in the RV every summer. They never go more than three months without seeing a grandchild.

It's not always easy to meet the demands. As you go on to second careers and other demanding pursuits in My Time, you may not be available for baby-sitting duties. The familiar juggling act of young parents gets re-created when you have young grandchildren.

Alice Rivlin, 72, senior economist with the Brookings Institution, who was director of the Office of Management and Budget in the Clinton administration, knows that dilemma. She describes the lock on her heart when she went to Grandparents Day at her granddaughter's school. It is the same school her son had attended a generation ago. And the same anxiety rises in her chest when she realizes the performance has gone on longer than expected and she is going to be late for a meeting downtown. As she battles Washington traffic to get to that meeting, she has to smile. Where is the book on the crisis of the working grandmother? The Second Shift for grandparents?

As Rivlin told her Bryn Mawr classmates at their fiftieth reunion, much progress has been made for women in the workplace. But the challenges to young parents have grown more complex. The work part may be easier for daughters today, but the life part is not. Women are still trying to do everything as they balance the competing demands of being "wives and lawyers, artists and soccer moms, community activists and whole people," said Rivlin.

Who understands this crunch? In many families, it's Hyper Granny who is guiding Super Mom. And, increasingly, Hyper Grandpops is helping out Super Dad. In the process, My Time parents and their adult children reconnect on a new level. As my daughter said when her son was born—*I get it, mom. We're on the same side now.* The two middle generations close ranks.

◆

Sometimes a grandparent is called on to do more. Longevity brings with it some cruel ironies. While the death of young children is rare, the longer you live the greater the chances are that you may lose an adult child. And sometimes the loss is not death but the trauma of illness or a family breakdown that leaves a child without the steady hand of a parent. That's when men and women in My Time take over.

About 3.7 million grandparents are helping to raise nearly 4 million grandchildren in the United States, reports the National Academy on an Aging Society. More than 1.3 million children are being raised solely by their grandparents, according to a 1998 Census Bureau report.

More than 80 percent of these parenting grandparents are under 65, most are married couples, and more of them live in the suburbs than in central cities.

You transform family loss by redefining the family. You are the steward of generations.

You never know when fate is going to turn on you.

The first half of Mary Hickey's life went smoothly, predictably even. A good marriage to a man almost a decade older. Four children. A prosperous existence in the Detroit suburbs. "I went from being an extremely dependent child controlled by my parents to a completely dependent young wife," says Mary, 67, a consultant in horticulture. In those days, she was a traditional stay-at-home mom, she says. She did volunteer work and raised her children.

Then, as she would later say to her son-in-law, the second half of her life began: "How old are you? 52! You know something? My world fell apart when I was exactly your age."

A whole cascade of jolts. In 1986, her father died. Her daughter Ellen was diagnosed with Hodgkin's disease—and was successfully treated. The next year began with joyful events: The weddings of Ellen and her older sister. And a magic trip to China with her husband. Except that his indigestion shortly after returning home turned out to be cancer. He died eight months later. "That was Dunkirk as far as I was concerned," she says. She was 52.

She emerged into a new role. She was no longer the dependent one; others were dependent on her—her mother who lived nearby, her expanding family with the addition of grandchildren. Mary turned a love of gardening into a career in landscaping. She had a few suitors.

In 1998, Ellen and her husband had a baby girl, Stafford, thanks to in vitro fertilization. Mary was there to help out. Six months later, as Ellen was nursing the baby, she complained that one breast was as hard as a rock. "For God's sake, go to the doctor," Mary said to her daughter.

Ellen was diagnosed with an aggressive breast cancer. Mary was there, helping her daughter through radiation and chemotherapy. Ellen spent only a few days in bed during her illness and went into remission. She began to travel again, taking the baby to visit her brother and sister. Then, on a trip with her husband to an antique show in Philadelphia, Ellen noticed that her waistline was too tight.

It was a fatal sign. The cancer had spread.

The call came on April 15: *Mom, this is what's happening . . . metastases to the liver.*

"I felt she was going to beat it," says Mary. "I had enough faith—blind faith. I did not think life could be so cruel." All through Ellen's illness, Mary was there. She tended to her daughter's daughter and bonded with her daughter's friends and comforted her daughter's husband. She went deeper and deeper into the love she bore for the daughter she was losing.

One day, as they were driving back from a hospital appointment, Ellen said to her: *Mom, I'm really worried that Stafford will forget me. I'm really worried that Stafford won't have the values that I feel are so terribly important in life and for her.*

Mary says she knew "things were shutting down." She remembers how she prayed: *God, tell me what to say.*

She turned to her daughter and said: *Ellen, do you trust me?*

Mom, of course I trust you.

Well, we will work things out.

Ellen celebrated her 40th birthday on May 21, 2000. Five days later, she died. Mary was there.

And she's still there. Ellen's husband asked her to stay and help raise Stafford. But Mary couldn't leave her mother and her whole life in Detroit. So she sets aside two weeks of every month to commute to Virginia to be with Stafford and her dad.

Out of sorrow has come the magic of her relationship with her granddaughter. "We dance. We skip. We play with her plastic kitchen."

Mary describes celebrating the child's 3rd birthday: "I said to her: *I really love you.* She eyeballed me. *I really love you too.*"

On Mother's Day, she goes to Stafford's school. Through Ellen, she has made a wide range of friendships with Ellen's contemporaries and with the mothers of Stafford's friends. "They keep me living in the twenty-first century. I'm bridging the gap between young and old," says Mary. And she's filling the gap for Stafford. And for herself.

"This is the incredible thing. One learns to juggle the impossible—exquisite pain and exquisite joy. One continues to laugh—right after crying," she says. "I used to be afraid of crying. I was terrified that if I let go, I would be a basket case. But now I know the importance of tears. They are cathartic—and give way to a tremendous surge of energy."

This energy infuses her relationship with other family members. She finds new closeness with her surviving adult children and other grandchildren. On the same day that she goes to Stafford's school she gets a Mother's Day card from her youngest daughter—who's comforting *her* daughter with a 102-degree temperature. "All she wanted to do was to crawl into my bed and snuggle with me. As I lay in bed with her for several hours, curled up beside her, I felt so content and fulfilled. I also spent a lot of time thinking about how you must have done the same for me when I was 3 and miserable with a fever. There was no place I wanted to be but curled up with you in your bed and very safe, loved, and comforted," she writes. "Our love and bond is so bone-deep it's almost too much to express in words. I had to become a mother myself to express it and really understand it."

Mary holds the card to her chest. She knows what's important in life. "There's no question I have a purpose. I'm struggling to keep my whole family together. I'm very focused. Life is very meaningful."

As family steward, Mary is leveraging her advantage of life experience. As she says: "I don't give a shit about superficial things anymore. I've been over the mountain too many times."

12

Confronting the Spiritual Crisis

The world is filled with the Absolute. To see this is to be made free.

TEILHARD DE CHARDIN

T HE MAN SITTING NEXT to me at dinner slowly begins to talk about it. He's cautious because he doesn't want people to get the wrong idea about him. But at 65, he's turning to religion. A conservative man, he has always been a member of a church—but now it's a full-time involvement. He's taken a special course in the bible. He's thinking about applying to divinity school. He is retired. His wife recently died of cancer. His children are grown. He wants to learn Greek and read the texts of the New Testament in the original.

He reminds me of another friend, a socialist philosopher at the opposite end of the conservative-liberal spectrum. He wants to learn Hebrew so he can read the bible in the original. Both men are hungry for knowledge, for original truth in texts that shaped the culture. And they are hungry for something else more personal. They are looking for spiritual nourishment.

When you get to My Time, you confront a crisis of the spirit. What is the significance of your life—of all life? How do you grapple with fate's mysteries?

You have a unique perspective. You've accomplished a long life span—yet you are not old. Traditionally, this kind of spiritual high-noon occurs at the end of life. But now the crisis can come in the prime decades from age 50 to 80. It's fused with the re-evaluation process of Second Adolescence. It is often part of a return to roots and the religious threads of childhood. Most important, it is also a going forward—a search for peace and confidence to guide you in the future. The pathway is different for each person. The challenge is universal.

Researchers point to a natural developmental process in old age called "life review." You go back over the past and find meaning in your life. You rework the script to turn it into a story. This process is enhanced when you review your life with another person—someone who is supportive and understanding. Life review has become a counseling approach for social workers, psychologists, and other psychotherapists who work with older people. But it is also something you can do yourself.

In conducting a life review, you put your life on the record and give it authority. "People go back and pull the threads together and make a narrative of their lives," says Margery Silver of the New England Centenarian Studies at Boston Medical Center. One woman, after reviewing her life, said to Silver: *You saved me from insignificance.*

"That was so breathtaking," says Silver.

Life review is an internal psychological process. If you are just reminiscing and presenting an oral history without trying to find meaning in the raw data of events, then it is not life review.

The concept of life review was first described by psychiatrist Robert Butler. As you go over the past, you address inner ghosts, make amends to yourself and others. You treat old wounds, recall lost loves. You transfuse pain into meaning. You celebrate the moments of joy. You begin to see the significance in your story and become grateful for the life you've had. As Sheryl Crow croons in "Soak Up the Sun:" *It's not having what you want/It's wanting what you've got.*

Life review is a healing process as well as a summing up. It involves "the progressive return to consciousness of past experiences, in particular the resurgence of unresolved conflicts which can now be surveyed and reintegrated," explains Butler in *Why Survive? Being Old in America.* In life review, you reframe previous incidents and put them in a different order. You find integrity in the new order. You answer the question: Did I matter? What is my legacy—to loved ones? To future generations?

In nursing homes and geriatric centers, life review is often a formal psychological process conducted by professionals in the mental health and social service field. Yet more and more researchers believe that life review is not limited to old age, but occurs at other turning points in people's lives.

Men and women in the prime of My Time are usually several decades younger than those in nursing homes. Outside the mental health arena, life review is a more do-it-yourself, informal passage. You take your own inventory. When you go to school reunions, you are conducting a kind of life review as you catch up and connect with former classmates. You can resurrect—and heal—old wounds at family occasions such as weddings. You may go into therapy for a deeper understanding of your personal script. Or turn to a specific religion.

It's all about finding a way to be *saved from insignificance.*

For many people, solitude seems to be a critical piece in the search for meaning. It's a dilemma: You need close relationships—and you also need alone time. Says my 90-year-old godmother who lives in New Mexico: "You need repose. Young people don't understand that. I love my time by myself. I read. I write. I take the dogs for walks. I think. I look out at the desert."

But it's hard to find a comfort level of solitude when you're just coming out of a busy life with family and work. You're surprised at how dependent you are on the built-in noise of children and colleagues. Silence can be very scary. Yet it allows you to confront issues that you've avoided for years. And as mental health professionals point out, psycho-spiritual growth usually takes place in times of discomfort—when you're feeling scared and needy.

You turn inward and look for a quiet space. You try it for a weekend. Maybe a month. Maybe longer. The need for solitude has spawned a thriving retreat industry—places to go to address spiritual questions, usually in the countryside, away from the honks of taxi-cabs. Sometimes the focus is on poetry or ceramics or dieting, but the agenda is to look inside. The purpose is to get away by yourself—usually with other people who are also getting away.

The need to spend time by yourself is also fueling the travel industry's new interest in the Independent Tourist—the man or woman who travels alone to discover new places inside and out.

Sometimes, wandering in solitude becomes a way of life. Joan Eldredge, 70, lives in a twenty-eight-foot Bounder motor home. She took her first trip alone decades ago in the wake of a divorce. As she describes it: "Here I was in this deserted campground, living in a tiny little pup tent that couldn't be locked, all alone, saying, Who am I?

"That first night I just sat in the tent and cried, letting go of my old civilized life, facing a new existence full of the unknown. It's a process of expanding your horizons, pushing your known limits, having the courage to take risks to live out your dreams."

Joan has been on the road ever since, seeking out the quiet places in a small motor home. "It's a feeling of coming alive, of leaving the noise behind and going where it's silent, really silent. Then you can hear your inner voice encouraging you to live a life of fulfillment, learning, adventure, and contentment."

You don't have to go into the wilderness to be alone and find a quiet spot. Annette Mitchell with Experience Corps, who works in an elementary school in Washington, D.C., created her place of repose in her garage. It's a room where she goes to listen to music, make clothes, and write in her journal—where she goes to reckon and regenerate.

You want to create an environment where it's safe to be alone.

Sometimes a period of solitude defines the transition to My Time. To break away from the past, you need to live alone—without being lonely or isolated. It's part of your dreaming phase to discover yourself, by yourself, as you wrestle with life's meaning.

Bill Alcorn, 67, lives alone in an old rambling, white clapboard farmhouse on an island in Maine. His companions are his dog, a husky-lab mix named Obie from "Star Wars," and two camel-colored Norwegian ponies, Falkar and Erik. He works on his place: a vegetable garden, a new barn, rolling fields, forests of spruce, and a tidal view of the Atlantic. He's had much success during his life on the mainland—a profitable wood company in southern Maine, three wives, four children, and eight grandchildren.

Five years ago, he thought his life was perfect. He sold his company. He was free to travel. He was in love with his third wife, an artist. Hip artist, hip guy—they took the magic trip to Bali and beyond.

Then his world fell apart. His wife left him. "I knew the relationship was not perfect. But I had no inkling this would happen. I was totally surprised," he says. "I cried and yelled—and screamed at the lawyer. The lawyer said: Cut your losses."

Stunned and wounded, Bill moved to the island, a lobstering community of about a thousand residents. It had been a place that he'd bought years ago for his family. Now it was a place of reckoning. "This is the first time I have lived by myself. It's been fantastic," he says. He wakes up at 6 A.M. "I take Obie for a jog. If it's hunting season, I stick to the shore and open spaces." Then back to the house for breakfast. "If it's a good day, I cut trees and make trails. I have a chain saw." He's building a boat—a wherry, a special rowing boat. He used to row in college—and he still likes to get out on the water. He's planted 450 seedlings, cleared 3 paddocks.

Once a day, he goes into the village—to the post office, the grocery store. Then, another walk with Obie in the late afternoon. "Back here for dinner. Nothing complicated—rice, pasta, fish, vegetables. Raw carrots," he says. The TV doesn't work. "I listen to the radio, watch an occasional video. I do some reading. I'm in bed by 9."

Slowly in the silence, on walks with Obie, and in rhythm with the tide, Bill conducts his own life review. What was it all about? How could he have been so unprepared for the death of his marriage? What has he accomplished? What about love? He feels it's essential to be alone to figure this out. "This place has always been very grounding for me. This is the place where I should be," he says. "I find it very fulfilling, educational."

You need alone time to do hard reckoning. Otherwise you are too distracted by the built-in intrusions of regular life and the demands of others. It's easy to avoid unsettling questions when you have more immediate priorities—going to meetings at work, driving in a carpool. You might not need to move to an island to be alone, but you do have to create your own space of solitude.

Bill looks back. Growing up in St. Louis, coming east to college and graduate school, moving around—Chicago, Des Plaines, settling in Maine. Getting the ponies brings him back to his boyhood when he was 10 years old and had a horse. "I rode him everywhere," he says. Then he discovered "girls and cars." He starts to laugh. Now he is back to horses—for a while anyway, during this phase when he is figuring things out.

He examines the long period when he was building up a business. Being ethical mattered. "I'm pretty forthright," he says. "My business ran on moral grounds. We were respected all through New England.

That's what I hope my epitaph will say: A man *respected*." Morality is important—and he wants to be where "my morality would be respected." Where he's trusted and can trust others.

He gathers his family around him. His sons come to visit. He's had some girlfriends and they come to visit, too. He plants beets and lettuce and keeps thinking. "I sometimes feel overwhelmed with projects," he says. Building a new barn, carving a pond out of the swamp, clearing another paddock. "Sometimes I plant great big trees, sometimes I plant only plug seedlings." But, as he says, "a big part of me is optimistic."

The future is unknown—but it beckons. Being optimistic, even partly optimistic, is crucial. It's also healing. In research on longevity, optimism is a recurring theme. Being optimistic is linked to survival and satisfaction. There's no denying sorrow. But you have hope—that a tree will grow, a child will grow up, a friend will hold your hand.

Doctors will tell you that attitude affects your immune system and influences recovery from disease. Psychiatrist Edward N. Hallowell wishes he could give out potions of hope along with medications and psychotherapy. "Doctors like me can't write a prescription for it," he explains in *Human Moment: How to Find Meaning and Love in Your Everyday Life*. But hope is a "vital necessity," he continues. "We don't know exactly where to turn when we run out. It's odd that we keep emergency stores of all kinds of things, but we don't usually keep an emergency store of hope."

What Bill is doing in his time of solitude is slowly building up a store of hope. That's part of the spiritual agenda, finding the hope you need to fulfill the promise of extra decades—hope in your own life and beyond.

◆

Sometimes the spiritual passage comes on as a crisis. You have to take a break from ordinary life to deal with it. The blows are too great to postpone the reckoning. You can't wait until you've finished the report or weeded the garden. You have to give it your full attention.

You begin with a change of scene.

One day, Margery Silver and her husband got in the car in Boston and headed west.

The previous decade had been good to Margery. A specialist in the psychology of aging, she had a high-powered job overseeing a network of eighty psychotherapists. The organization, founded by a group of psychologists, provided mental health services to nursing homes.

Then came two jolts. The organization was bought out by a company that changed the culture of care to a bottom-line business. "It reached the point that I was not able to provide quality services to patients. I was being asked to exploit my therapists," she says.

And her husband was diagnosed with Parkinson's disease. He was 58. "We had to make choices," she says.

But they weren't ready to make life-changing decisions. They needed time alone. Margery knew she could no longer work for the new company, but she didn't know what she wanted to do. And they had to think about new living arrangements. They decided to take a trip—"to have some fun, to get away and regroup. To rethink things," she says. They had savings to draw on. They were both in a stopping place and could take a few months out of their lives. And later, they might not be able to travel. Margery quit her job. Her husband was able to leave his law practice for several months. Then they let fate shape their journey. "We had a lot of flexibility. We made no advance reservations. We visited friends along the way and headed for places we wanted to see."

Driving east from Palm Springs, California, they passed a sign: "To Mecca." They looked at each other and said *We've got to go to Mecca*— and turned off the road. Mecca turned out to be nothing but a cross-road, a gas station, and a grocery store. To get back on the highway they had to take another route. "It was stark but beautiful countryside. Gray rock formations without a soul in sight," she says. "I don't know how to describe it—it was just wonderful." The whole trip "was being able to find moments like that—moments of peace and awe and wonder—serendipitously."

That's what you're looking for in the spiritual search: *Moments of peace and awe and wonder*—moments to break through the routine, to conduct your own life review and find new purpose. Moments where you give up control and let experiences flood in. Margery Silver celebrated her 60th birthday on the road. After she returned, she had the clarity to focus on her *what next?* She switched fields from psychotherapy and developmental psychology to neuropsychology and found a whole new career in the study of centenarians.

Meanwhile, she and her husband moved into a retirement community connected to a college that focuses on intergenerational contact and intellectual development—an environment that nourishes and supports them both.

Looking back on those months of travel, she says: "The most significant part of the trip to Mecca was the trip back to our main road."

✦

Behind the search for meaning is one constant—the shadow of death. In the Middle Ages, cathedrals were built and death was omnipresent; you prepared for the end from the beginning—because life was short. As the life span extended, you could delay the moment of reckoning, but when it came, death was usually imminent. Erik Erikson described the psychological task in the final stages as overcoming despair by striving for *integrity*—pulling your life together, integrating different parts, and finding meaning in the whole story.

The focus was on getting prepared to die. As Harvard researcher George Vaillant explains in *Aging Well*: "Erikson suggests that one of the life tasks of Integrity is for the old to show the young how not to fear death."

My Time completely changes this focus. With the emergence of this new stage in the life cycle, the spiritual imperative shifts to life, rather than death.

You still have to prepare for death—but you probably won't die for a while. You get ready for death . . . in order to live. "It's accepting your life as it was in preparation not for death, but for this long potential span of life ahead of you," says Margery Silver. "It's taking stock of your life, taking knowledge from it to go on. Erikson saw it as preparation for death. Now it isn't," she continues. "You're not looking at an end. You're looking at a beginning."

This is the paradox of My Time. In order to live fully in these extra years, you have to be ready to die.

Certainly the urgency of death hovers over the bonus decades. Injuries occur and diseases come out of the blue, no matter how many miles you jogged or what food you ate or what books you read or how many people you loved. Still, the chances are you will survive an illness for many years. You may have a weak heart, a synthetic knee, a hearing aid. You may go for regular checkups to see if an artery has closed up or a cancer has come back. But you live.

One of the striking findings from the centenarian studies is how resilient and engaged people can be in late life. "The 100-year-olds were living pretty much in the present," says Silver, co-author of *Living to 100*. "These are people who have come to terms with their lives. As far as death went, that was something they took for granted. They said they were ready to die."

Yet they were very much alive. Margery Silver was a guest lecturer for a course on the life span, and she brought to the class a 101-year-old woman. At the time, Margery was 70. The class instructor was 48. The kids were 20. There were four generations in the room. "The students were blown away," she says. Here was the new reality of longevity. "For young people to have those experiences—that's going to change things."

How do you get ready to die—when death is not imminent?

The context is historic as well as personal. Who are you? Where do you fit in the larger universe? At 50 you've already lived longer than most people did in previous centuries.

By this time, you've had little meetings with death—losses in health, setbacks in work, the end of relationships. You've experienced the deaths of loved ones—a parent, for example, or a close friend. You know that you are part of a long human chain that stretches beyond time and place. But still, it is a sense of your own mortality that galvanizes your spiritual search. As Butler says of this struggle: "Death is crucial."

Harvey Rich has always considered himself a spiritual person—and his search for the spiritual originates in a background of death. It was shaped, he says, by his "complicated family history regarding religion and survival. That history was tied up with death. My people were Jews, and Jews died. It was that simple. My mom nurtured me on that fact without saying a word." Family members were lost in the Holocaust. Even before the catastrophe of World War II, his grandmother had come to the United States, "found sweat shops and a barely good-enough husband who impregnated her too many times," he continues. "She got cancer and died.

"I was weaned on the fear that I could be ended—terminated—annihilated—and join those who died before me. That fact drove my search for peace of mind and that, in turn, drove my search for the spiritual."

His search took him to the Roman Catholic Church for a period when he worked with the nuns in a hospital. Then he came back to his Jewish roots, but "I couldn't accept much of the daily practice of my faith either. So I was cast out—a bit like Ishmael—into the world searching for the spiritual."

The search was "like a hum in me," he says. It cropped up suddenly in those transcendent moments of life—"making love, holding my babies, coming to terms with my son's diabetes, my own impending blindness," he says. "Always there was this hum and it echoed off the background of death."

There were times when he could not deny death—in his patients, in family members. "I shuddered like everyone else. But my shudder went so deep and so far back—back to the cries of my mom and the silent screams of the millions," he says. He refused to be overcome by a fear of death. He would make friends with death—and fool death into letting him live a long time. "I lived with death as some people lived with God."

All through adulthood, he was on guard in the little meetings with death. And then, one day not too long ago, "death was silent," he says. The fear was gone. As a psychoanalyst, he was surprised by that. What had happened inside him to dispel death?

He looks back at his transformation in My Time—when he started to lose his eyesight and stopped practicing to write *In the Moment: Celebrating the Everyday*. In the writing process, he conducted his own life review. As Harvey describes the process: "The old people, who had gone on to die, sat with me in my solitude and told me their stories—again. I could hear their accents and see their poor clothes and even smell them. I sometimes cried. I sometimes laughed. I was in awe of what was happening to me. I hadn't realized what memory really was. I hadn't realized that memory had a depth—a profundity—that could not be measured by my science or anyone's neurochemistry. It was the *meaning* of memory that gave it this extra dimension."

The next time death knocked on his door (another procedure on his eye), he didn't shudder. By telling stories and putting meaning into memory, he began to understand that "death, and the fear of death and the comfort with death, was all about connections," he says. "If I could be that connected to all who came to me and told me their stories, then I was equally connected to the time ahead of me. I had discovered something that I could witness and believe. It's about connections. I was connected to the time before and the time ahead. I was part of a human process—a spiritual process. The collective connections were what I had sought. I could call it God or the spiritual; I was with it and it was in me.

"And I no longer feared death, because I would be *beyond death*."

By finding meaning in memory, he was saved from insignificance. Death had lost its terror.

That's one of the goals in My Time—to get *beyond death* in order to live.

◆

It's not always possible. For some, the spiritual crisis is complicated by a paralyzing medical crisis. The person may be overwhelmed by severe depression or other mental illness. One of the symptoms of depression is a prolonged sense of hopelessness. You feel that your life has no significance and you lose the will to live.

This puts you on the edge of tragedy.

As a health columnist, I receive many letters from readers. One day, a handwritten letter, unsigned with no return address, arrived in my mailbox at the *Washington Post*:

"I'm 65—female—a great-grandmother. At some point this year I will finally end my life. I've planned, read and worked to get to this point since I was 16. I've hated every day of my life as far back in life as I can go."

The woman looks back. "Getting pregnant put things on hold. My children needed to be raised. That has been done. I've thought long and hard," she wrote. She has apparently gotten some treatment but calls it "mental health BS."

"I'm not crazy. Maybe tired. I raised 7 kids alone. I deserve to be tired. So take all your mental [health] babble—. It is not worth the time or trouble." She has made careful preparations. "I've collected the sleeping pills, a good bottle of Scotch, hose for the car, plastic cover to keep fumes in and enough painkillers to stop an elephant. . . . I have music to listen to," she wrote. "Bills will be paid. Letters written and I will finally be free. Free from this earth that is so full of meanness and hate."

There is no way to trace her. I wrote a column in the newspaper to try to reach her. I never heard from her again.

If I could have found her, I would have tried to get her good mental health care to screen for depression and relieve her suffering. The right therapist, the right medication, the right support. After that, there would be plenty of time to deal with the existential questions she raised: What is the meaning of life? Is it worthwhile?

Most suicides take place in the context of untreated (or mistreated) mental illness, researchers point out. There are two peak periods of greatest risk: ages 15 to 24 and 65 to 85—roughly the upheavals of first and second adolescence. Overall, more people in the United States kill themselves every year than are murdered.

You have to be alert to the symptoms of depression and other mental disorders. Some people have a first episode after age 50. In a significant number of cases, depression develops in combination with other illnesses such as heart disease. Depression can also be a first sign of Alzheimer's disease. Whatever the origin, depression needs to be treated.

My Time is marked by life-changing events that can lead to despair. Every year, roughly one million Americans experience the death of a spouse. Between 20 and 30 percent develop a clinical depression within six months, points out Charles F. Reynolds III, a specialist in geriatric psychiatry at the University of Pittsburgh.

Sometimes people are hit with multiple losses—the loss of a spouse, the loss of a job, the loss of health. They lose the roles that have given their life meaning. "When those roles are removed, they feel a real sense of devastation and emptiness. We see that all the time," says Reynolds.

Retirement is often experienced as a loss. "It's terrifying," he continues. "For some, work is a major focus of life. With the loss of work, there's a loss of person-hood. It's important to find replacements that can lead to hope and integrity instead of despair and emptiness."

Grieving is different from depression. It's normal to grieve after a loss. But it's not normal if your mood is consistently low or sad, day after day. If you're not eating, not sleeping. If life has no meaning. A lot of people make the mistake of thinking that depression is a normal part of living past 50. But that is an ageist myth. Depression is an illness to be treated.

✦

You want to feel safe. You want physical security—and emotional security. Part of the spiritual search is to build up an internal defense system. Many people in My Time turn to nature to find a safe place inside themselves. For some, it's mountains; for others, it's the sea. Or a shaded park in the city.

Mary Page Jones, 63, could have just gone to church to have a spiritual life. She is the daughter of a minister . . . and the wife of a bishop. But her spiritual life is intensely personal—an alchemy of background and boldness, nature and solitude.

Her life started out in a hurry. A Virginia girl, she married at 21 and had two daughters. After seventeen years, the marriage ended in divorce. She went to work. For a while, she was holding down four jobs "just to pay the bills," she says. She finished college after age 40. "I went to that place in life where everything is survival. How many hours are there in a day when I can make money?"

She made it through the desperate years and gave herself a present: a trip to Wyoming.

It changed her life. "Something about the Teton mountains drew me," she says. "I was liking that part of me that could withdraw, that could not go to parties. I had started pulling back." She was supposed to start a new job when she returned home to Virginia. Instead, she decided to move to Wyoming. Some of her friends thought she was crazy. But Mary Page had started her search for inner security. "I've never been good with *shoulds* and *oughts*. There's a whole heavy load of what you're supposed to do and how you're supposed to act. In Wyoming, I was free to be. It was a place where no one knew me. I found out who I was. I didn't have all that baggage."

She found work to support herself and she looked at the mountains. "I'd sit on the porch on weekends and watch the trees. If there was a storm, I'd watch that," she says. She looked back on her past and got rid of wondering what other people think. The "ego people," she calls them. She found that place of acceptance—"accepting the fact that I'm a size 14," accepting "the person I've become instead of trying to be the person I wanted to be."

She'd look out at the mountains—*from whence cometh my help*. Her religious roots got mixed up with her personal reckoning. "It was so fulfilling," she says.

And then she took another leap into the future. She remarried at age 52 to a widower and former bishop in Wyoming. By then, Mary Page had been single for more than a decade and she knew how to hold on to her spiritual center. "I'm no longer living in the fear of my identity being sucked away," she says.

And finally she took a leap that radicalized her future on another continent. When her husband was offered a position at St. George's College in Jerusalem, Mary Page got involved in the peace movement in the Middle East. Working with Palestinian and Israeli women to end the violence on common ground has become her purpose in My Time. She now runs an e-mail clearinghouse on the status of the conflict. "I am single-visioned," she says.

All the while, she has kept looking at the mountains—clarifying this vision of peace with her spiritual supports of solitude and nature.

Since her husband's retirement several years ago, they have been able to travel more. She goes back to Wyoming and stares at the Tetons. She goes to Cyprus and sits on a patio. "I look out to the mountains or the Mediterranean. Nothing between us but fields. That's my solitude. I don't write. I don't do. I just be." She travels through the Judean desert. "I love the desert. It's the raw me in the desert."

Not long ago, she and her husband took a trip to Alaska. "Just driving through the mountains," she says. "There was not a village, not a town, and you better have a full tank of gas. The mountains were covered with snow. It was God's presence. It was fabulous. I find God in nature. That brings me to a safe place."

Alaska, the Middle East, Wyoming . . . Mary Page has found that "safe place" of spiritual strength. "I've always come up to the abyss and stepped over. A lot of it is my faith. When I step into the abyss, my experience is that I am always caught. Something good happens. I never operate out of fear."

Mary Page has earned her faith in life.

Psychologist Carl Jung tells the story of his travels in Africa when he reached the end of the line of the Uganda railroad. Beyond was unexplored territory. Who could not fear the unknown? An "elderly Englishman," wrote Jung, "joined me." The man had been in Africa for forty years. "May I give you a piece of advice?" he asked. Jung encouraged him. "You know, mister," he said, "this here country is not man's country, it's God's country. So if anything should happen, just sit down and don't worry."

Sit down and don't worry. It's God's country. As Jung described the man's psychological state, "not man but God was in command here," he wrote.

Mary Page *sat down* in her solitude. By transforming the traditional beliefs of her childhood into a personal faith, she has found safety in *God's country*—and new purpose in her marriage and her cause.

✦

Some people believe in God or a divine power; some do not. Some aren't sure.

And some make religion a career in the bonus decades.

Bernie Hillenbrand, 78, always wanted to be a priest. He grew up poor in upstate New York—twelve to fourteen feet of snow every year. His father was unemployed for eight years during the Depression. His parents fought—"a bullheaded Kraut and a red-headed Irish girl," he says. When his father was 38, he put a rifle in his mouth and blasted his brains out all over the bathroom. Bernie had the church. He had school. He grew up knowing he would leave his past. He would go to college. He would not be poor.

He accomplished his goals. He went to war; he was in combat and lost partial use of his hand. He went to college. He married well and had four children. He came to Washington and, at age 30, took over the National Association of Counties (NACO)—turning it into a powerful political voice. He was Mr. County Government with 130 employees and a busy social calendar studded with the Capital's Glam Crowd.

Then it was over. In his mid–50s, his world imploded. He divorced and remarried—and left the Catholic Church. And a few years later, his organization nearly collapsed in a financial crisis. "It was abrupt—like Enron," he says. His organization was financing the construction of a new building—hidden cost overruns threatened to wipe out the association. The scandal made headlines and ended Bernie's career.

"I didn't have a hint," he says. "I thought everything was going along fine. Suddenly. . . . " His voice trails off. "That shook me. The organization had been my mission in life. I had neglected my family," he says. The scandal was "the greatest trauma of my life," he continues. "I'd been so proud of my reputation. I made every effort to protect it. Now, all of a sudden, I didn't have any reputation."

Everything he had built up in his public career has been torn down. What was he left with?

"All I had was my relationship to God. My relationship to God has meaning. And my relationship to people," he says.

At age 60, Bernie reinvented himself. He went to Wesley Theological Seminary at American University and became a minister. "I was the oldest in the class. I got used to being the oldest in the way that once I was the youngest," he says. The courses provided an intellectual framework of religion, but "with me, it's highly personal. God is a personal thing. I think it's inside you. It lives inside everybody else. That's the only place you're equal. You're equal not in height or weight, but in—one person, one soul."

That's Bernie's style—one on one. Today, Bernie shapes his ministry around a message of love and connection. "I'm known as the holy hugger," he quips. Part of his work has been counseling veterans at Walter Reed Army Medical Center in Washington, DC. One patient wanted to go home to die. He lived in West Virginia by a little stream. He wanted to fish in the stream. Bernie asked him: *Are you afraid to die?* He said: *No.* He had lived with his cancer for some time. "We just talked about death. We didn't talk about God. He could feel that I could feel what he was going through."

This is what being a minister is all about, continues Bernie. "Empathy, connecting with others. . . . It's caring for someone else as much as you care for yourself. If you can't do that, I don't know how you live."

Bernie knows about death—his father's suicide, the deaths of his buddies in the war. "I've had a constant sense I'm living the lives of other people," he says.

With this sense of mission, he has accomplished much in My Time. The boy who wanted to be a priest is a minister. The man who lost his reputation in scandal has found dignity in caring for others. And he wonders what he'll do next. He always had this Irish notion that he'd be dead at 50. But now he's 78, in good health, in a good marriage. "I have 20 years to go," he says with a smile.

✦

The old line *Aging is not for sissies* takes on new meaning when you have to plan for forty or fifty years after you celebrate your 50th birthday. Sometimes you may feel like the Cowardly Lion in the *Wizard of Oz*: Where do you find courage?

That's an important task—psychologically and spiritually. As theologian Paul Tillich outlined a half-century ago in his lectures on "The Courage to Be" at Yale University: "The courage to be is the courage to accept oneself as accepted in spite of being unacceptable," he said. "Accepting acceptance though being unacceptable is the basis for the courage of confidence." Tillich continued: "It is the paradoxical act in which one is accepted by that which infinitely transcends one's individual self."

In other words, you accept yourself (with all your unique flaws) and you are accepted by something larger than yourself. This double acceptance is a spiritual search engine and source of courage.

You need courage to regenerate. Courage allows you to be inventive. Courage makes it easier to take risks. And taking risks may be a key to making the most out of My Time.

My aunt by marriage is a glamorous woman of 93 who wears scarves and hats and has thirteen great-grandchildren. At the age of 68, Elmira Ingersoll became a widow. She looked at what her life had been—a fairly conventional adulthood on Long Island—and then she did something very different. She got together with a friend who had also lost her husband—and ended up creating a spiritual retreat for themselves and others. In the process, they expanded their family circle and deepened their friendship.

One warm October day on a trip to New England, the two women were driving through Connecticut and they stopped to look at property on a lovely lake with the gold and crimson of fall leaves reflected on the water. On the way back to Long Island, they decided to sell their houses, pool their resources, and make the move there—together.

"That's when we took the big risk. One never grows without risk. Having been able to take that risk—it promotes a lot of change. It could have been difficult. We've been very blessed, very fortunate. It's still unfolding—since we took that risk. We did it suddenly," she says with a twinkle in her green eyes.

But the path to that boldness took many years. Elmira was 18 when she met the man she would marry on a ship returning home from England. She was traveling with her parents and when he came over to their table and asked her to dance, she turned to her father and said: "May I, Daddy?"

They danced the whole voyage. "It was like dancing with Fred Astaire," she recalls. "It was all so romantic." He was 11 years older, sophisticated. He wooed her hard once they returned to New York and wrote a song for her entitled "Honest Eyes." After two years, they married. But that meant two things: She was still pretty timid and she didn't go to college as planned. That left her with a "feeling of inadequacy all my life," she says. Making up for college has been the easy part. "I've taken courses all my life. I'm hungry for knowledge and I still am," she says. Finding her courage was harder.

In the middle years, she had four children and led the Long Island life. But the young girl who asked her father's permission to dance began to assert herself. She had to. By the time the children had left home, her life was fracturing. "A lot of social stuff," she says. "Too many cocktail parties. We didn't have labels like alcoholism then." Her husband was not happy in his work—a family paint business. "There was no passion in it. In his soul, he was a musician. He wanted to be writing music. The way he handled that—he drank too much," she says.

Elmira needed courage to break the impasse in their lives. She turned to Subud, an international spiritual movement originating in Indonesia that helps people connect with the "divine power that can heal and purify," according to the Subud website. Elmira merged the rituals of Subud with her Protestant roots.

Her mother thought she had joined a cult. But Elmira was no longer timid. She persuaded her husband to move to a smaller place, farther away from the country club and the cocktail parties. Her husband was in shock—*You'd leave our home?* She persisted and convinced him. After the move, "we began a new part of our marriage," she says. She was 54.

Her husband was wary of her novel spiritual commitment, but "he saw that it had meaning to me," she says. "I began working from a different place within me." She used her new faith to heal her marriage. They grew closer together. They traveled; they enjoyed their children's families. He discovered the pleasures of gardening, a passion they shared.

When he developed lung cancer, she nursed him. One afternoon, as he lay dying on the bed, he asked her to perform the Subud exercise of purification. "I took off my shoes. I danced and sang around the room," she recalls. Afterward he said to her: *That was quite an experience.* He died a short while later. "He left knowing we had this connection," she says.

Elmira held on to this connection and the healing power of her faith. The timid 18-year-old girl had found her courage.

When Elmira and her friend saw the property by the lake, they saw possibility. The chance to create a whole new life. And they did.

They built a wing onto the house so that they had a common living area with separate studio apartments on the side. Before long they started to hold retreats for people of all ages who needed to spend some quiet time by the lake. Soon they were holding conferences on everything from music and philosophy to yoga, tai chi, and poetry. Over the years, their home has become a spiritual center for themselves and the community.

It is also their legacy. They have found others to carry on their mission and keep the center open for those in need of a spiritual retreat. Harmony House on Cedar Lake will endure after they are gone.

Elmira is someone who blossomed in her bonus years. She has been blessed with good health and financial security. Not everyone at my aunt's age is so fortunate. You need some good fairies in My Time—a basic level of health so that you can function physically and mentally, and a basic level of economic support from public and private sources to protect you from impoverishment.

Many people have suffered losses in the recent downturn of the economy. Government programs such as Medicare, Medicaid, and Social Security are in flux. Still, most Americans can count on these two fairies when they arrive at My Time. That's the evolutionary bonus of longevity. The challenge is to use these assets and extend the decades in this productive stage.

The spiritual process of reckoning and renewal sets the agenda in My Time. Each of us has our own pace, our own purpose. The rigors of Second Adolescence demand that you take an activist approach and not just slide along from adulthood to the end-game of old-old age.

You strip away the layers of habit and even hypocrisy that eased your way through the first half of adulthood. You stop listening to other people's voices and pay attention to your own. You now have the time and freedom to discover a more basic truth about your self, your relationships, and your work. You find your spiritual strength. You change as everything—and everyone—around you is changing.

For all those facing the bonus decades, this is an extraordinary story of personal renaissance.

Elmira stands out as a pioneer in her generation—but she is a harbinger of what is likely to be the common scenario for those who are now in their 50s.

"Looking back, I'd say the 80s were my best decade," she says. "I was so free. I was so content."

Freedom. Contentment. Purpose.

That is the promise of My Time.

Another Jolt!

Feeling light within, I walk.

NAVAJO NIGHT CHANT

Little did I know when I started working on this book that it would be my own awakening. Each time I sat down and talked to a person about this stage in life, I got a jolt. The questions I posed ricocheted back to me. The stories illuminated a richness in human experience that I had never imagined. It was dazzling.

For decades I have lived on the journalistic edge that allows me to cut through the daily fare of evil and mayhem, bureaucratic foolishness, and the pomp of politics.

But the story of My Time unfolds in a different dimension. It goes beyond the headlines of pain and power. It is a modern saga of possibility and the power of relationships.

As I roamed around, searching for stories and doing interviews, I was struck by the positive energy in this new stage in the life cycle. Several impressions stand out.

How good people are. Sure, there are snakes and dirty players, abusers and betrayers. There is corporate scandal, government corruption, family dysfunction, and the violence of war. But most of the men and women I interviewed were just plain decent. They had a strong moral sensibility. Perhaps the past fifty years of a rising standard of living and increased health span are helping to foster a large *decent* majority that is silent in the noise of news.

How strong people are. Despite horrible losses—or maybe because of them—these My Timers regenerated. Altogether they suffered every kind of trauma—the death of loved ones, life-threatening illness, divorce, job loss and financial decline, moments of despair, and the limitations of disability. For the most part, they repaired and renewed.

How generous and loving people are. The impulse to give and tend others seems to take off in My Time whether it's reading *Charlotte's Web* to a grandchild or building houses for a needy family or running a clinic to serve the uninsured. What a resource this burgeoning population is for the country!

But are these profiles extreme examples of the good life after a certain age? What percentage of people aged 50 to 80 actually regenerate? The question comes from a man who is 70 years old. We are sitting on the deck of a friend's house, a group of us all over 50, all talking about what we want to do—*next.*

There is no national survey that monitors renewal rates in personal development. But there is indirect evidence that people are flourishing in this period. According to studies by the National Council on the Aging, people over 65 say they have fewer health problems and are less concerned about money, loneliness, and crime than they were twenty-five years ago. More than 90 percent say they are happy and look forward to more bonus decades. About a third say "These are the best years of my life." African-Americans and Hispanics are more likely to say these years are best, notes the Council's president James Firman.

Social scientists know what makes for happiness and well-being. All the research points to two factors: having a purpose and being connected to others. Finding purpose and cementing relationships after 50 usually involve some process of change.

We start talking around the table about people we know in My Time—the couple who "retired" from the government and now teach in a city school, the colleague who went back to school, and our hosts who got married in their 50s, a second marriage for both.

Everywhere I go, I get a buzz. A man comes up to me in the subway to ask for directions, and we talk. Turns out he's coming up to 50, going through a divorce, and just started working for a small firm after being downsized from a corporate giant. "You're writing about me," he says. "I want to know what happens."

Sometimes you don't realize you're in a rut until you get out of it. After each interview, a blocked piece inside me broke loose. My horizon suddenly expanded with these narratives of possibility. I connected with the people I interviewed in a deep, personal way. So many welcomed me into their homes and into their lives. I came away invigorated. I had gained a second family—a wide My Time web of kinship.

We keep up with e-mails and phone calls. Jimmie Grace Van Vacter has moved again—from Alaska to Hawaii. Connie Kehoe has turned her interest in the young warrior from her Civil War ancestor to her father-in-law, an infantry man who fought in Europe in World War II. Barney Tresnowski was diagnosed with prostate cancer and underwent surgery. "I am again aware of my own mortality," he writes. But he regenerates. "I keep working at Legal Assistance," he continues. He keeps listening to tapes while he exercises.

There's no stopping in My Time. I see it in my own corner—scripts ending and beginning—*Hello, Goodbye, Hello*—lives taking off again and again.

I keep up with the husband I loved and lost. About five years after the breakup, he gave up the booze. "I haven't had a drink in three years," he tells me. I weep and rejoice. Too late for what we had in the past—but never too late for a new life. Remembering is laced with tenderness as we e-mail back and forth.

I visit my 91-year-old stepmother in an extended care facility. She has gotten very thin and weak. The doctors have ruled out any life-threatening illness. Since my father died some twenty years ago, she and I have become close. At age 70, she began another chapter in her life in public service for her adopted city of Boston. A daughter of Mississippi, she became the matriarch in Massachusetts of green space—preserving ancient elm trees on Commonwealth Avenue, restoring Copley Square, guarding the skyline to let in sunlight, resurrecting distinctive old buildings, and planting flowers wherever she could find a spot of dirt. But now she was suffering.

I take her hands in mine. "I'm afraid you've given up," I say. She looks at me, almost surprised. "Do you really think I can get better?" she asks. "Yes," I reply. The doctors agree. She has a resilient body and mind. How much more time? None of us knows. But she has good reason to hope for more bonus years. Her mood improves as she gets ready to go home and tackle more projects.

I go dancing. A quick trip to Austria for the wedding of my godson and his Austrian bride. So much hope as we dance by the lake in Krumpendorf, round and round the ballroom, holding on to each other, keeping the beat, from Strauss waltzes to hard rock, twirling and grinding, two cultures merging, the clan expanding, round and round, childhoods ending, the future beckoning. My friend Heddy, the mother of the groom, takes over the dance floor in her smashing gown of royal blue—laughing, gyrating. She is so happy, so healthy, so vibrant. She widens the dancing circle with her husband, her siblings, her friends, her new Austrian relatives. We are all so happy, so healthy, so vibrant.

Finally I go to my sacred spot in Maine, a rock on the shore, and look out on the water. The book is done and this family place is the harbor for my wandering soul. I remember tea time with Granny and sailing with Daddy. I think about my sister and brother. I can replay the weddings of my daughters in the field. As the sun sinks lower over the Camden Hills, I dream of adventures yet to be.

Maine is my annual ritual of renewal. But it's a deeper regeneration this year. I have learned so much. As an osprey flies overhead, I hold on to my extended My Time family—Juanita Jackson singing spirituals, Peter Barnes bicycling in New Zealand, Sandy Scott laughing, Mary Hickey crying (and laughing, too), Harvey Rich facing blindness, Keith Laken confronting impotence, Jim and Jayne Taylor sailing in the Caribbean, Mary Kunze learning Italian. These My Timers are messengers of hope and possibility. They have shown me again and again how to make the most of the bonus years.

As the sky explodes in swirls of salmon, pink, orange, yellow, I am so grateful. I know the joy of love, the blessing of friendship, the grace of opportunity.

What's next?

I can hardly wait.

Selected Bibliography

Robert N. Butler, *Why Survive? Growing Old in America*, Johns Hopkins University Press, 2003.

Robert N. Butler, Myrna I. Lewis, Trey Sunderland: *Aging and Mental Health*, 5th edition, Boston, MA, Allyn and Bacon, 1998.

Gene D. Cohen, *The Creative Age: Awakening Human Potential in the Second Half of Life*, New York, Avon Books, Inc., 2000.

Marc Freedman, *Prime Time: How Baby Boomers Will Revolutionize Retirement and Transform America*. New York, Public Affairs (Perseus Books Group), 1999.

Phyliss Moen, editor, *It's About Time: Couples and Careers*, Cornell University Press, 2003.

Thomas T. Perls and Margery Hunter Silver, with John F. Lauerman, *Living to 100: Lessons in Living to Your Maximum Potential at Any Age*, New York, Basic Books, 1999.

Theodore Roszak, *Longevity Revolution: As Boomers Become Elders*, Berkeley, CA, Berkeley Hills Books, 2001.

John W. Rowe and Robert L. Kahn, *Successful Aging*, New York: Pantheon, 1998.

George E. Vaillant, *Aging Well: Surprising Guideposts to a Happier Life, from the Landmark Harvard Study of Adult Development*, Little, Brown and Company, 2002.

Resources

AARP
601 E Street, NW
Washington, D.C. 20049
1–800–424–3410
www.aarp.org

Civic Ventures
139 Townsend Street, Suite 505
San Francisco, CA 94107
415–430–0140
www.civicventures.org

Elderhostel
11 Avenue de Lafayette
Boston, MA 02111
1–877–426–8056
www.elderhostel.org

Experience Corps
2120 L Street NW, Suite 400
Washington, D.C. 20037
202–478–6190
www.experiencecorps.org

Habitat for Humanity International
121 Habitat Street
Americus, GA 31709
1–800–422–4828 (1–800-HABITAT)
www.habitat.org

International Longevity Center (ILC)
60 East 86th Street
New York, NY 10028
212–288–1468
www.ilcusa.org

National Council on the Aging (NCOA)
300 D Street, SW, Suite 801
Washington, D.C. 20024
202–479–1200
www.ncoa.org

National Institute on Aging
Building 31, Room 5C27
31 Center Drive MSC 2292
Bethesda, MD 20892
301–496–1752
www.nia.nih.gov

Index

AARP, 84

Adolescence (Hall), 30

adolescence, Second Adolescence vs., 23–27, 30–32, 38, 64–65, 69

Aging Well: Surprising Guideposts to a Happier Life (Vaillant), 14, 107, 151, 191, 239

Ahrons, Constance, 186

Alcorn, Bill, 235–37

Alzheimer's disease, 130, 131, 139

Amiel, Henri-Frederic, 50

andropause, 25

anxiety
  dreaming and, 6–7
  My Time and, 21
  Second Adolescence and, 126

Augustine, St., 36

authenticity, 203, 204–05

Baltimore Longitudinal Study of Aging, 52

Barnes, Peter, 52–56, 57

Berkman, Lisa, 23, 25–26, 166–67, 171, 172, 207

Borden, Libby, 125–30

Browne, Bliss, 59–62

Brundtland, Gro Harlem, 27

Bush, Barbara, 34

Bush, George H. W., 33–34, 35

Bush, George W., 20

Business Council for the United Nations, 152

Butler, Robert N., 21, 145, 156, 157, 232–33, 241

Campbell, Joan Brown, 193–94

Camus, Albert, 41

Care-A-Vanners, 107, 110, 113

career consolidation, 14–16, 20, 25, 108

Carson, Nancy, 71–73, 74

Carter, Jimmy, 6, 32–33

Carter, Rosalynn, 32–33

A Chair for the Mother (Williams), 117

change
  legacy and, 146
  My Time and, 13–14
  retirement and, 77
  risk-taking and, 98

Second Adolescence and, 23–24, 70

Charlie Wilson's War (Crile), 214

Chrono Rad (chronological radical), 10

Churchill, Winston, 105

civic engagement, 108, 110

Civic Ventures, 108

Civil War, 16–17

Clinton, Hillary, 21

Cohen, Gene D., 14, 20, 91–92, 124, 132, 135, 136, 152, 15, 70–71

commitment, 14–15

compartmentalization, 198, 200

compensation, 14–15, 17, 109–10

competence, 14–15, 109

Conservation International, 127

contentment, 14–15, 55–56, 122, 134–145, 254

continual caretaker, 114–15

Cornell Employment and Family Careers Institute, 26

Cornell Lifetime Well-Being Study, 90

Costa, Paul T., Jr., 51, 178

courage, 13, 110, 251

Cowan, Carolyn Pape, 31, 210–11

Cowan, Philip A., 31, 210–11, 25

The Creative Age: Awakening Human Potential in the Second Half of Life (Cohen), 15, 135, 152

creativity
  loss and, 42, 135–36
  maturity and, 15
  My Time and, 124
  uncertainty and, 18

Crile, George, 214

crisis
  dreaming and, 66–67
  loss and, 57

da Vinci, Leondardo, 152

death
  fear of, 242–43
  preparation for, 240–41
  spiritual crisis and, 239–43
  urgency and, 240

De Chardin, Teilhard, 231

denial, 24

Dent, Charles C., 152

Department of Education, 124

Department of Health and Human Services, 8

depression, 50, 244–45

De Saint-Exupery, Antoine, 183

Dinesen, Isaac, 145

docu-fiction, 157

Dodds, Bob, 132–35

doers, 41, 48

Drake, Danille, 203

dreaming
  anxiety and, 6–7
  crisis and, 66–67
  focus and, 75–76
  identity and, 74–75
  reinvention and, 65–66, 74–75
  retirement and, 71
  Second Adolescence and, 24–25, 31–32, 63–80
  time and, 71
  uncertainty and, 68–69

Dreaming of Love and Fateful Encounters (Person), 194

drifters, 41, 48

education
  health and, 130–31
  life expectancy and, 130–31

My Time and, 123–44, 124–25
  next career and, 130
Eldredge, Joan, 234
Elizabeth I, 29
empathetic leadership, 15
empowerment, 31
England, 29
Erikson, Erik, 14, 107, 239, 240
Everything to Gain (Carter and
  Carter), 32
Experience Corps, 117, 120–21

family
  career consolidation and, 14
  creating, 207
  marriage and, 208
  My Time and, 207–30
Firman, James, 7, 84–85, 109
Freedman, Marc, 108
friendships
  health and, 171–73
  importance of, 165–67
  loss and, 174
  men and, 172, 173–74
  My Time and, 165–82
  parenting role of, 177–78
  recovery of, 167–71
  reminiscing and, 169
  singleness and, 180–81
  stress and, 174
  women and, 172–74
Fry, Sandra, 167–71

Gates, Bill, 115
generativity, 15, 91, 107, 115, 151
Gide, André, 23
Giles, Marian Taylor, 193
Girl Scouts, 38–39

Gollob, Herman, 19
Goodman, Ellen, 172
Goodnight, Paul, 149
Goodrich, Nancy, 167–71
Gottesman, Al, 174–77, 179, 181
Graham, David, 152–56
Graham, Katharine, 156
grandparenting, 62, 224–231
Gray, C. Boyden, 33–35
Greene, Everett A., Sr., 18–19
grief. *See* loss

Habitat for Humanity, 106–07, 110
Hall, G. Stanley, 30–31
Hallowell, Edward N., 237
Handbook of the Life Course (Moen),
  24, 26
Harvard Study of Adult Development,
  14, 132, 151–52
health
  crisis of, 55
  education and, 130–31
  friendships and, 171–73
  Second Adolescence and, 8–9
  volunteering and, 108
health span, 9, 10
Heraclitus, 146
Hickey, Mary, 227–30
Hillenbrand, Bernie, 247–49
"Honoring the Legacy", 149–50
*Human Moment: How to Find
  Meaning and Love in Your
  Everyday Life* (Hallowell), 237

identity, 108
  adulthood and, 14
  dreaming and, 74–75
  sexual, 192–94

volunteering and, 115
work and, 74
I Know Just What You Mean
    (Goodman and O'Brien), 172
Imagine Chicago, 59–61
Ingersoll, Elmira, 250–52
In Retrospect (McNamara), 156
integrity, 15, 91
International Longevity Center, 21,
    156, 225
Internet, 184
*In the Moment: Celebrating the
    Everyday* (Rich), 178, 242
In the Next Galaxy (Stone), 136
intimacy, 14, 108

Jackson, John and Juanita, 146–51
Jeffords, Jim, 20
Johnson, Lyndon, 153
Jones, Mary Page, 245–47
Jong, Erica, 3
Jung, Carl, 247

Kahn, Robert L., 140, 166
Keeper of the Meaning, 15, 132,
    151–52
Kehoe, Constance Messerly, 16–18
King, Martin Luther, Jr., 83
Kitterman, Bob and Marge, 105–07,
    110–14
Kunze, Mary, 63–64, 66–69,
    192–93

LaBier, Douglas, 215–16
Laken, Keith and Virginia, 216–23
leadership, empathetic, 15
legacy
    autobiography and, 156

change and, 146
creating, 146, 151–52
generativity and, 151
memoirs as, 150, 156–58
My Time and, 145–61
promise and, 160–61
struggle and, 145–46
Lewis, Myrna, 21
life empowerment, 33, 115–16, 121,
    132
life expectancy
    education and, 130–31
    Second Adolescence and, 30–31
    volunteering and, 108
    work and, 89–90
life review, 232–33
life span, 9
life wealth, 113
Lipton, Judith Eve, 173
*Living to 100: Lessons in Living to Your
    Maximum Potential at Any Age*
    (Silver), 68, 240
Logan, Kay, 180
longevity
    loss and, 227
    memoirs and, 157
    My Time and, 8–9
    regeneration and, 4
    romance and, 183–84
    Second Adolescence and, 30–31
    social revolution and, 10
loss
    catastrophic, 50
    creating, 58–62
    creativity and, 42, 135–36
    crisis and, 57
    dealing with, 44–45
    depression and, 50, 244–45

friendships and, 174
longevity and, 227
of love, 191–92
My Time and, 45
psychological growth and, 50
reinvention and, 46–48
relief after, 57–58
Second Adolescence and, 41–62
of self, 58
stress and, 51
sudden, 49
types of, 50–51
love. *See* romance

MacArthur Foundation Study of Aging
    in America, 9, 25, 166
McNamara, Robert, 156
Mahler, Gustav, 196
*Making Love Again: Hope for Couples
    Facing Loss of Sexual Intimacy*
    (Laken and Laken), 220
Mandela, Nelson, 87
marriage
    family and, 208
    gender differences in, 211–12
    men and, 211–12
    My Time and, 184
    Second Adolescence and, 26
    serial, 212–13
    women and, 211–12
Mattingly, Pat, 27–30, 204
maturity
    creativity and, 15
    discovery and, 210
    phases of, 15
Matuszeski, Bill, 76–80, 208–10
McGovern, George, 192
Me and Shakespeare (Gollob), 20

memoirs, 150, 156–58
The Memory Bible (Small), 130
men
    andropause and, 25
    friendships and, 172, 173–74
    marriage and, 211–12
    My Time and, 74
    sexual identity and, 194
menopause, 25
midcourse, 24
Mitchell, Annette, 235
Moen, Phyllis, 24, 26, 90–91
Morrison-Bogorad, Marcelle, 123–24,
    131
Moses, Grandma, 135–36
motivation, 109
My Time
    anxiety and, 21
    breaking away and, 23–40
    challenges of, 73–74
    change and, 13–14
    creativity and, 124
    education and, 123–44, 124–25
    empowerment of, 191
    family and, 207–30
    friendships and, 165–82
    goals of, 181
    legacy and, 145–61
    longevity and, 8–9
    loss and, 45
    marriage and, 184
    men and, 74
    mortality and, 8
    potential of, 9–10
    psychological tasks of, 91, 122
    reinvention and, 4–8, 11–13
    romance and, 183–205
    singleness and, 185

spiritual crisis and, 231–53
volunteering and, 105–22
women and, 67–68
work and, 83–103
See also Second Adolescence

National Academy on an Aging
    Society, 227
National Association of Counties
    (NACO), 248
National Council on the Aging
    (NCOA), 7, 52, 57, 84
National Institute of Mental Health
    (NIMH), 139
National Institute on Aging, 51, 124,
    131, 178
National Press Club, 84
NBC, 6
Necessary Losses (Viorst), 50
New England Centenarian Studies,
    212
next career
    education and, 130
    volunteering and, 110
Nin, Anais, 179
Novelli, William D., 84
Nun Study, 139

O'Brien, Patricia, 172
omni-potential, 31

Pauley, Jane, 6
Person, Ethel S., 194, 196–97
Personal History (Graham), 156
Peter D. Hart Research Associates,
    108, 114
Picasso, Pablo, 123
Pincus, Stephanie, 213–14

Plato, 63
Plaut, S. Michael, 193
posttraumatic stress disorder, 50
Preston, Dorcas, 185, 187–91, 192
*Prime Time: How Baby Boomers Will
    Revolutionize Retirement and
    Transform America* (Freedman),
    108
Procter, Mary, 208–10
public service. *See* volunteering
purpose
    education and, 123–44
    legacy and, 145–61
    volunteering and, 105–22
    work and, 83–103

Raitt, Bonnie, 6, 20–21
re-enchantment, 197, 210
regeneration, 4, 32–33
Reid, Heddy, 181–82
reinvention
    dreaming and, 74–75
    loss and and, 46–48
    psychosocial dimensions of,
        15–16
    retirement and, 83–85
    risk-taking and, 11
    Second Adolescence and, 4–8
    trigger for, 10–13
Reitkopp, Nancy, 167–71
Religion, 61, 63–64, 107, 149–151,
    153, 188, 232, 242, 246,
    249–250, 252–253
retirement
    change and, 77
    children and, 102
    dreaming and, 71
    early, 17

as endpoint, 7
official, 18, 210–11
plan for, 94–95
preparation for, 71–72
reinvention and, 83–85
Second Adolescence and, 3–4
volunteering and, 108
work and, 83, 89–92, 114
Reynolds, Charles F., III, 244
Rich, Harvey L., 11–13, 177–80,
    241–42
risk-taking
    change and, 98
    growing and, 251
    not fearing and, 110
    reinvention and, 11
    responding to tragedy and, 48
    romance and, 194, 197–98
    turning into opportunity and,
        101–103
Rivera, Aida Nydia Munoz, 140–44
Rivlin, Alice, 226–27
Robinson, Mary C., 117
Rockefeller, John D., 115
Roethke, Theodore, 63
romance
    authenticity and, 203, 204–05
    Internet and, 184
    longevity and, 183–84
    My Time and, 183–205
    re-enchantment and, 197, 210
    risk-taking and, 194, 197–98
    sexual identity and, 192–94
Rowe, John, 9–10, 140, 166
Rowe, Jonelle, 7–8

Samuelson, Robert J., 90
Scott, Alexandra Korff, 42–50

Second Adolescence
    adolescence vs., 23–27, 30–32, 38,
        64–65, 69
    anxiety and, 126
    awareness of, 24–25
    breaking away and, 23–40
    change and, 23–24, 70
    chaos and, 75–76, 77
    denial and, 24
    dreaming and, 24–25, 31–32,
        63–80
    emotional changes of, 25–26
    empowerment and, 31
    fear and, 4
    friendships and, 177–78
    getting to, 3–21
    health and, 8–9
    life expectancy and, 30–31
    longevity and, 30–31
    loss and, 41–62
    marriage and, 26
    personal life and, 26
    physical changes of, 25
    regeneration and, 32–33
    reinvention and, 4–8
    retirement and, 3–4
    uncertainty and, 129
    urgency and, 26–27, 42
    women and, 74
    See also My Time
September 11 attacks, 21, 50
Shinhoster, Richard, 83–84, 85–89
Silver, Margery H., 57–58, 68, 212,
    232, 237–39, 239–40
singleness
    friendships and, 180–81
    My Time and, 185
    women and, 185

Small, Gary, 130
Smith, Anne, 167–71
social capital, 166
solitude, 233–35
The Soul in Balance (Scott), 47, 49
spiritual crisis
    death and, 239–43
    life review and, 232–33
    My Time and, 231–53
    solitude and, 233–35
Stafford, William, 35
Stone, Ruth, 136
stress
    friendships and, 174
    loss and, 51
Successful Aging (Rowe and Kahn),
    140, 166
suffering. *See* loss
suicide, 243–44
Sullivan, Nancy, 92–94
Sunderland, Trey, 139

Taylor, Jayne, 99–101
Taylor, Jim, 95–103
Taylor, Shelley E., 172
*The Tending Instinct: Women, Men,
    and the Biology of Our
    Relationships* (Taylor), 172
Teresa, Mother, 207
Tillich, Paul, 249–50
Tocqueville, Alexis de, 63
Torres, Verna, 167–71
tragedy. *See* loss
Tresnowski, Bernard, 36–38
Trotsky, Leon, 165

U.S. Department of Education, 28
UCLA Center on Aging, 130

uncertainty
    creativity and, 18
    dreaming and, 68–69
    Second Adolescence and, 129
urgency
    death and, 240
    Second Adolescence and, 26–27, 42

Vaillant, George E., 14, 15, 25, 95, 107,
    115, 132, 151–52, 191–92, 239
Van Susteren, Lisa, 24–25
Van Vacter, Jimmie Grace, 4–6
Viorst, Judith, 50
volunteering
    benefits of, 108–09
    compensation and, 109–10
    competence and, 109
    health and, 108
    identity and, 115
    life expectancy and, 108
    motivation and, 109
    My Time and, 105–22
    next career and, 110
    pitfalls of, 114–15
    redefinition of, 109–10
    retirement and, 108
    work and, 109

WAAW (Washington Attractive
    Accomplished Woman), 71
Warren, Earl, 35
*When Partners Become Parents: The
    Big Life Change for Couples*
    (Cowan and Cowan), 210–11
Whistler's Mother, 10
Why Survive? Being Old in America
    (Butler), 156, 233
Wilderness Society, 127

Williams, Emory, 136–37, 138, 140, 156–57
Williams, Janet, 136–39
Williams, Vera B., 117
Wilson, Charlie, 214–15
women
  competitive edge for, 67–68
  friendships and, 172–74
  marriage and, 211–12
  menopause and, 25
  My Time and, 67–68
  Second Adolescence and, 74

sexual identity and, 194
singleness and, 185
Wooley, Mary, 38–40
work
  identity and, 74
  life expectancy and, 89–90
  My Time and, 83–103
  necessity of, 3–4
  retirement and, 83, 89–92, 114
  volunteering and, 109
World Health Organization, 27
A Year in Chautauqua, 149